WORDS OF WELFARE

WORDS OF WELFARE

The Poverty of Social Science
and the Social Science of Poverty

SANFORD F. SCHRAM

Foreword by Frances Fox Piven

UNIVERSITY OF MINNESOTA PRESS

Minneapolis / London

Published by the University of Minnesota Press
111 Third Avenue South, Suite 290, Minneapolis, MN 55401-2520
Printed in the United States of America on acid-free paper

Second printing, 1996

Library of Congress Cataloging-in-Publication Data
Schram, Sanford.
Words of welfare : the poverty of social science and the social
science of poverty / Sanford F. Schram.
p.   cm.
Includes bibliographical references and index.
ISBN 0-8166-2577-8 (hc)
ISBN 0-8166-2578-6 (pb)
1. Public welfare — United States.   2. United States — Social
policy.   3. Poverty — Government policy — United States.   4. Policy
sciences.   I. Title.
HV95.S37   1995
361.973 — dc20   94-37312

To Lillie Schram

Contents

Foreword

FRANCES FOX PIVEN

The essays that follow focus on the interpretations or meanings embedded in American poverty policies, and in the social science research that is linked to those policies. Sanford Schram thinks these interpretations, or "discursive practices," are at the very core of what policy and policy science are about, that our understandings of poverty are "constructed" by policy discourse. I want in this foreword to explain why I think Schram's approach is illuminating.

Let me first remind the reader of the contrast between Schram's "postmodern" approach and the dominant model of policy science, which treats poverty policies, like all policies, as scientifically informed interventions by government. Presumably the objective is to alter the taken-for-granted conditions named poverty, or dependency, or underclass culture. The means, or strategies, of intervention are ostensibly derived from scientific studies of empirical cause-and-effect relations that identify the sorts of interventions, usually in the form of economic incentives and disincentives, that can be expected to reduce poverty and the cultural deficiencies associated with poverty. In other words, the dominant model regards policy as the rational and scientifically based manipulation of specific aspects of the circumstances of the poor to achieve the articulated goal of reducing their poverty.

This model is transparently inadequate, if not entirely misleading. Consider the debacle called welfare reform that unfolds in Washington as I write these words. Presumably the reform proposals originate in the work of a policy team led by David Ellwood and Mary Jo Bane, brought to Washington by the Clinton administration as preeminent policy scientists with an extensive record of research and publication dealing with the ostensibly complex relations among welfare policy, poverty, and patterns of family formation. On the face of it, this should be an excellent example of rational and scientifically based policy making. By the standards of that model, however, the proposals are entirely bewildering.

The puzzle begins with the administration's trumpeting of the AFDC program as somehow a major and growing problem of American society. Why? It is in fact a relatively small program, however it is measured. Fewer than 5 million adults are on the rolls, and, until the recent recession, the number had not risen since the early 1970s. Measured as a proportion of the poor, or as a proportion of single-mother households, the numbers on the rolls have in fact shrunk. And program costs are modest, to say the least, amounting to about 1 percent of the federal budget.

Or consider the further claim that welfare is a problem because it encourages women to become "dependent" on government handouts, instead of earning their own way. In fact, the administration's own data show that three-quarters of the applicants for welfare remain on the rolls for less than two years (although they may reapply at some subsequent time when they again confront financial emergencies). And even while they are "dependent" on AFDC, many women continue to work, packaging income from welfare and wages for the simple reason that neither provides enough for survival, partly because both welfare benefit levels and wage levels have fallen dramatically over the past two decades.

Or what about the much-heard claim that welfare is a big problem because it encourages out-of-wedlock births, which in turn are said to lead to impoverished female-headed households, where children are more likely to become dropouts, delinquents, drug users, and eventually welfare dependents themselves? Out-of-wedlock births have indeed increased, but the increase has occurred in all strata of the society. True, there are proportionately more out-of-wedlock births among the poor, for the simple reason that there are fewer men in these communities who have the income or stability to be reasonable husbands. Welfare benefits cannot be the cause of this trend, because they have in fact fallen sharply, and so has the proportion of poor single mothers who receive benefits. Moreover, interstate comparisons suggest that higher AFDC benefit levels are associated with lower, not higher, recipient birthrates. Nor is there evidence that out-of-wedlock births are associated with the string of pathologies attributed to them when other conditions, such as poverty, are taken into account. Similarly, international comparisons do not show any correlation between the relative generosity of social benefits and the rate of out-of-wedlock births, or between out-of-wedlock births and such problems as delinquency. If anything, countries with more generous benefit systems report far lower rates of single-parent family formation than the United States, despite similarly rising rates of out-of-wedlock births. And finally, irony of ironies, some of the most-cited research demonstrating that welfare benefits in the United States have little to do with out-of-wedlock births was authored by the administration's own esteemed policy scientists, Ellwood and Bane.[1]

Or think how odd the "solutions" are if we hold to the model of policy making as the design of rational and scientifically based interventions to solve an articulated problem. The main solution is to force women into the labor market. The administration proposes to limit cash assistance to twenty-four to thirty months over a lifetime, so as to force women into the job market or, if that fails, into a state-run workfare program called WORK. But again, why? As Schram makes clear, the habit of policy scientists is to focus narrowly on selected variables to be manipulated by policy, ignoring most of what is going on in the world. If they were to lift their heads they would notice that the labor market is already saturated with people looking for jobs. Indeed, average unemployment levels have risen steadily for more than four decades, and the problem is worsening as the globalization of production, together with the reorganization of production in the mother countries, leads to the massive shedding of workers. Time limits will indeed push more poor women into the search for work, but the jobs they get will be jobs that other people will not get.

The policy scientists also claim that employment would not only overcome the habit of dependency, but lift people out of poverty. This also makes little sense, if we take the scientists at their word, for the reason that unskilled jobs pay even less than the welfare package of benefits and food stamps. The wages of nonsupervisory workers have been falling for more than two decades, and the wages of unskilled workers are falling fastest. In the 1960s, a minimum-wage worker with a full-time steady job could indeed earn enough to bring a family of three above the poverty line. In the 1980s, that same worker and her family fell $2,000 short of the poverty line. And more and more jobs are part-time and temporary, and without benefits. In fact, if the policy scientists turned policy planners have their way, they will flood the bottom of the labor market with women scrambling for work, exerting more downward pressure on wages and working conditions.

I could go on. Another oft-repeated claim is that welfare reform will reduce out-of-wedlock births and strengthen families. Aside from a proposal to require minor parents to live at home, which most now do in any case, it is difficult to see what cause-and-effect relationships explain how forcing poor mothers into the labor market (and doing nothing about unemployed men) will reduce out-of-wedlock births. As for strengthening families, the reverse would be more likely, as poor single mothers try to juggle work and child-care responsibilities without welfare supports. In a word, current efforts to "reform" welfare make no sense if they are scrutinized in the light of the dominant model of policy making as the scientifically based manipulation of variables to achieve an explicit goal or end state.

So, what is it all about? Schram thinks we need a different model to understand welfare policy and policy research. What we should attend to, he says, are the discursive practices of policy, which help to construct the very problems that are supposedly being mitigated. Drawing on the earlier and seminal work of Murray Edelman,[2] he proposes that the important and neglected dimension of welfare policy is symbolic, and the symbols or interpretations constructed by welfare policy discourse are transmitted both by words and arguments about policy and by welfare practices. Thus, we cannot understand welfare policy and policy science simply as interventions by government to alter objective conditions, by manipulating the balance of incentives and disincentives attached to work or welfare, for example. Rather, policy and policy science are about interpretation, and policy about the poor is about "reencoding 'the poor' as the marginal 'other.'"

This perspective seems to make immediate sense when we think of the ancient policies for dealing with the supplicant poor, including the lash, the brand, and other rituals of public humiliation. Or think of the nineteenth-century poor law system, with its elaborate arrangements for consigning the supplicant poor to hellholes called "houses of industry." But these Durkheimian rituals for reencoding the poor as the marginal other are not just a feature of the past. They also are at the heart of the contemporary welfare policy debate. Viewed as an effort to construct meanings, the administration's initiatives begin to make sense, albeit a grim and even cynical sort of sense. This is not so much an effort to do something about poverty or welfare as it is an effort to construct a national narrative about the nature of economic and social change in the United States. The administration has brought welfare to the center of the political stage in order to point to poor women, especially minority women, as the source of America's troubles. Welfare and the women who depend on it have been cast as the locus of a kind of moral rot, as the cause of changing gender and family norms (family breakdown, "illegitimate" births), for example, or of poverty and an eroding work ethic (dependency, work disincentives), or of crime, drug use, and so on.

The narrative ought to sound familiar. It is an only slightly updated version of the nineteenth-century view that poverty is the result of moral breakdown, and moral breakdown is encouraged by helping the poor. Crusaders looked about them, saw the vast misery and disorganization created by industrial conditions, and concluded that the problem was that a too-liberal charity was encouraging the immorality of the poor. "Scholars proclaimed in unison," Polanyi tells us, "that a science had been discovered which put the laws governing man's world beyond doubt."[3] It was at the behest of these "laws" that poor relief was restricted to the workhouse, and this policy then proclaimed as the solution to widespread misery. Today's reformers are following in lockstep.

The marginalization of the poor is accomplished in part through words about policy, especially the words of political leaders searching for easy ways to divert widespread public discontent over the shocks of economic decline and changing social mores. It matters that a David Duke, running for governor of Louisiana in a hatemongering campaign, fingers welfare recipients as somehow the main problem of the state; or that Ronald Reagan recites anecdotes about "welfare queens" and poor people who buy vodka with food stamps; or that Daniel Patrick Moynihan grandly proclaims to the press that whereas unemployment was the defining issue of preindustrial society, dependency is becoming the defining issue of postindustrial society. And it matters that Bill Clinton uses the platform of the presidency to explain that poverty is a problem of family values and individual irresponsibility.

For the most part, policy scientists have reinforced rather than countered these political definitions. To put the matter simply, research requires money, and the issues taken up by policy researchers are inevitably the issues for which funding is available. Bounded as they are by the exigencies of government and corporate financing, policy researchers in the area of welfare and poverty have largely constricted their research agenda to questions about the impact of welfare on work and family patterns. As an exercise in the construction of meaning, this narrowing of the inquiry is itself an amazing feat, for it manages to set to one side the massive changes that have occurred in the U.S. economy, in patterns of settlement, and in social mores. No matter what the empirical findings, the questions themselves underline the main political argument that somehow it is welfare that is linked to poverty and changing family patterns.

The marginalization of the poor is not just the result of words about policy. It is also the result of the policies themselves. Welfare policies and practices have meanings, and these meanings help to define and organize the social world. Thus, the intricately different programs divide people into intricately differentiated categories — the able-bodied unemployed, impoverished adults without children, poor single-parent families, the aged or disabled poor, the "insured" aged or disabled — helping to construct different identities and different interests. Then each of these program-constructed categories of people is dealt with differently: each program confers different rights on prospective beneficiaries, subjects them to different procedures for determining and maintaining eligibility, and each program provides beneficiaries with different levels of economic support.

Widely shared political understandings are generally thought to be an important influence in shaping policies. Thus, it is often said that emphasis on individual self-reliance in American political culture explains the meanness of our policies toward the poor. Schram's point of view turns this banality on its head, reversing the relationship between policy and political culture. Policy is no doubt to some extent shaped by widely held understandings, but it also helps to shape those understandings. By segregating the poor into different programs, U.S. welfare policy reinforces the separation of the poor from working- and middle-class Americans, and also creates divisions among the poor. Moreover, once separated by the programs, the poor are also more likely to be denigrated by the treatment accorded them. Benefits are less likely to be a matter of right and more likely to be discretionary, subject to the successful hurdling of bureaucratic inquisitions and runarounds and continuing bureaucratic surveillance, all of which shapes the understandings of both the people who endure this treatment and the people who in a sense are the public audience for it. Finally, and very important, recipients receive benefits that keep them very poor, ensuring their marginalization in an affluent and materialistic society.

In sum, welfare policy and practice are also a text, and their impact over time on political culture is large. By marginalizing and stigmatizing the poor, welfare policy constructs an explanation of economic misfortune that locates the blame in the victims of misfortune. And, of course, over time, the political culture shaped by welfare policy as text helps to pattern future welfare policies. It is this kind of symbolic politics that Sanford Schram helps us to understand. Never has it loomed larger, not only molding the lives of its marginalized and impoverished victims, but distorting the political culture of a nation that is audience to the dark drama.

Preface and Acknowledgments

This collection of essays represents the distillation of several years of work, several different approaches to research, and several locations for writing. Over the course of this intellectual, academic, and geographic journey, I have benefited greatly from the efforts of numerous people.

I had been writing about welfare and poverty for more than ten years when, in 1987, after finishing a year working on these issues at the Institute for Research on Poverty at the University of Wisconsin-Madison, my increasing frustration with both the entrenched nature of poverty in the United States and the narrow range of politically viable discourse on the subject led me to reconsider my approach to the topic. Something else very much related was at work as well. I had found that, at least in my own particular case, publishing work on these topics involved making a particular set of forced choices and accepting a special set of imposed constraints. The process of getting my work out to others almost always at least implicitly involved having to choose whether I was, for lack of better terms, a "critic" or a "scientist." Being both as much as neither did not help me with the editorial review process. Given that scientists are more valued than critics, I found myself often being asked to eliminate "political" considerations from my writing in order to publish statistical findings. On the other hand, more "critical" pieces often were subjected to treatment that involved eliminating specific statistical presentations on the grounds that they too could be subject to criticism. This sort of unreflective antiempiricism seemed to suggest a disinterest in getting involved in policy contests and a contentment with disengaged, abstract theorizing. These sorts of editing experiences highlighted the discursive constraints under which social scientists operate when trying to write about welfare and poverty. With successive articles being prepared for publication through such cleansing processes, I became more and more interested in writing about those discursive limits themselves and suggesting how social science can move beyond them in politically engaged ways. The result is this collection of essays.

Earlier versions of parts of chapters 3 and 4 appeared in *Rethinking Marxism*; chapter 5 is based on work I coauthored with Theresa Funiciello, which previously appeared in different form in *The Reconstruction of Family Policy*, Elaine A. Anderson and Richard C. Hula, editors; chapter 6 is based on an article that appeared originally in the *American Journal of Economics and Sociology*; chapter 7 was first published in slightly revised form in *Polity*; chapter 8 is based on an article that appeared originally in *Policy Sciences*; and a different version of Chapter 9 appeared in *Social Text*.

I started writing on these topics in the Adirondacks of northern New York in the congenial setting of Potsdam College of the State University of New York. I continued my work at Macalester College in St. Paul, Minnesota, which proved to be a most invigorating setting for sharing ideas. I finished the manuscript while on leave from Macalester and in residence at the La Follette Institute of Public Affairs at the University of Wisconsin-Madison, a very special place where scholars concerned about these issues can find supportive and informed people.

Throughout these efforts, I have had the pleasure of working with people from various backgrounds. Many were most willing to comment on my work even when in some instances they disagreed with much of what I had to say. Economists, policy analysts, political scientists, sociologists, literary theorists, and community activists—people with different political orientations and different approaches to understanding and attacking poverty—were willing to discuss criticism even when it was pointed in their direction. My experience in working on this book therefore has been reassuring even as I confronted the depressing reality of persistent poverty in the United States. Although my investigations forced me to confront pervasive theoretical and practical obstacles, the willingness of people to consider my criticisms proved that deliberate change was still possible. As much as we disagreed, I remain most appreciative of the time Michael Wiseman, Sheldon

Danziger, Robert Hauser, Robert Moffitt, Irv Garfinkel, Robert Haveman, and Larry Mead each took to discuss my project. Robert Moffitt also graciously supplied the data I report in chapter 9. Although I do not think I have convinced any of them to change the way they do business, I found their willingness to join the issue itself uplifting.

I have also benefited greatly from the responses of colleagues who have taken the time to read selected chapters or even the whole manuscript. In particular, I want to express my gratitude to the members of our writing group at Macalester College who have been so critical in helping me complete this project. This group of committed scholars has continued to challenge me intellectually. They are the best colleagues a scholar could hope for — serious, dedicated, willing to ask hard questions, and always supportive: Juanita Garciagodoy, Ruthann Godollei, Mahnaz Kousha, Cecilia Martinez, Michal McCall, Darrell Moore, Mary Romero, Geoff Sutton, Leslie Vaughan, and Joelle Vitiello. They were particularly helpful on chapters 3, 4, and 6. And the cookies were always fresh.

Lynn Appleton, Alan Draper, Ken Hoover, Joe Kling, Joe Peschek, Pru Posner, Brian Schmidt, Martha Schmidt, Anne Sisson Runyan, Todd Swanstrom, and Carl Swidorski read selected chapters. More than colleagues, these friends knew me well enough to point out habitual lapses in thought and writing. All continued to challenge me right to the very end to make good on my promise to demonstrate a self-reflective, politically engaged social science. Their efforts in this regard will be forever appreciated. I also thank Deborah Stone for commenting on chapters 7–9, especially because her own work has been so inspiring for me. Gordon Fisher generously provided a line-by-line review of chapter 5 and very helpfully offered an indepth history on the development of the poverty line.

Chuck Green, Michal McCall, Dan Spicer, and John Tambornino each read the entire manuscript, and each provided extensive commentary that greatly improved it. Without their suggestions this book would be a pale shadow of its present self. Their dedication to my project as well as the level of insight they brought to it was more than any scholar should ever expect from colleagues. I am also most glad that Chuck Green was willing to translate his handwriting in person, making it possible for me to get more of his insights than I could glean from his scrawl.

My coauthors on earlier works deserve mention as well. Gary Krueger, Phil Neisser, Mark Prus, Pat Turbett, Peg Schultz, and Dan Spicer collaborated with me on various investigations related to chapters 8 and 9. Gary Krueger's efforts were particularly influential concerning statistical issues.

Gary is an excellent econometrician, a wonderful teacher, and a good friend. I learned much from our work together, and I am sure glad that Gary got a blackboard for his office, so we did not have to go down the hall each time he wanted to demonstrate another econometric principle. Paul Wilken and Pat Turbett coauthored articles that I relied upon for chapter 6. Although lacking a handy blackboard, these two methodologists also proved most capable in analyzing statistical data on welfare and poverty. My collaboration with Phil Neisser provided an opportunity for me to benefit from his close reading and keen understanding of literature related to family discourse. Dorothy Dodge and I jointly studied the food shelves of the Twin Cities and prepared several reports on them. I rely on some of our findings for my discussion of the political economy of food shelves in chapter 4. Dorothy's tireless efforts on behalf of the shelves has served as a model for how to combine social science and politics. Theresa Funiciello was my coauthor on two articles that served as the basis for part of chapter 5. Table 5.1 in that chapter, which costs out the buying power of the welfare grant in New York State, was originally Theresa's idea. Most often during long-distance telephone calls and through the mail, Theresa and I have worked to challenge and support each other in our research. She continues to be an inspiration to me, even if I almost never get to see her anymore.

Frances Fox Piven, who read the entire manuscript, and Murray Edelman, who read selected chapters, both have gone beyond offering helpful suggestions. Both have served as models for me in my work. Each has produced a body of scholarship that in its own way demonstrates what a politically engaged social science of poverty can be. Three other political scientists, again each in his own way, inspired me — John Gunnell, Joseph Zimmerman, and Michael Shapiro: Joe as a mentor who since my graduate school days has continued to educate me about the intergovernmental complexities of social policy; Jack also as a mentor from those early days who has continuously helped me think seriously about the academic character of contemporary theory and the issues involved in trying to relate philosophy to politics and theory to practice; and Michael, who commented on all of the chapters in this book, as a writer whose elegantly crafted works inspire the possibility of interrogation as a discourse. Another source of inspiration has been Lisa Freeman, director of the University of Minnesota Press. She has continued to convince me that an alternative social science of poverty is worth demonstrating. She had the vision and the ability to help make it happen. Pat Gonzales, Todd Orjala, and Laura Westlund, also at the Press, ably assisted in the production of the manuscript, and Judy Selhorst helped in the editing.

Closer to home, colleagues in political science — Bruce Baum and Ahmed Samatar at Macalester and Maria Cancian, Don Culverson, Dennis Dresang, Peter Eisinger, Karl Kronebusch, and Joe Soss at Wisconsin — have gone well beyond commenting on my writing to challenging me in numerous stimulating discussions about the issues I have raised. Don in particular forced me to rethink many of my arguments with his in-depth knowledge and keen insights about the issues of race, poverty, and social science. His intellectual performances have continually helped refine my own thinking, and his friendship has been a tremendous source of support. Don more than anyone else encouraged me to pursue the line of argumentation I have chosen for these essays. He also suggested numerous ways to strengthen the argument. Other Macalester colleagues — Anna Meigs, Jeff Nash, Peter Rachleff, and particularly Norm Rosenberg — also proved to be a constant source of intellectual stimulation. My gratitude to all these people greatly exceeds the frustration they caused me by getting me to think seriously about what I was doing.

A major wellspring of inspiration, stimulation, and challenge has come from students at both Macalester and the University of Wisconsin-Madison. On numerous occasions we have exchanged ideas on topics covered in this volume. If I ever needed to be convinced about the critical relationship between teaching and research, my welfare seminar has done that many times over. In particular, I want to express my appreciation to Amy Hanauer, Kristin Kelly, and Judy Olmanson for the provocative discussions we had individually and collectively regarding numerous issues addressed in this book. Nicole Lindstrom, Sisonke Msimang, Chad Stegman, and Zeke Shortes performed admirably in assisting me in my research efforts. I also want to express my deep appreciation to Jean Beccone and Jeanne Stevens, librarians at Macalester College, for their assistance in providing data and other source material.

Even closer to home (as we most often know it), my son Ryan has proven to be a constant source of intellectual stimulation and a fount for ideas concerning this manuscript. It may sound despiriting that a teenager might actually enjoy discussing these issues; it also may sound a bit boastful for me to suggest that my son actually contributed to a scholarly volume. Yet, a teenager he is in many wonderful ways; and as to the value of the manuscript, that will have to be determined by others. Contribute, however, he did — especially by recommending critical changes in the introduction. Over the past year, it has been great fun for us to spend hours discussing shared readings on postmodernism, and I am glad the manuscript has provided us this opportunity to learn together. My younger son, Jonathan, has been his own kind of inspiration, delighting me with his playfulness just about whenever I needed a break from the drudgeries of writing. His role is no less significant, if different.

Joan Schram, more than anyone else, however, has made this manuscript possible. Life partners, we have shared much together, especially our concern about the well-being of children. A dedicated and caring Head Start teacher, Joan continually provides me with evidence about the "real" world—a place social scientists need to visit with greater frequency. Once there, I can only hope they will find as much support as I have found in writing this book. If that is the case, then the prospects for a more politically efficacious social science will be bright.

Introduction

Wisely or not, a special social science subject labeled policy analysis attends
to the needs of functionaries, not of citizens.
Charles E. Lindblom, *Inquiry and Change*

The capture of the social science agenda by government combined with the
capture of poverty research by economists to confine the scope of debate
within market models of human obligation and interaction. For all its
emphasis on innovation, poverty research remained preoccupied by the
oldest question in the history of social welfare. For more than two
centuries, critics, reformers, and administrators all have asked: Does social
welfare leave the poor less willing to work? Although the economists who
dominated poverty research disagreed on answers, they asked the same
questions. Rarely did they examine their assumptions about the role of
market incentives on human behavior or the limits of market models as the
basis for public social obligations. In the process, they either ignored or
belittled the few alternative frames proposed.
Michael B. Katz, *The Undeserving Poor*

Three themes inform this text. First, welfare policy research is insufficiently
attentive to how it is implicated in perpetuating the problems of welfare
and poverty.[1] Even when allowing challenges to the factual basis of social

policies, the discursive practices of welfare policy research help reproduce the ideological premises of such policies. Very frequently written in what I call an economistic-therapeutic-managerial discourse, much of welfare policy research is reduced to providing the state with technical information on how to regulate the behavior of persons living in poverty. Inattentiveness to the political implications of these discursive constraints serves only to reinforce the myth of autonomous social science.[2]

Second, my concerns about discourse are not limited to literary exercises about "how to do things with texts."[3] Instead, interrogating discourse provides a way to challenge structures of power that constrain what is politically possible. I believe that highlighting the ways in which discourse helps construct what is taken to be real, natural, and true creates resources for working toward alternative arrangements.[4] Such a perspective allows for questioning how welfare policy discourse helps construct the ostensibly pregiven problems it is supposed to address.[5] Welfare policy has therefore not only material consequences in terms of the benefits it supplies.[6] It also has symbolic consequences in reinforcing prevailing understandings of "the poor," "welfare dependency," "dysfunctional families," and so on. In fact, attention to discourse helps show how the symbolic and the material are interrelated, as in a welfare policy that provides inadequate benefits under demeaning circumstances to a denigrated subpopulation.[7]

Third, a self-reflective social science of poverty interrogates the political character of social scientific information not so as to create political paralysis, but instead to use such information to promote political change. Both the false objectivity of scientism and the refusal to utilize empirical information are insufficient bases for a politically efficacious social science of poverty. Yet if the social science of poverty is going to be politically effective, it is going to have to address how it is already implicated in politics.

Politics: The Stigma of Social Science

Charles Lindblom suggests that policy analysis has come to serve the needs of the state at the expense of citizens.[8] Michael Katz tells us that at least in the case of welfare, this is no accident, for policymakers in the 1960s consciously sought to encourage research by economists who could help them understand poverty in ways that would enable them to manage it better.[9]

Within the institutional setting of the university and allied research centers (such as the Institute for Research on Poverty at the University of Wisconsin-Madison and independent organizations like the Urban Institute in

Washington, D.C., and the Manpower Demonstration Research Corporation in New York City), poverty research over the past three decades has become a discourse in need of interrogation.[10] Most often done by social scientists, largely economists, who wanted to use social science data analysis
techniques to shed a helpful light on the problems of poverty and welfare,
this research frequently expressed an unexamined acceptance of the relevance of economic assumptions to its chosen topics. Although done in the
name of increasing knowledge that could help solve problems, such research also often assumed the prevailing behavioral bias of contemporary
social science, that focusing on the behavior of the poor was the key to
solving those problems.[11] Invoking the discursive practices of science, especially social science and most especially economics,[12] such research left
unexamined its bias of conducting research from a tacit managerial perspective. This bias assumed that such studies were unproblematically done
to empower state managers and policy makers to manage better the poverty/
welfare problem.[13]

Questions abound: Is welfare taking best understood as a decision regarding the "labor/leisure" trade-off as specified in "human capital" theories of behavior? Can such decisions be modeled in econometrically tested
data? Are additional factors that might complicate this equation accounted
for in such models? Does explaining welfare taking according to such a
discourse prove helpful in trying to ameliorate poverty?

In 1983, Robert Moffitt published an article titled "An Economic Model
of Welfare Stigma."[14] Liberal in his intentions, scientific in his idiom, scrupu-
lously meticulous in his use of data, Moffitt sought to question whether
there was a "stigma" associated with welfare taking. The "disutility of participation" was operationalized in the data. In the process, Moffitt put a
coefficient estimate on the effects of stigma in deterring welfare taking. In
what was to become just another inventive move among many for Moffitt,
econometrics extended the range of welfare-related phenomena that could
be explained by the paradigm of economic rationality.

Moffitt's article is a paradigmatic case of what is good and bad about
the social science of poverty.[15] This research, like many other major studies
in this field, has frequently been tied to federal funding and was designed
to further the government's attempts to understand poverty and welfare so
that it can manage them better.[16] Today, the ties between research and antipoverty policy making are fused in the Clinton administration, where the
top advisers for welfare reform are the Harvard University poverty researchers David Ellwood and Mary Jo Bane. Their studies on the period of

time people receive public assistance and the effects of welfare on family structure and living arrangements have been translated into key concerns of welfare reform in recent years: imposing time limits for receiving public assistance and changing policy to discourage teen mothers from living independently.[17] The Clinton administration's attempts to reform welfare grow out of their empirical research, as well as the work of others, and are therefore inextricably tied to the structural constraints of welfare poverty research as it has evolved in the academy, under government funding and written with the exclusionary practices of an economistic-therapeutic-managerial discourse. The state structures welfare policy research and welfare policy research reinforces the state. Welfare reform cannot help but then perpetuate the established orientation of trying to change people's behavior so that they will be more willing to respond to the right incentives, forgo being dependent on the state, and thereby ease managerial anxiety about welfare burdens.

The ascent of Ellwood and Bane to positions of influence in the Clinton administration suggests that it is empirical work that authorizes people as experts, and knowing about such things as how long people are on welfare becomes the basis for authorizing judgments about who should receive assistance and under what conditions.[18] It is arguably Ellwood and Bane's empirical research more so than Ellwood's policy prescriptions in his book *Poor Support* or Bane's experience as commissioner of social services in New York State that first brought them to the attention of policy makers as authorities on welfare reform.[19] Welfare policy discourse is today driven by empirical questions about state-centered concerns regarding what incentives at what costs will get persons living in poverty to behave in certain ways.[20] Less important are broader normative questions about welfare policy.

A troubling chiasmus has emerged: the social science of poverty reflects the poverty of social science. The social science of poverty is impoverished in its ability to provide structural or even poststructural critique of the current state of affairs. Therefore, even if it were the case, as it almost surely is, that most poverty analysts are liberal by political persuasion, Democratic by party affiliation, and desirous of ensuring their research can provide a factual basis for welfare policy, the social science of poverty is conducted in ways that greatly constrain its ability to be a source for alternative policy approaches.[21] The net result is that existing welfare policy, with all its limitations, is affirmed in general even as it is challenged in the specific.

Take the recent study by Philip Robins and Paul Fronstin on the increasingly popular idea circulating among states of discouraging mothers on welfare from having additional children.[22] Their timely piece of research shows that reforms enacted in states such as New Jersey that deny additional benefits for each child born while the mother is on welfare are not based in fact. Although Robins and Fronstin did find a correlation between the basic benefit level and the family size decisions of whites, Hispanics, and high school dropouts, they found no correlation between increments in additional benefits and the probability of having an additional child. They, however, frame their analysis in the prevailing discourse of poverty research and limit their conclusions to suggestions about programmatic efforts to get single mothers to complete high school. Liberal policy research that pokes holes in the shibboleths that inform welfare policy results in the reinscription of a behavioral orientation that focuses on changing the behavior of the poor as the primary way to overcome poverty.

The economistic-therapeutic-managerial discourse of welfare policy research paves the way for analysts like Charles Murray, who, in his highly popular Reagan-era tract *Losing Ground,* could narrate the lives of his hypothetical couple, Harold and Phyllis, as self-interested, income-maximizing individuals who decide whether to stay together or separate, go on welfare or take work, strictly in terms of a calculus that parallels the economist's labor/leisure trade-off.[23] Lost is attention to the broader structural context, and forgotten is the possibility that without changing culture and economics, how value is created and allocated, poverty will persist.

What are the consequences of studying poverty and welfare in terms of such a discourse? What gets left out and what gets insinuated into poverty research done in these terms? I want to suggest that the answer to both is politics. Explicit attempts to be political are discouraged at the same time that poverty research gets conducted in a depoliticizing way that fails to question how it is implicated in existing political arrangements. Scientists claim not to "do" politics, even if they are trying to be politically relevant and even if there are political implications to the discursive practices they invoke. Yet, if they do not attend to the politics of how they conduct their policy science, who will?

Discource and Structure

This, then, is not strictly a question of discourse per se. Poverty research as a special field of applied social science exists because it was created to serve state managers and existing political-economic arrangements.[24] From government grants and contracts to a political realism that reinforces the need to impress those in power, the discursive practices of poverty research anticipate the prevailing structures of society writ large. Research gets written in ways that reinforce that structural context. Welfare policy discourse in turn promotes exclusionary practices in poverty research. Seeking to inform a policy discourse that limits alternatives serves only to impoverish the social science of poverty. Policies that are implicated in the perpetuation of poverty come to impoverish poverty research. Poverty research comes to reinforce poverty.

Helen Longino has sought to deflate the myth of autonomous, objective science by suggesting that science is always constructed out of values internal to any specific field of scientific endeavor, such as standards of method and evidence (i.e., constitutive values) and values external to that science associated with the broader cultural context (i.e., contextual values).[25] Similarly, I want to suggest that the microdiscourse of the social science of poverty is influenced by the macrodiscourse of the broader society.[26] No more autonomous than any other discipline, poverty research discourse is no pure unalloyed good, but instead is infiltrated by the prevailing discursive structures of the broader society, all the more so as poverty research strains to achieve policy relevance. This problem interests me as more than a way of debunking the alleged autonomy of social science or as a means for highlighting how power operates in the exclusionary practices of scientific discourse. It opens the possibility for promoting a postmodern, poststructural, postpositivistic poverty research retrofitted for the postindustrial era.

Postmodern Policy Analysis

As disputes about the term recede, it is possible to see postmodernism as a cultural sensibility that is increasingly incorporated into popular and academic thought.[27] This sensibility takes many forms, but in common is the appreciation that reality as we know it is socially constructed and discursively constituted—that is, that there is a politics to how we go about making sense of the world and the ways in which we communicate our understandings to others.[28] This postmodern sensibility stresses perspectivism. In other words, we always understand things from a partial (in the senses of both incomplete and biased) perspective. This particular perspective also stresses textual mediation, which suggests that our understandings of the world are always mediated through texts and that we need to be attentive to how discursive practices help constitute the partial perspectives we rely on for making sense of the world. The preferred technique for doing this, called *deconstruction,* involves pointing out how any text must necessarily invoke various discursive practices without which its coherent character would collapse. To deconstruct a text is not to repudiate it, for all texts, if we read them closely enough, deconstruct themselves.[29] Yet deconstruction has allowed investigators to highlight the constitutive practices of any texts, to make these moves visible, and to interrogate them.

Postmodernism includes a poststructural orientation that encourages the dematerialization of structures into discursive practices.[30] This poststructural perspective denies structures their materiality as real entities that can be experienced independent of discourse. This refusal to accept the autonomy of material structures is why Michel Foucault concentrated his energies on what he called "genealogy" or "eventualization"—the practice of showing how discursive practices make it possible for some things and not others to happen.[31] Dematerializing structures involves interrogating them as prevailing systems of interpretation. These stabilized structures of interpretation serve as the basis for structuring the activities of daily life, which in turn cycle back and reproduce these stabilized structures of interpretation, be they the social structure, the economy, the state, or whatever. From this perspective, value gets created when discursive structures are stabilized sufficiently to serve as the basis for enabling people to value some identities and interests over others. Identities emerge out of textually constructed differences. Preferring one identity over others converts difference into "otherness." Preferring other distinctions marginalizes a host of other interests, things, places, and so on.

The oft-quoted postmodern maxim "Il n'y a pas de hors-texte" (There is no outside-the-text) is, however, no excuse for ignoring the broader social context, including culture, institutions, and markets.[32] Instead, it is to suggest that there is no "inside-the-text" either; that is, there is no realm of autonomous textuality. Discourse versus structure, text versus institutions, and the like become falsified binaries. Attention to how structure and institutions help impart meaning is a necessary part of the deconstructive enterprise.[33] Such exercises provide a means for challenging value-allocating interpretive structures. Yet this is only the initial move in the politicization of the material world—that is, an important first step in highlighting the discursive structures that make it possible for things to happen the way they do. Getting people to resist the structural insistences of prevailing discourses is, however, no simple second act. Discursive politics may start with dematerialization; however, mobilizing enough people to destabilize the reproduction of embedded structures entails moving beyond reinterpretation.

Articulating alliances and building coalitions involve taking structures, even if they are discursively constituted, seriously. A politically directed social science of poverty therefore necessarily interrogates prevailing discourse, but treats it as structure firmly enmeshed in the reproduction of daily life of researchers and citizens alike. Another false dichotomy that finds its legitimation in a pragmatic orientation geared for achieving political efficacy, "discursive/material," like its cousin "symbolic/substantive," has its uses.

Not so much rejecting as deconstructing positivistic approaches to policy analysis, postmodern policy analysis involves highlighting how policy analytic work is implicated in its own representations of reality. Postmodern policy analysis is therefore not so much "antipositivistic" as it is "postpositivistic." A postpositivistic orientation to policy analysis rejects the artificial distinctions that have plagued policy analysis, such as between theoretical and empirical, objective and subjective, interpretive and scientific work. It recognizes that the "assumptions which provide epistemological warrant for empirical policy analysis are highly contentious" and that "empirical policy analysis masks ... the valuative dimensions of its own technical discourse."[34] From this perspective, policy analysis is at best insufficient and at worst seriously misleading if it fails to examine the presuppositional basis for what are taken to be "the facts" of any policy. As an alternative, postmodern analysis examines how policy is itself constitutive of the reality against which it is directed. Postmodern policy analysis, therefore, may be defined as those approaches to examining policy that emphasize how the initiation, contestation, adoption, implementation, and evaluation of any policy are shaped in good part by the discursive, narrative, symbolic, and other socially constructed practices that structure our understanding of that policy, the ostensible problems to be attacked, the methods of treatment, the criteria for success, and so on.

The value of a policy analysis such as the one I have just characterized is better appreciated when policy is seen from a critical viewpoint as not just a response to preexisting problems, but something that is central to their formulation. Modernist perspectives assume the materialist base of society as given. The discursive practices in which state actors are implicated are not taken to be critical constitutive factors that go into helping bring about and reproduce that material reality. This perspective maintains, for instance, that poverty is a preexisting problem. The decline of the two-parent family, for example, is from the dominant liberal perspective a relatively autonomous reality not dependent on the actions of the state for its trajectory from a once marginally troubling development to the now quickly accelerating crisis in the social fabric of postindustrial society. The dominant liberal perspective allows for an indictment of existing public policy on the grounds that it fails to address the material or structural sources of the problem being attacked. Conservatives stress how welfare as a material benefit is implicated in the problem. Yet such a perspective fails to address the extent to which the discursive practices involved in the analysis and making of public policy are themselves contributing factors helping to constitute the reality being addressed. Modernist perspectives do offer critical possibilities for showing, for instance, how welfare policy is a form of denial, in the sense that it defers recognition of how the problems of poor families today are intimately connected to the structural shifts implicit in the postindustrial transition under way in the United States. Such perspectives, however, fail to highlight how welfare policy is a form of denial in another sense, in that it denies how the state's discursive practices are themselves critically involved in helping to constitute and reproduce the very problems those policies ostensibly are designed to attack.[35] Denial here could be understood psychoanalytically, politically, and in a variety of other ways. Yet the most important for my purposes is an understanding of denial as the result of discursive practices that repress their role in helping reproduce arbitrary distinctions of identity and otherness that work to marginalize some people and disadvantage them in their attempts to gain access to resources. "Self-sufficiency" versus "dependency" and other dichotomies are ratified in a contemporary welfare policy discourse that reinforces institutionalized practices that work against those who are considered "dependent" or in some other way undeserving.[36] Attentiveness to the political implications of these discursive practices is critical if we are to understand how politics, welfare policy discourse, and poverty research are intimately tied together.

A Policy Hybrid: Neither Pseudo nor Cynical

Disciplinary discourses operating within broader discursively constituted cultural, social, economic, and political structures help establish what can and cannot be said about a topic such as poverty. Examining the discursive constraints operating on poverty research provides ways not just of questioning the limitations of such work but also of offering a more politically efficacious social science. This is not done in ignorance of the pitfalls of similar moves by either the critical-minded or the empirically oriented. A politically self-conscious social science of poverty must attend to a wide variety of issues, all of which involve examining the political implications of research: theoretical perspective, methodology, the issue of who gets to say what about whom, the question of audience, and discourse. This is not an antiscientific approach, but one that suggests that being scientific means critically examining the constitutive practices of that scientific work and recognizing their political implications. Attempting to achieve a more robust conception of objectivity, such work strives to account for the value-laden character of ostensibly factual research.

In the chapters that follow, I seek to illustrate how the hybrid of a more politicized empiricism not only makes for a better social science, but also provides a way for social scientific work to engage politics more effectively.[37] Such a social science, in my mind, must necessarily try to negotiate the not-always-clear path between scientism and politicization.[38] A politically efficacious social science is neither pseudo(science) nor cynical (politics).[39] While rejecting chimerical social science, with its pretensions of objectivity and apolitical impartiality, politically engaged social science would avoid the cynical and censorious attitude that all social scientific work must be subject to political manipulation if it is to be politically efficacious. The essays that follow are in service of a social science of poverty that is neither pseudo nor cynical.

~

Interrogations

CHAPTER ONE

Suffer in Silence: The Subtext of Social Policy Research

"Differences between liberal and conservative researchers were not as significant as their shared preoccupation with the perverse effects of relief. To be sure, liberal researchers demonstrated that conservative charges were overblown, and their remedies extreme. But liberals and conservatives could readily agree that poor relief generated "dependency," and that funnelling women into the labor force was the remedy.... The result ... is that ... much of the literature on relief—whether the arid moralisms and pieties of nineteenth-century writers or the ostensible "value-neutral" analyses of twentieth-century professionals and technicians—merely serves to obscure the central role of relief agencies in the regulation of marginal labor and in the maintenance of civil order.
Frances Fox Piven and Richard A. Cloward, *Regulating the Poor*

By the 1990s, the social science of poverty was caught up in the growing obsession with "welfare dependency" and its alleged deleterious effects on work and family.[1] Welfare policy research did not stand outside the political debate; instead, it was consumed by it. Reading its agenda off the preoccupations of policy makers, it was relegated to providing technical advice on fine-tuning existing policy.[2] Laurence Lynn Jr. has written:

Policy analysts now serve a highly constrained and expedient status quo. If problems have solutions requiring a challenge to entrenched interests and significant new resources, they will reach the decision agenda only in symbolic form. Policy analysts have become the technicians of political compromise.... Thus many policy analysts have been coopted into the symbolic treatment of poverty by the sponsors and clients of their work.[3]

In what follows, I demonstrate the politically questionable character of the connection between welfare policy research and welfare policy making. Contemporary welfare policy research is created by the government and has come to be written in a discourse that reinforces state interests about how to understand "the poor." The structural connection has been reproduced in the discursive practices of welfare policy researchers. Reports on welfare policy research are written in an economistic-therapeutic-managerial discourse (ETM) that imputes to the poor the identity of self-interested, utility-maximizing individuals who need to be given the right incentives so that they will change their behavior and enable the state to manage better the problems of poverty and welfare dependency.[4] This discourse concentrates almost exclusively on disembodied information on individual behavior as the primary way to isolate the causes of poverty and develop solutions.[5]

Welfare policy researchers often frame research and interpret data in ways that do not account for these biases. Examination of bias is most often limited to technical matters regarding rational models of behavior and decision making.[6] Left unexamined are how the external contextual values of society as well as the internal constitutive values of the discipline together work to undermine the field's autonomy and bias its efforts.[7] And because such research is often written in the objectivistic language of science, it is open to appropriation by others. Welfare policy research masquerades as neutral and autonomous data-confirmed knowledge, only to remain impotent when appropriated. Welfare policy research, like research in other disciplines, fails to conform to the myth of autonomous science. Prominent examples from the field offer reasons for challenging how ETM undermines the political autonomy of welfare policy research and reinforces its subordination to the late-modern welfare state.

The Late-Modernity of Welfare Policy Research

The late-modern welfare state is the primary repository for the disciplinary practices of the modern age. Modernity is an age ordered according to social norms and institutions that are derived from a particular dilemma: the emancipation of the individual from tradition and other forms of conventional authority re-creates pressures for community.[8] Modernity's most influential thinkers have turned again and again to questions of the self as a site for resolving this dilemma, generating a preoccupation with promoting a self-regulating self—that is, an autonomous, rational, self-sufficient self who can be counted on to use her or his freedom to conform to the imperatives of society and contribute to its overall well-being.[9] Under these conditions, the state becomes preoccupied with what Michel Foucault calls the problem of governmentality—that is, with coordinating social exchanges among selves constituted so as to ensure the stability of the order.

Conformity to the ideal of a self-regulating self is contingent upon access to the means of realizing standards of individual competence implied in such an ideal. Yet, in late-modern deindustrializing America, the inability to conform and the pressure to do so intensify simultaneously, complicating the politics of the welfare state.[10] The politics of late-modernity are in no small part preoccupied with this postindustrial variant of modernity's initial dilemma. Given that this is a market-centered society—where value is preeminently market value, and where worth, including self-worth, is most significantly determined in economic terms—pressures build to prove that one is not just autonomous and rational but also economically self-sufficient and productive.[11] The politics of late-modernity are therefore centrally concerned with evaluating which selves qualify as valuable members of the economic order and what the state should do in response. Welfare politics is therefore a paradigmatic politics of the late-modern state.

The late-modern welfare state can be said to be a set of managerial practices designed to reform poor persons therapeutically so that they will respond to the right economic incentives.[12] Welfare policy research in the dominant mode, not surprisingly, is fashioned out of a discourse tied to the needs of that state. Much of welfare policy research employs econometric analysis to inform those with policy-making and managerial responsibilities about how to change poor people's behavior to make it more economically productive.[13] This field has sought to promote an ostensibly autonomous and objective social science that can "speak truth to power" on matters regarding poverty and welfare. Yet the ability of researchers working in this mode to influence policy is very much contingent upon the extent to which their work is consonant with the prevailing assumptions among state actors about welfare and poverty.

In the Name of the State: Welfare Policy Discourse

Liberals and conservatives continue to debate "welfare dependency," but noticeably without attention to their shared discursive practices.[14] Yet it is these discursive practices that hold much of the politics of welfare policy research. On the surface, the research reflects the best available ideas, models, and explanations of poverty problems, backed up by the best available quantitative data.[15] Although such research has the potential to make it harder for unsubstantiated myths and shibboleths to serve as the basis of welfare policy,[16] the spate of state actions in the late 1980s and early 1990s regulating the sexual, marital, parental, and work habits of welfare recipients suggests that this is by no means always the case.[17] Instead, welfare policy research has often been treated by policymakers as irrelevant to attempts to regulate the behavior of the poor.[18] When policymakers do take welfare policy research into account, it is largely limited to technical considerations related to fine-tuning existing programs.[19] Welfare policy research in the dominant mode is thus both politicized and depoliticized.

There is, then, a politics to welfare policy research. It is not, however, a politics in the conventional sense of liberals versus conservatives. It is instead a depoliticizing politics that reduces the problems of poverty and welfare dependency to the rational calculations of economically minded poor people who have been encouraged by the wrong incentives to engage in counterproductive behavioral pathologies, such as teenage pregnancy, out-of-marriage births, welfare dependency, drug abuse, and crime.[20] The discourse ensures that welfare policy researchers will be able to participate in contemporary welfare policy making, but only on the basis of a politically tendentious subtext. All the while aspiring to scientific impartiality, welfare policy research achieves political credibility not by its objectivity, but by its consistency with the prevailing biases of welfare policy discourse. Free from neither the biases of scientific social science nor the interests of the policy-making process itself, welfare policy research is autonomous in only the most relative sense of the term.[21]

The Relative Autonomy of Welfare Policy Research

The discursive constraints of welfare policy research suggest that the myth of autonomous and objective social science needs to be questioned.[22] Those whose research is legitimated in the policy-making process engage in an exclusive discourse that precludes a wide variety of perspectives and concerns.

For instance, I know of no research estimating the extent to which welfare taking is associated with attempts to escape abusive relationships.[23] Welfare policy discourse also requires that researchers forgo much of what they might like to say in order that they still be considered legitimate. This is the double bind of welfare policy research. On the one hand, as Bruno Latour has emphasized, it is in "doing science … that most new sources of power are generated."[24] On the other, science is most effective when it is a site for the production of knowledge/power that aligns itself with the political and economic arrangements of the "capital/state axis."[25] In an age that valorizes science, social science research has its role to play in promoting power practices. Contrary to the idea of social science as a realm of autonomous thinking that can critique and inform public policies, social science is thoroughly rooted in these relations in contradictory ways. Social science has its greatest impact when it is uncritically accepting of the discursive context already operating in society. Social science proves to be at its most policy efficacious when it reinforces the dominant biases that often serve as the backdrop for its own statistical interpretations. Adolph Reed Jr. captures this well:

> Policy professionals function in a world of shared norms, conventions and allegiances that can override other commitments; the community's belief structure also exalts this technicist mystique, i.e., the belief that careful search for consensually agreeable facts will produce consensus on policy. These circumstances overdetermine a tendency toward avoiding sharp criticisms of others' interpretations, as well as a tendency toward not venturing very far from the conventional wisdom or the common sense of the moment or what passes for it.[26]

On the surface, welfare policy research in the dominant mode appears to have achieved the status of an autonomous realm of applied knowledge. Scientific, with a legitimating base in economic and behavioral models, geared toward therapeutic intervention, directed at policy, and having achieved its own legitimacy and autonomy, welfare policy research appears to be the paragon of a politically engaged social science informed of a pragmatic spirit and dedicated to making change happen. Yet it is perhaps the overriding irony of welfare policy research that in practice it is all too rarely autonomous, if for no other reason than that its genesis is the state.[27]

The Genesis of Contemporary Welfare Policy Research

The ascendancy of ETM in welfare policy research is attributable in part to the dominance of economics in the social sciences. It is also in part attributable to prevailing understandings of science. Yet, another part of the story is found in the role the state played in creating welfare policy research as a field that could serve its purposes. Robert Haveman, a leader in both practicing and chronicling welfare policy research, notes that there was a moment in the 1960s when policy analysts could start to believe that "logic, data, and systematic thinking were to compete with, if not dominate, 'politics' in the making of public decisions."[28]

Yet Haveman has also emphasized how the relationship of poverty research to antipoverty policy was actually inverted — that is, public policy transformed social science, rather than the other way around. The Johnson administration's War on Poverty called for a new kind of social research geared to promoting the experimentation and innovation necessary for mounting new antipoverty initiatives. In the process, the study of poverty was taken over by a new group of social scientists who were willing to study controversial topics of culture, race, and poverty in terms consistent with the economic initiatives of the government in Washington. Michael Katz has written that "the angry protest following Daniel Patrick Moynihan's 1965 report, *The Negro Family: The Case for National Action,* helped bury both the culture of poverty and the black family as acceptable topics in liberal social science and to pass the leadership in poverty research to economists. Economists met the government's need for systematic data, predictive models, and program evaluation."[29] This dependent relationship helped produce a new field of academic study that entrenched an economistic-therapeutic-managerial discourse in poverty research. Haveman notes: "From its outset, the War on Poverty was conceived of as an economic war; the designs, the debates, and the evaluations were all conducted in economic terms. Economics was the central discipline in both the action and the research components of the war."[30] In the process, poverty became the property of economists, "a technical subject to be discussed only by experts."[31]

The innovations of welfare policy research, however, reinscribed age-old obsessions about the deleterious effects of welfare dependency, thereby forfeiting the ability to check the prejudices that served as the basis of so much social policy:

> By placing government policy on a scientific basis, poverty researchers
> hoped to transcend politics and ideology. In the end, although they won
> several battles, they lost even the intellectual war.... the capture of the
> social science agenda by government combined with the capture of poverty
> research by economists to confine the scope of debate within market
> models of human obligation and interaction. For all its emphasis on

innovation, poverty research remained preoccupied by the oldest question in the history of social welfare. For more than two centuries, critics, reformers, and administrators all have asked: Does social welfare leave the poor less willing to work? Although the economists who dominated poverty research disagreed on answers, they asked the same questions. Rarely did they examine their assumptions about the role of market incentives on human behavior or the limits of market models as the basis for public social obligations. In the process, they either ignored or belittled the few alternative frames proposed.[32]

Neutered Analysis For a Managerial State

There is more politics to the discourse of welfare policy research. Besides promoting an economistic-therapeutic-managerial orientation to understanding welfare and poverty, ETM engenders research that is easily open to political appropriation. The myth of autonomous social science helps promote research that aspires to be objective and neutral. This orientation actually undercuts its autonomous stance in two ways. First, researchers are discouraged from bringing a particular perspective to setting the research agenda. The agenda comes to be set by what topics are pressing in the policy-making process. The welfare policy researcher is relegated to the position of an underlaborer supplying research findings on predetermined topics such as "welfare dependency." Second, research findings on such topics are presented in the language of objective social science, leaving them open to appropriation by interpreters who use them for various political ends.

Reagan-era examples of appropriation took place with studies on the effects of "work incentives" in the main cash assistance program for the nonaged poor — Aid to Families with Dependent Children (AFDC). Since the late 1960s, states deducted the first $30 and the next one-third of earnings in redetermining eligibility of welfare recipients. The major studies found small effects on work.[33] Preferring to require work rather than to reward it, the Reagan administration used these findings in 1981 to justify limiting the earnings disregard to the first four months of taking welfare.[34] Incentives allegedly only encouraged welfare recipients to maximize their combination of welfare and earnings rather than to try to become self-sufficient strictly through employment. Yet this interpretation de-emphasized the role of the low-wage labor market in leaving recipients in limbo between welfare and full-time employment. Technical research on the effect of work incentives on earnings overlooked that with improved job prospects such incentives might promote more work. Studies on the Reagan changes also indicated no real effect on work effort.[35] This "no effect" consequence was touted as proof that the Reagan reforms were not draconian. The suggestion that the Reagan revision of the disregard did not affect work effort, however, overlooked the fact that many people continued to work as much as they did before they lost the disregard, because of their commitment to working, the pride derived from having a job, or just the dire need to retain the income they gained from employment. Appropriators instead chose to interpret technically neutral analyses to fit their preconceived politics.

A different sort of example is David Ellwood and Mary Jo Bane's 1984 federally funded study on the impact of AFDC on family structure and living arrangements. They found that

> welfare appears to have a dramatic impact on the living arrangements of young single mothers. In a low benefit state, young mothers who are not living with a husband are very likely to live in the home of a parent. In high benefit states, these women are much more likely to live independently....
>
> There is relatively strong evidence in our data that benefit levels influence divorce and separation rates to some degree. Among very young married mothers, the impact may be quite sizeable. Among most other women, the impact appears to be rather small....
>
> We found little evidence that AFDC influenced the child-bearing decisions of unmarried women, even young unmarried women....
>
> Differences in welfare do not appear to be the primary cause of variation in family structure across states, or over time.[36]

This ostensibly neutral research targeted "welfare dependency" as a problem, with welfare as the cause and family structure as the effect, rather than the other way around. The strongest findings, however, were on the least controversial matter: living arrangements.[37] Yet even this was framed as an issue of concern. Ellwood and Bane conclude "More research and attention needs to be focused on the desirability of encouraging young single mothers to remain at home or to establish independent households. Here is a place where policy really does make a difference."[38] By 1994, Ellwood and Bane were members of the Clinton administration, which responded to growing concerns about teen pregnancy by joining an increasing number of states in proposing restrictions on aid to teen mothers living independently.[39] No need for appropriators here; Ellwood and Bane could do that on their own, because their technical research was already co-opted, given its focus on addressing the state's preset interest in reducing "welfare dependency," without consideration of the broader political-economic context that was working to put poor families at greater risk.

Ellwood and Bane's most influential work, however, was subject to all kinds of appropriation. It suggested that large numbers of welfare recipients at any one point in time were in the midst of a long spell of welfare taking.[40] This research contradicted most analysts' belief at the time that people relied on welfare only episodically.[41] Although these statistics are very slippery, conservatives were quick to seize on them.[42] In the end, this research proved influential in forging a "new consensus" on welfare among policy makers that "welfare dependency" was a significant problem.[43]

The appropriators overlooked critical measurement issues that might have explained the new findings; instead, the results were attributed to improved research methods.[44] The methodological issues, however, highlight how the implied context structured the research design and interpretation of the results. For example, earlier studies stressed the frequency and length of welfare spells for the population over time, whereas the newer studies added consideration of statistics for the welfare population at any one point in time. Given that families who remain on welfare for short periods enter and leave the welfare system more rapidly, looking at the rolls at any one point in time would reveal a larger proportion of long-term recipients than would an examination of the rolls over time. Whereas Ellwood found that 65 percent of those on the rolls at any one point in time were in the process of receiving welfare for eight or more years, he also found that only about 30 percent of all families that ever received AFDC did so for eight or more years.[45] In terms of the total population, about one-seventh (15 percent) lived in families where AFDC income was received during at least one year between 1970 and 1979, but only 2.2 percent of individuals lived in families that received income from AFDC in eight or more years.[46] "In other words, looking at the rolls over a period of time shows a high degree of transiency, but looking at them at a point in time emphasizes persistent use."[47] When Ellwood emphasized the latter, he reflected an interest in "targeting" long-term users for special services, but whether long-term use was really a prevalent problem was more of an open question than the people who used Ellwood's research would allow.[48]

Another issue was whether people who "slipped" on and off welfare during a period of time should or be considered as having had continuous stays on welfare. Mark Greenberg has noted that "the often-misunderstood point . . . is that [Ellwood] did not seek to, and did not measure total time on AFDC; [he] only sought to measure years in which AFDC was received."[49] Therefore, although there might be honest differences about whether episodic multiple use of welfare implied long-term dependency, it was a serious mistake to suggest that Ellwood's research implied anything about the extent of continuous welfare use. More recent work shows a different picture than that painted by Ellwood's appropriators. Using monthly data from the National Longitudinal Survey of Youth (NLSY), LaDonna Pavetti found that a monthly analysis "produces a distribution with many more short spells of welfare [and] fewer long spells."[50] Pavetti adds that 70 percent of all recipients who begin a spell of welfare will have spells that last for two years or less; only 7 percent of recipients who begin a spell of welfare receipt will have a spell that will last for more than eight years. Comparisons with earlier studies indicate that monthly data reveal far greater transiency in the welfare population, and that yearly data overstate extended continuous use.

Further, additional research suggests that welfare use lags well behind eligibility. According to Rebecca Blank and Patricia Ruggles:

> Single mothers use AFDC in 62 to 70 percent of the months in which they are eligible, depending on the eligibility estimate used.... A substantial proportion of those leaving assistance programs appear to remain eligible to participate, but apparently choose not to do so. For AFDC, 50 percent of those leaving the program are still eligible at the time of exit, 30 percent are still eligible after 12 months.... Only 28 percent of those women who experience an eligibility spell will ever take up AFDC.... Most of these eligibility spells without take-up are very short spells. Twenty-three percent of them close within 1 month, another 21 percent of the remaining spells close within 2 months, another 13 percent of the remaining spells close within 3 months.... Despite the on-going preoccupation of many public officials with high AFDC and food stamp caseloads, these results indicate that only a minority of those who become eligible for these programs actually use them.[51]

Although extended use may exist to some extent, there are evidently numerous instances of nonuse as well.

Ellwood may have focused his research on trying to isolate the extended-use population so that they could be targeted for special services—a logical topic given policy makers' concern about "welfare dependency." And there is evidence from these studies that among AFDC recipients, single, especially never-married, mothers are much more likely to use welfare for extended, continuous periods of time.[52] Yet, although identifying this and related populations may very well have been Ellwood's intention, his efforts at targeting were misappropriated by commentators and policy makers to

feed the growing preoccupation with abuses associated with "welfare dependency." Ellwood's work, however, had created the seeds of its own mis-
use. Its alleged objectivity was in good part derived from the fact that it reflected the prevailing assumption that extended welfare use implied abuse
of the system of public assistance. Extended welfare use was an issue to be
quantified. In this context, the "length of stay" had meaning beyond time
in the arid moralisms of promoting "self-sufficiency." The mitigating factors
of labor markets and other circumstances were not a central component of
this implied perspective. Unexamined was the postindustrial economy,
with its declines in manual labor, decreases in wages, relocation of facto-
ries, and still other disruptions, which could have accounted for the longer
welfare stays found in the Ellwood studies.

Conservatives, however, were not content to let it rest at that. More ammunition for reinforcing a "new paternalism" in social policy was in hand.[53]
The use of welfare could now more firmly be interpreted as an abuse that
has to be unlearned. Extended welfare stays must imply something about
people's growing willingness to be dependent on assistance.[54] Even more
troubling, the use of this research did not stress that some recipients were
working while receiving welfare.[55] Instead, narrowly focused studies were
translated into definitive evidence of people forgoing work and abusing
welfare.

What is perhaps most troubling about this debate over the frequency
and duration of welfare "spells" is that none of the combatants, liberal or
conservative, considered welfare taking as anything other than some disembodied act that recipients choose to start and end as they see fit. Given
the ascendancy of ETM in welfare policy research, it is basically impossible
to suggest that welfare taking may often be a commendable attempt by
women in particular to cope with difficult domestic and economic circumstances. In downplaying the impact of social, economic, and administrative forces that push and pull recipients in and out of the welfare system,
such an approach may overlook several important causes of both extended
and episodic welfare taking. For example, about two million recipients annually are affected by the administrative practice known as "churning,"
whereby welfare agencies periodically drop recipients from the rolls incorrectly or for technical violations and then allow them to return after corrections have been made.[56] Thus, it may be that welfare recipients would
be on the rolls for longer spells than present research indicates but are not
for reasons other than the recipients' own choosing. If we discount churn-

ing, conservatives may be right that welfare taking persists for longer periods than much research suggests.

Yet, discounting churning is just what is wrong with the shared perspective of liberal and conservative analysts. Concentrating on producing neutral information on poor people's behavior, much research generates data that can be easily appropriated for various political ends. Neglecting to account for the broader political-economic context of this behavior, such research often overlooks how the current system of public assistance perpetrates its own deleterious practices at the expense of the people it ostensibly is designed to serve. Lacking pressure to account for that broader context, welfare research is free to become an experimental science.

The Politics of an Experimental Science

Haveman has stressed that one of the great achievements of public policy's transformation of social science in the 1960s was the subsidization of large-scale experiments to assess the effects of welfare on work, childbearing, and family formation among the poor.[57] Most noteworthy have been the guaranteed income experiments of the 1960s and 1970s and the workfare demonstrations of the 1980s.[58] Experimentation has more recently achieved an unprecedented role in the making of social policy. New federal rules on "waivers" for how states administer AFDC programs require experimental evaluation of these changes.[59] Most of these experiments involve behavioral inducements and penalties designed to get recipients to leave welfare, such as two-year time limitations for the receipt of welfare, rewards for getting married, penalties for having additional children while receiving public assistance, and denial of aid to teen mothers living independently.[60] Experimentation has arrived as an institutionalized part of welfare policy making.[61]

This undoubtedly has occurred, but what is significant about it may have more to do with legitimating the idea that people in poverty can be unconsenting subjects of government-sanctioned experiments. There is an insidious, if unintended, subtext to the rise of this new "social experimentation," though what I have in mind is hardly the conservative critique against "social engineering" as hopelessly idealistic and meddlesome. From the income maintenance experiments of the 1960s to the workfare demonstrations of the 1990s—that is, from liberal-minded experiments about a guaranteed income to conservative-minded programs requiring work for benefits—

welfare policy research has been implicated in a pernicious but pervasive logic: the poverty of poor people is a mysterious thing, attributable in good part to their individual behavior, worthy of being medicalized in terms of experimental interventions that are designed to test the viability of various schemes for changing their behavior. Policy makers might have a hard time justifying this sort of nonconsensual "experimentation" when providing benefits for the nonpoor; however, there is little political opposition to treating the poor as a special group for whom such experimentation is appropriate.[62]

Paralleling a long-standing American tradition that has assumed the propriety of experimenting on marginalized populations, especially poor persons of color, the idea of social welfare experiments reinforces attitudes concerning other more aggressive treatment of the poor, such as their use in the testing of new medicines and for the study of the effects of untreated sexually transmitted disease, and even forced sterilization.[63] Recent revelations about experiments by the U.S. Department of Energy examining the effects of radiation on unsuspecting low-income pregnant teenagers further underscore this tradition of assuming that persons in poverty are more readily available for nonconsensual experimentation.[64] Proposals concerning the mandatory use of contraceptive implants to reduce pregnancy among welfare recipients bring together social experimentation and more medicalized experiments on the poor.[65] Under such circumstances, even the best-intentioned social experimentation potentially reencodes "the poor" as the marginal "other." Experimentation, at the least, reinforces the idea that the goal of welfare policy research is to produce decontextualized information about the distinctive behavior of the poor so that the right mix of incentives and penalties can be introduced in order to get the impoverished to change their behavior. Experimentation is entirely consistent with ETM and the way it constructs the poor as deficient subjects of the welfare state.

The Underside of "Underclass"

The racially coded "underclass" is probably the most glaring example of how ETM encourages the production of disembodied information that has profound political implications. William Julius Wilson, Isabel Sawhill, and many others have offered statistical analyses of what they call they "underclass"—"a subgroup of the American population that engages in behaviors at a variance with those of mainstream populations," often indicated by such "dysfunctional" behaviors as dropping out of school, female heading of families with children, welfare "dependency," and adult male unemployment or underemployment.[66] Adolph Reed Jr. has noted: "Instead of clarifying or correcting the impressionistic generalities and simple-minded prejudices . . ., social scientists have legitimated them with an aura of scientific verity, surrounding them in an authenticating mist of quantification."[67]

In the quest to be politically relevant, welfare policy researchers have often accepted the idea that there is an "underclass," that is, a distinct group of poor people with behavioral deficiencies. In the quest to provide "useful" quantitative information, they often fail to examine sufficiently the political implications of the use of this term.[68] This is not a matter of how the word sounds in polite company; instead, it is an issue for how research gets framed and results get interpreted. The concept of an "underclass" encourages locating the causes of poverty in individual pathology.

Even when authors seek to explain "the underclass" in terms of societal racial prejudice, the discourse is unavoidably almost always one of pathology.[69] In *American Apartheid*, Douglas Massey and Nancy Denton marshal census tract data to reject William Julius Wilson's argument for declining racism. Yet their analysis also suggests that racism has helped produce an underclass concentrated in poor, African American neighborhoods. Even if racism is the primary cause, the underclass is afflicted with behavioral pathologies. Massey and Denton underscore how segregation has systematically worked to undermine social, educational, and economic opportunities for African Americans; however, like so many other analysts today, they resort to suggesting that segregation produces behavioral pathologies that must be discouraged. The study of the underclass may easily end up serving to rationalize state disciplinary practices, if for no other reason than that such research reinforces the idea that individual behavioral pathologies lie near, if not at, the heart of the problem of poverty today. Irrespective of what scholars such as Massey and Denton intend, the study of the underclass may easily end up serving to reinforce the idea that individual choices rather than constraining structures are the primary causes of contemporary poverty.[70] Lou Turner addresses this issue forthrightly:

> As much as they are at pains to critique the neoconservative "culture of poverty" arguments, Massey and Denton succumb to just such a tendency in their discussion of the "personal failings," "individual shortcomings," "normative" behavior and "oppositional culture" in the Black community. Their distortion of "being black" as a form of social deviance because of its oppositional nature represents a depoliticization of Black consciousness.[71]

Welfare Policy Research as Facts from Nowhere

More information, by itself, may not be better. More information, disembodied from the relevant structural context and expressed in a discourse that concentrates poverty in behavior, may mean more misguided regulation of the poor.[72] Imagine it the other way around, and the implications of producing decontextualized social scientific information about the poor become painfully apparent. As Alan Wolfe quotes Martin Nicolas:

> What if the machinery were reversed? What if the habits, problems, secrets and unconscious motivations of the wealthy and powerful were daily scrutinized by a thousand systematic researchers, were hourly pried into, analyzed and cross referenced, tabulated and published in a hundred inexpensive mass circulation journals and written so that even the fifteen-year-old high school drop-out could understand it and predict the actions of his landlord, manipulate and control him?[73]

The bulk of welfare policy research evaluates discrete empirical findings about individuals, devoid of consideration of contextual factors.[74] There is a lack of critical reflection about how such individualistic explanations reflect about political biases of ETM. Like a shell removed from the beach, an anthropological artifact in a museum, or the proverbial quotation out of context, the discrete data of welfare policy research are rarely interpreted in terms of the racial, gender, and class contexts of daily lived experience, but instead are disembodied facts superimposed on their subject matter. When the broader context is invoked, it is often still part of an equation for predicting individual behavior. For instance, Wilson hypothesizes in *The Truly Disadvantaged* that inner-city ghetto neighborhoods that are "overwhelmingly socially disadvantaged" produce "concentration effects" while losing their ability to act as a "social buffer" and thereby inculcate bad values and fail to discourage deleterious social attitudes and practices.[75] In response, studies soon began appearing that tested for "neighborhood effects" on work effort, family formation, welfare taking, criminal activity, and so on.[76] Rather than examining issues of community development, researchers had reduced these issues to just another variable for predicting behavior and fashioning better models for informing attempts to change those behaviors.

In spite of the best of intentions not to "blame the victim" or to individualize structural sources of poverty, liberal welfare policy research often necessarily is subordinated to the exclusionary practices of ETM. The implications are profoundly conservative, as liberals themselves have openly agonized.[77] The sources for this contradiction are the double bind of wel-fare policy research. Analysts who want their research to contribute to the diminishing of poverty and related problems must write in ways that con-form to the accepted rhetorical, analytic, and methodological standards of contemporary welfare policy research. Implicitly believing that science, ob-jectivity, and the dispassionate presentation of new factual information will in the end improve our collective ability to make things better, analysts to varying degrees accept the discursive constraints of welfare policy research.[78] Their hope is that more information, in whatever form, even if expressed in terms of common conceits about "the underclass," "broken families," and "marital instability," will help add to the efforts to "solve" the paradox of poverty in an affluent society. Liberals therefore continue to write in this way even if the information they produce reinforces the idea that indi-vidual behavior is a prime cause of poverty.

Yet conservatives find ETM most congenial for the stories they want to tell about the poor. In *Losing Ground,* Charles Murray presents his hypo-thetical couple, Harold and Phyllis, as self-interested income maximizers who make decisions about work and welfare according to a labor/leisure trade-off.[79] Although Murray uses this logic to suggest that welfare is more counterproductive and has more work disincentives than most liberal ana-lysts will accept,[80] his reading of welfare taking as a purely economic mat-ter, devoid of contextual considerations such as economic dislocation, the deterioration of inner-city neighborhoods, and abusive gender relation-ships, could not be more consistent with prevailing discourse. Murray's fit with ETM highlights how its subtext lends itself to a disciplinary welfare regime.

Until Another Discourse

Reflecting the concerns of the late-modern state, ETM encourages an un-derstanding of the poor as deficient, given their failure to conform to dom-inant opinion about what it means to be an autonomous, rational, self-sufficient member of society. Welfare policy research invoking this discourse helps reinscribe the poor as threats to societal order. Seeking to be politi-cally relevant, such work gets to be so only to the extent that it produces knowledge that is politically consonant with existing state-power relations. This dilemma encourages muted, neutered policy analyses that are prone to exploitation in a variety of ways, sometimes even contrary to the origi-nal purposes of such research.

Only when efforts are made to resist the exclusionary constraints of welfare policy discourse do we begin to get a glimmer of what a politically self-conscious welfare policy research might look like. The promotion of alternative discourses, with different understandings of "autonomy," "rationality," and "self-sufficiency," can initiate new avenues of research, including such understudied topics as the frequency with which women take welfare to escape abusive relationships at home and on the job. In another discourse, we can begin to examine the role that welfare taking plays not in promoting "dependency" but in serving as a source of individual and collective empowerment by those for whom society has left no other means to cope. Until then, the narratives articulated in terms of the prevailing discourse of welfare policy research will leave the poor to suffer in silence.

CHAPTER TWO

Discourses of Dependency

The Politics of Euphemisms

The notion that you change a situation by finding a newer and nicer word
for it emerges from the old American habit of euphemism, circumlocution
and desperate confusion about etiquette, produced by fear that the concrete
will give offense.
Robert Hughes, *Culture of Complaint*

Needs-talk appears as a site of struggle where groups with unequal
discursive (and nondiscursive) resources compete to establish as hegemonic
their respective interpretations of legitimate social needs. Dominant groups
articulate need interpretations intended to exclude, defuse, and/or coopt
counter interpretations. Subordinate or oppositional groups, on the other
hand, articulate need interpretations intended to challenge, displace, and/or
modify dominant ones. In neither case, are the interpretations simply
"representations." In both cases, rather, they are acts and interventions.
Nancy Fraser, *Unruly Practices*

The sounds of silence are several in poverty research. Whereas many
welfare policy analysts are constrained by economistic-therapeutic-managerial discourse, others find themselves silenced by a politics of euphemisms.
The latter suggests that if only the right words can be found, then political

names & things (Mutare vel.)

change will quickly follow. This is what happens when a good idea goes bad, when the interrogation of discourse collapses into the valorization of terminological distinctions.[1]

Recently, I attended a conference of social workers who were part of a network of agencies seeking to assist homeless youths. A state legislator addressed the group and at one point in the question-and-answer period commiserated with one professional about how the by then well-accepted phrase *children at risk* ought to be dropped, for it is pejorative. The legislator preferred *children under stress* as a more "politically correct" euphemism. Much discussion ensued regarding how to categorize clients so as to neither patronize nor marginalize them. No one, however, mentioned the reifying effects of all categorization, or how antiseptic language only exacerbates the problem by projecting young people in need onto one or another dehumanizing dimension of therapeutic discourse.[2] No one suggested that although isolated name changes may be a necessary part of political action, they are insufficient by themselves. No one emphasized the need for renamings that destabilize prevailing institutional practices.[3] Instead, a science of renaming seemed to displace a politics of interrogation. A fascination with correcting the terms of interpersonal communication had replaced an interest in the critique of structure. A comfort in dealing with discourse in the most narrow and literal sense had replaced an interest in the broader discursive structures that set the terms for reproducing organized daily life. I was left to question how discourse and structure need to be seen as connected before reflection about poverty can inform political action.[4]

The deconstruction of prevailing discursive structures helps politicize the institutionalized practices that inhibit alternative ways of constructing social relations.[5] Isolated acts of renaming, however, are unlikely to help promote political change if they are not tied to interrogations of the structures that serve as the interpretive context for making sense of new terms.[6] This is especially the case when renamings take the form of euphemisms designed to make what is described appear to be consonant with the existing order. In other words, the problems of a politics of renaming are not confined to the left, but are endemic to what amounts to a classic American practice utilized across the political spectrum.[7] *Homeless, welfare,* and *family planning* provide three examples of how isolated instances of renaming fail in their efforts to make a politics out of sanitizing language.

Reconsidering the Politics of Renaming

Renaming can do much to indicate respect and sympathy. It may strategically recast concerns so that they can be articulated in ways that are more appealing and less dismissive. Renaming the objects of political contestation may help promote the basis for articulating latent affinities among disparate political constituencies. The relentless march of renamings can help denaturalize and delegitimate ascendant categories and the constraints they place on political possibility. At the moment of fissure, destabilizing renamings have the potential to encourage reconsideration of how biases embedded in names are tied to power relations.[8] Yet isolated acts of renaming do not guarantee that audiences will be any more predisposed to treat things differently than they were before. The problem is not limited to the political reality that dominant groups possess greater resources for influencing discourse. Ascendant political economies, such as liberal postindustrial capitalism, whether understood structurally or discursively, operate as institutionalized systems of interpretation that can subvert the most earnest of renamings.[9]

It is just as dangerous to suggest that paid employment exhausts possibilities for achieving self-sufficiency as to suggest that political action can be meaningfully confined to isolated renamings.[10] Neither the workplace nor a name is the definitive venue for effectuating self-worth or political intervention.[11] Strategies that accept the prevailing work ethos will continue to marginalize those who cannot work, and increasingly so in a postindustrial economy that does not require nearly as large a workforce as its industrial predecessor. Exclusive preoccupation with sanitizing names overlooks the fact that names often do not matter to those who live out their lives according to the institutionalized narratives of the broader political economy, whether it is understood structurally or discursively, whether it is monolithically hegemonic or reproduced through allied, if disparate, practices. What is named is always encoded in some publicly accessible and ascendent discourse.[12] Getting the names right will not matter if the names are interpreted according to the institutionalized insistences of organized society.[13]

Only when those insistences are relaxed does there emerge the possibility for new names to restructure daily practices. Texts, as it now has become notoriously apparent, can be read in many ways, and they are most often read according to how prevailing discursive structures provide an interpretive context for reading them.[14] The meanings implied by new names of necessity overflow their categorizations, often to be reinterpreted in terms of available systems of intelligibility (most often tied to existing institutions). Whereas re-naming can maneuver change within the interstices of pervasive discursive structures, renaming is limited in reciprocal fashion. Strategies of contain-ment that seek to confine practice to sanitized categories appreciate the discursive character of social life, but insufficiently and wrongheadedly.

I do not mean to suggest that discourse is dependent on structure as much as that structures are hegemonic discourses. The operative structures reproduced through a multitude of daily practices and reinforced by the efforts of aligned groups may be nothing more than stabilized ascendent discourses.[15] Structure is the alibi for discourse. We need to destabilize this prevailing interpretive context and the power plays that reinforce it, rather than hope that isolated acts of linguistic sanitization will lead to political change. Interrogating structures as discourses can politicize the terms used to fix meaning, produce value, and establish identity. Denaturalizing value as the product of nothing more than fixed interpretations can create new possibilities for creating value in other less insistent and injurious ways.

The discursively/structurally reproduced reality of liberal capitalism as deployed by power blocs of aligned groups serves to inform the existentially lived experiences of citizens in the contemporary postindustrial order.[16] The powerful get to reproduce a broader context that works to reduce the dissonance between new names and established practices. As long as the prevailing discursive structures of liberal capitalism create value from some practices, experiences, and identities over others, no matter how often new names are insisted upon, some people will continue to be seen as inferior simply because they do not engage in the same practices as those who are currently dominant in positions of influence and prestige. Therefore, as much as there is a need to reconsider the terms of debate, to interrogate the embedded biases of discursive practices, and to resist living out the invid-ious distinctions that hegemonic categories impose, there are real limits to what isolated instances of renaming can accomplish.

The Political Limitations of Euphemisms

Renaming points to the profoundly political character of labels. Labels oper-ate as sources of power that serve to frame identities and interests. They predispose actors to treat the subjects in question in certain ways, whether they are street people or social policies. This increasingly common strategy, however, overlooks at least three major pitfalls to the politics of renaming.[17]

Each reflects a failure to appreciate language's inability to say all that is meant by any act of signification.

First, many renamings are part of a politics of euphemisms that conspires to legitimate things in ways consonant with hegemonic discourse. This is done by stressing what is consistent and de-emphasizing what is inconsistent with prevailing discourse. When welfare advocates urge the nation to invest in its most important economic resource, its children, they are seeking to recharacterize efforts on behalf of poor families as critical for the country's international economic success in a way that is entirely consonant with the economistic biases of the dominant order. They are also distracting the economic-minded from the social democratic politics that such policy changes represent.[18] This is a slippery politics best pursued with attention to how such renamings may reinforce entrenched institutional practices.[19]

Yet Walter Truett Anderson's characterization of what happened to the "cultural revolution" of the 1960s has relevance here:

> One reason it is so hard to tell when true cultural revolutions have occurred is that societies are terribly good at co-opting their opponents; something that starts out to destroy the prevailing social construction of reality ends up being a part of it. Culture and counterculture overlap and merge in countless ways. And the hostility toward established social constructions of reality that produced strikingly new movements and behaviors in the early decades of this century, and peaked in the 1960s, is now a familiar part of the cultural scene. Destruction itself becomes institutionalized.[20]

According to Jeffrey Goldfarb, cynicism has lost its critical edge and has become the common denominator of the very society that cynical criticism sought to debunk.[21] If this is the case, politically crafted characterizations can easily get co-opted by a cynical society that already anticipates the political character of such selective renamings. The politics of renaming itself gets interpreted as a form of cynicism that uses renamings in a disingenuous fashion in order to achieve political ends.

Renaming not only loses credibility but also corrupts the terms used. This danger is ever present, given the limits of language. Because all terms are partial and incomplete characterizations, every new term can be invalidated as not capturing all that needs to be said about any topic.[22] With time, the odds increase that a new term will lose its potency as it fails to emphasize neglected dimensions of a problem. As newer concerns replace the ones that helped inspire the terminological shift, newer terms will be introduced to address what has been neglected. Where *disabled* was once an improvement over *handicapped,* other terms are now deployed to make society inclusive of all people, however differentially situated. The "disabled" are now "physi-cally challenged" or "mentally challenged." The politics of renaming pro-motes higher and higher levels of neutralizing language.[23] Yet a neutralized language is itself already a partial reading even if it is only implicitly biased in favor of some attributes over others. Neutrality is always relative to the prevailing context. As the context changes, what was once neutral becomes seen as biased. Implicit moves of emphasis and de-emphasis become more visible in a new light. "Physically" and "mentally challenged" already begin to look insufficiently affirmative as efforts intensify to include people with such attributes in all avenues of contemporary life.[24]

Not just terms risk being corrupted by a politics of renaming. Proponents of a politics of renaming risk their personal credibility as well. Proponents of a politics of renaming often pose a double bind for their audiences. The politics of renaming often seeks to highlight sameness and difference si-multaneously.[25] It calls for stressing the special needs of the group while at the same time denying that the group has needs different from those of anyone else. Whether it is women, people of color, gays and lesbians, the disabled, or even "the homeless," renaming seeks to both affirm and deny difference. This can be legitimate, but it is surely almost always bound to be difficult. Women can have special needs, such as during pregnancy, that make it unfair to hold them to male standards; however, once those differ-ent circumstances are taken into account, it becomes inappropriate to as-sume that men and women are fundamentally different in socially signifi-cant ways.[26] Yet emphasizing special work arrangements for women, such as paid maternity leave, may reinforce sexist stereotyping that dooms women to inferior positions in the labor force.

Under these circumstances, advocates of particular renamings can easily be accused of paralyzing their audience and immobilizing potential sup-porters. Insisting that people use terms that imply sameness and difference simultaneously is a good way to ensure such terms do not get used. This encourages the complaint that proponents of new terms are less interested in meeting people's needs than in demonstrating who is more sophisticated and sensitive. Others turn away, asking why they cannot still be involved in trying to right wrongs even if they cannot correct their use of terminology.[27] Right-minded, if wrong-worded, people fear being labeled as the enemy; important allies are lost on the high ground of linguistic purity.

Euphemisms also encourage self-censorship. The politics of renaming discourages its proponents from being able to respond to inconvenient infor-mation inconsistent with the operative euphemism. Yet those who oppose it are free to dominate interpretations of the inconvenient facts. This is bad politics. Rather than suppressing stories about the poor, for instance, it would be much better to promote actively as many intelligent interpretations as possible.

The politics of renaming overlooks that life may be more complicated than attempts to regulate the categories of analysis. Take, for instance, the curious negative example of "culture." Some scholars have been quite insistent that it is almost always incorrect to speak about culture as a factor in explaining poverty, especially among African Americans.[28] Whereas some might suggest that attempts to discourage examining cultural differences, say in family structure, are a form of self-censorship, others might want to argue that it is just clearheaded, informed analysis that de-emphasizes culture's relationship to poverty.[29] Still others suggest that the question of what should or should not be discussed cannot be divorced from the fact that when blacks talk publicly in this country it is always in a racist society that uses their words to reinforce their subordination. Open disagreement among African Americans will be exploited by whites to delegitimate any challenges to racism and to affirm the idea that black marginalization is self-generated.[30] Emphasizing cultural differences between blacks and whites and exposing internal "problems" in the black community minimize how "problems" across races and structural political-economic factors, including especially the racist and sexist practices of institutionalized society, are the primary causes of poverty.

Yet it is distinctly possible that although theories proclaiming a "culture of poverty" are incorrect, cultural variation itself may be an important issue in need of examination.[31] For instance, there is much to be gained from contrasting the extended-family tradition among African Americans with the welfare system of white society, which is dedicated to reinforcing the nuclear two-parent family.[32] A result of self-censorship, however, is that an important subject is left to be studied by the wrong people. Although analyzing cultural differences may not tell us much about poverty and may be dangerous in a racist society, leaving it to others to study culture and poverty can be a real mistake as well. Culture in their hands almost always becomes "culture of poverty."[33] A politics of renaming risks reducing the discussants to only those who help reinforce existing prejudices.

In another context, however, *culture* becomes the preferred term for those who want to get rid of "the trope of race."[34] The radically naturalizing otherness implied by race ensures marginalization for those who are relegated to the "other" half of any racial divide. Displacing racial categories becomes a critical first step in any politics that seeks to overcome racial divisions. *Negro* is replaced by *black*, which is replaced by *African American*. If such moves are tied to attempts to dislodge the institutionalized context for interpreting what the terms describe, as has in fact been the case with displacing the trope of race, then they may very well have significant political effects.[35] Yet interrogating the discursive practices of racism is still only a first step. The politics of racial justice cannot rest with terminological victories. It must push on to disclose how the invidious distinction implied by "race" or its substitutes can be re-created given the prevailing discursive context of a racist society.[36] While recognizing race as a politically tendentious trope, Henry Louis Gates Jr. has noted, "To declare that race is a trope, however, is not to deny its palpable force in the life of every African-American who tries to function every day in a still very racist America."[37]

Welfare, Homeless, and Family Planning: Three Euphemisms

The politics of renaming often combines naïveté and cynicism. Renamings often tilt toward being naively cynical, cynically naive, or both. Naively cynical renamings are dedicated to displacing ascendant categories with euphemisms designed to put something that is currently denigrated in a new, more positive, light. Naively cynical renamings try to challenge dominant understandings; however, they often fail to account for how they get interpreted within the context of prevailing power relationships. Cynically naive renamings, in contrast, do not seek to challenge prevailing understandings but instead depict what is being described as consonant with dominant understandings and as acceptable on those terms. The dilemma for renamings is whether to try to challenge or accept prevailing systems of intelligibility. Renamings face a double bind: those that do tend toward pariah, those that do not tend toward parvenu.[38] Most renamings, such as "the homeless," "welfare," and "family planning," however, in practice involve both the strategic quality of naive cynicism and the accommodationist character of cynical naivete.

Take the controversy surrounding the label *homeless*.[39] *Homeless* characterizes "street people" in a new light in terms of what they lack—housing.[40] *Homeless* has a euphemistic quality in that it calls attention to the plight of people on the street without labeling them as personally deficient. As "the homeless" have grown in number, more people have participated in efforts to address their needs. The name change may have played a role in helping to create that public support.[41] Yet it also may have contributed to a focus on the problems of the more "visible," if highly diverse, population of people on the streets, to the neglect of the broader problem of poverty.[42]

How one estimates the homeless population determines whether one sees housing is the key to addressing the needs of most homeless.[43] If one limits the estimate to people on the streets and in temporary shelters, then a high proportion of the homeless population is made up of single males, a good proportion of whom have histories of drug addiction or mental illness.[44] Many are young, without education, training, or supportive family ties. A surprising number have been in foster care.[45] But if one estimates the homeless population more broadly, to include those who have resisted living on the street or going into the shelter system, then a higher proportion of the homeless population consists of families whose low incomes make housing unaffordable.[46] Under the latter estimate, housing is more easily presented as the key to addressing the homeless problem, whereas under the former estimate, more work is needed to show that housing, rather than mental health and drug treatment services, should be the central component in any attempt to address this population's needs.[47] The former estimate is the more popular one with policy makers; it makes "the homeless" a population that needs services rather than more expensive housing programs.[48]

Yet, regardless of the estimates, the politics of renaming the homeless has evidently backfired.[49] The characterization "homeless" encourages limiting discussion to housing, and this leaves the characterization open to charges of being misleading, a label strategically crafted to put the homeless in a positive light. It also discourages advocates for the homeless from entering struggles over how to discuss their other needs. The resulting void is filled by others who are willing to read the homeless as pathological. Under these circumstances, those interested in disciplining the homeless get to dominate discussions about services, often emphasizing highly coercive therapeutic settings.[50] Rather than housing or supportive services, the homeless face the prospect of getting neither. Emphasizing *homeless* as a catchall name for a very diverse population of people risks returning social service provision to the medieval hospital: an all-purpose dumping ground for the criminal, the poor, and the mentally ill as well as the sick.[51] Thus, the homeless face the prospect of getting neither housing nor supportive services.

Conservative critics such as William Tucker and Thomas Main have been able to put homeless advocates on the defensive by arguing that many of the people in the shelters in New York City and elsewhere are not really homeless, but are simply using shelters to avoid paying rent or as a way to get access to better housing.[52] There may well be evidence that in some cases, for short periods of time, people use the shelters in these ways, especially if they are poor families with children, short of needed funds for basic necessities, and especially if they are new to a city or are otherwise in transition from one home to another. Rather than suppressing these "facts" about the homeless, it would be better to get the word out on how many types of people need to use the shelter system even if they are not, strictly speaking, homeless, but simply poor and desperate. When the *New York Times* ran a story in 1991 about shelter inhabitants, it was accused by some homeless advocates of pushing only the Tucker-Main version of the homeless story.[53] The newspaper's actions may have been a result of the unwillingness of homeless advocates to discuss the variety of people in shelters for fear of making the homeless look less deserving.[54]

The dominance of some stories for interpreting information about the homeless was critical in the downfall of Nancy Wackstein in 1991, Mayor Dinkins's point person on the problem of homelessness in New York City. The Dinkins administration was committed to closing down the infamous welfare hotels that provided unsafe and unsanitary living conditions for homeless welfare recipients at very high cost. In order to bring the number of such hotels down to zero, the administration created in 1990 the Alternative Pathways program, which would set aside 2,000 of the approximately 8,000 anticipated openings in public housing during the coming year for families in shelters. This meant the prospect of incurring no small amount of grousing from many of the 189,000 people on the waiting list for public housing in New York City and the estimated more than 100,000 "doubled up" with friends and relatives.[55] William Grinker, the former Koch administration welfare chief, warned that people who were not homeless would simply declare themselves homeless and go into the shelters in order to bump others in line. He predicted a surge in the shelter population. At the time, Wackstein denounced his analysis as cynical. A year later, the number of families in temporary apartments, shelters, and even the welfare hotels was increasing, after declining since 1987. Alternative interpretations could have emphasized the lack of adequate housing for many poor "nonhomeless" people. Instead, Grinker was seen as right and Wackstein as wrong. She said as much when she resigned later that year.[56]

Even more controversial was the 1991 task force chaired by Andrew Cuomo that Dinkins established to examine what to do about the homeless problem.[57] The Cuomo task force would eventually recommend a series of small service-oriented shelters with apartmentlike facilities for the home-less—just like the ones Cuomo's own nonprofit agency was building. Al-though this conflict of interest is itself suggestive of how some policy for the homeless gets made, more important was the empirical research Cuomo had done to justify his recommendations. Many homeless advocates in-sisted that lack of affordable housing was the root of the homeless prob-lem.[58] This perspective discouraged the promotion of stories about the personal maladies afflicting many homeless individuals on the grounds that emphasis on drug problems and mental illness would distract atten-tion from the affordable housing issue.[59] More conventional housing, not service-oriented transitional residences, was the solution. But Cuomo re-fused to play along. His commission produced a report that suggested that as many as two-thirds of the single individuals in shelters and on the streets were addicts or deinstitutionalized mental health patients, and one-third of the adults in homeless families in shelters were suffering from drug and alcohol problems.[60] With such empirical evidence, Cuomo could push aside cries for affordable conventional housing and reframe the homeless debate in terms of providing therapeutically oriented transi-tional housing.[61]

Given these sorts of stories, alternative narratives are needed. For in-stance, most homeless persons are not mentally ill or drug addicts.[62] Many who are have become so after being on the street, rather than the other way around, thereby making lack of access to housing the primary factor initiating their "homelessness." Further, many people are homeless even if they avoid both the shelters and the streets and instead double or triple up with friends or family members.[63] In addition, addicted individuals can perhaps be better served if they reside in affordable conventional housing and receive treatment elsewhere.[64] These stories were not stressed in the Cuomo data.[65] It was no surprise, then, that his data were interpreted as supporting more business for his agency,[66] or that once again the homeless were seen as needing something other than housing. It was no surprise either that people were willing to continue to accept the conflation of "homeless-ness" with "begging," even if most "homeless" do not beg and many beg-gars are not homeless.[67] Renaming the homeless has not reduced their marginalization; macrodiscursive structures rework "homeless" as another category of alien others, even as microdiscursive practices provide some basis for resisting those structures.[68] Michael Katz has written about the limits of deploying a term like *homeless*:

Homelessness.... is a social category, not a defining quality of persons. Those poor people with nowhere to live vary greatly in their characteristics. To collapse them into one category by abstracting one aspect of their lives is to subordinate their individuality; to mark them as different, and because they need help, as inferior to the rest of us; and to leave them with a label that can turn as quickly into a stigma as into a plea for help. Yet, without the creation of this category, public sympathy on behalf of those poor people included within it would not have swelled, many fewer volunteers would have responded, and poor people would have suffered even more.... Is there a way to energize public action that does not stigmatize and isolate? Is there in America a way to foster a discourse about poverty based on human dignity and community rather than on invidious categories and marketbased models of public policy? The late 1980s provided little reason for optimism.[69]

Welfare is a different sort of example of the uneven results of euphemistic politics. Whether called *the dole, poor relief, public assistance,* or the formerly positive-sounding *welfare,* it has most often historically been interpreted negatively as a "dependency" that is to be discouraged.[70]

William Julius Wilson has suggested that liberals for many years engaged in self-censorship and were reluctant to discuss the growing problem of welfare dependency, especially among African Americans.[71] Wilson argues that the extensive criticism heaped on Daniel Patrick Moynihan in 1964 and 1965 for his *The Negro Family* (known as the Moynihan Report) discouraged liberals from discussing the topic out of fear of being labeled racists who wanted to blame the black family for its own problems.[72] Only after the problem began to reach crisis proportions, Wilson notes, did liberals finally begin to enter this taboo terrain. Adolph Reed Jr., however, rejects Wilson's contention and asserts that many people continued to discuss the issues of poverty after the fallout from the Moynihan Report.[73] They simply did not focus on deleterious behaviors as the primary causes of increased poverty and welfare dependency. Although liberal self-censorship may not have been apparent, something more troubling may have been at work. Liberals, in a cynically naive fashion, have been for a long time too willing to read "welfare" in terms of the prevailing context of liberal capitalism.

Most liberals have never really challenged the interpretive context that sees "welfare" as "dependency." Instead, liberals often read "welfare" nonjudgmentally, but interpreted extended welfare use as a sign of individual deficiency.[74] In recent years, many liberals have more explicitly embraced the critique of welfare dependency (as discussed in chapter 1). Some embrace it on the pragmatic grounds that emphasis on these points of division and conflict in society makes for ineffectual politics and impedes necessary coalition building.[75] Others believe that the Democratic party has made itself politically vulnerable by pushing affirmative action and redistribution policies.[76] "Race, rights, and taxes" have made the Democratic party a political pariah. The only alternative is to work within the confines of the conservative-dominated discourse that characterizes poverty and welfare dependency as largely problems of individual failing. Democrats who promote a politics of personal responsibility are the only ones who can succeed electorally. Whether Bill Clinton's success was an example that confirms or refutes this thesis is another banal example of the obfuscations of electoral politics.

Consequently, a new form of liberalism has become all that is feasible within such a one-sided discourse. "Neoliberalism" is a non liberal liberalism retrofitted to the current period's constricted political horizons of limited economic possibility and heightened stress on individual responsibility.[77] It cannot help but be part of the anxious rhetoric that expresses concern about how to enforce discipline in order to perpetuate the existing social arrangements in the face of postindustrial change. Neoliberalism calls for reduced government, fewer entitlements, and an end to the rights revolution in the face of cultural backlash by the "New Right." The net result has been that all political actors have had to at least pay homage to established institutions: the sanctity of the family, the universal applicability of the work ethic, and the autonomy of the market. Ignored are the limited nature of dominant notions of the family and the cruelty of a work ethic for unskilled workers who have been made unemployable by a postindustrial economy.[78] No text has helped produce a toxic text — one with lethal consequences for such problems as the growing numbers of poor, female-headed families.

What would have been better would have been an ongoing willingness to discuss the rise in female-headed families, with an eye to providing intellectually responsible and politically efficacious readings of this phenomenon.[79] Such readings would have highlighted the structural context, emphasizing how race, gender, and class work to lower the chances of success for the black family.[80] Such readings would highlight how welfare policy has systematically offered inadequate or often no benefits for poor families, which tend, coincidentally, to be disproportionately black and to constitute a much larger proportion of black families (approximately 30 percent in recent years) than white families (approximately 8 percent).[81] Such readings would have highlighted how welfare policy also tends to provide inadequate or often no support for two-parent families, making it hard for poor two-parent families to succeed. The majority of poor two-parent families receive no public assistance.[82] Such readings would have highlighted how the problem itself has not really continued to increase linearly over time, like some out-of-control crisis, but instead actually declined in the late 1960s, perhaps in response to increased government support and economic growth, and began to increase only with the deterioration of the economy and the retrenchment of public assistance in recent years (I will return to this topic in chapter 9). Yet, given the acceptance of the prevailing context, "welfare" by another name still means "dependency."[83]

For conservatives, "family planning" is a stark example of "social engineering." Yet, as Linda Gordon notes, Planned Parenthood, the dominant organization for providing such services for more than fifty years, assiduously sought to ensure that family planning, from contraception to "marriage" counseling, was seen as consonant with the dominant discourse of family.[84] At various turns this has proven most difficult, particularly when contraception was shown to be at least as important to the unmarried as the married, or when abortion was finally determined to be part of women's right to privacy. More important, the integration of women's reproductive rights into family discourse has at times meant the subordination of efforts to achieve gender equality in order to rationalize reproductive freedom as consistent with family values.

Family planning is a politically significant misnomer. The term obscures that fact that the most politically significant services offered in the name of "family planning," such as pregnancy counseling for unmarried teenagers, are often provided when the planning of a family is exactly what does not happen, or is what the young women want to avoid. Reproductive freedom includes the right not to have a family. The better response, however, is not to deny the need for the services implied by "family planning," but instead to legitimate them on their own terms. Rather than subordinate the laudable social goal of reproductive freedom, it is better to resist the tendency to tie reproductive freedom to the family ideal. Although there are bound to be moments in any struggle where the tie to dominant discourse may be strategically advantageous, the contradictions that come with achieving reproductive freedom in the name of family suggest that this is a tie that binds retrogressively.

Planning is its own misnomer here. Families are often ill equipped for planning, and planning for families is something that many people do poorly, for a variety of reasons that have more to do with the inadequacies of their circumstances than with the people themselves. Poverty, lack of education, youth, and many other factors make some people more dependent on attempts to engage post hoc in retrospective family planning. "Family planning" often deals with problems of poverty well beyond the family. Yet, perpetuating the profamily orientation within the context of allegedly rational "planning" would reinforce the idea that family structure is the key to solving the problems of poverty. This same family discourse justifies coercive intervention in other areas of public assistance, including the growing popularity of the idea that welfare recipients should be encouraged or required to submit to contraceptive implants.[85] The dilemma for "family planning" advocates is how to legitimate their services within the dominant discourse on families without emphasizing family over other, more critical, causes of poverty.

While under assault by the right as antifamily, advocates of the Planned Parenthood variety have risked falling prey to profamily rhetoric as a way to eke out some legitimacy for reproductive rights. "Family" is the all-too-convenient card for rationalizing many social practices—some good, some reprehensible. It can irresponsibly justify almost all that is done in its name as well as limit consideration of practices that deserve to be affirmed in their own right even if they cannot be justified as serving the allegedly greater good of "the family." Abortion, in particular, as a critical form of reproductive freedom, especially for people living in poverty, needs to be justified on its own account, as feminists have demonstrated, as integral to realizing the social goods of gender equality and a more just society.[86]

Discourse and Structure in the Politics of Renaming

The politics of renaming highlights the relationships of discourse to structure and ideology to power.[87] The limits of euphemisms suggest that these renamings often reinforce a broader, institutionalized, and structural context that is supported through the daily actions of aligned groupings exercising power to effect outcomes consistent with their interests. Yet the power plays reinforcing prevailing structures also operate to encourage selected interpretations of a wide variety of acts of signification. These structures help create a "social logic" that constrains interpretation of even the most imaginative of renamings. Whereas the structural conditions that constrain policy discourse are themselves discursively constituted, they in turn produce material constraints that limit notions of what is feasible and practical under the existing arrangements. Therefore, displacing the self-sufficiency of the "breadwinner" will not on its own make "dependents" more worthy. Even if "bread" itself is shown in good part, if not the whole loaf, to be symbolic, that will not by itself lead people to eat some other symbol. Gaining leverage for political change involves appreciating not just how material structures can be denaturalized. Political change comes with also appreciating how material practices serve to constrain seriously the extent to which discursive moves will have any tractability in public settings. Only when the power plays supporting such structural conditions are resisted can alternative discursive moves gain political salience.[88] Action to improve the lives of poor people involves instituting changes in institutional practices so that people will be motivated to think more inclusively or be willing to entertain the idea that it is rational for them as well-meaning, if not self-interested, individuals to promote the well-being of marginal groups. The existing institutional infrastructure currently works against such thinking.

The United States today is organized by power blocs of aligned groupings around a postindustrial culture that has materialistic consequences.[89] This culture does much to engender privatization, that is, the idea that most issues are best handled privately, through market exchanges. A central feature of this culture is the idea of exclusive consumption, by each on his or her own. Even self-worth comes to be designated by what one consumes. Postindustrial consumerism is also associated with the deterritorialization of the political economy in an increasingly integrated global system of exchange. National loyalties, citizenship, and the civic bond in general are obliterated in this global political economy. The state-centered discourse of reciprocal rights and obligations evaporates in the face of pressures for everyone to extract value on his or her own from an economic system that moves beyond the boundaries of the nation-state.[90] The Third World exists within the First World, the homeless with the symbolic analysts, and in this brave new world (dis)order, the latter need not assume responsibility for the former. Deterritorialization of the political economy reduces the institutionalized pressure to think about how the state can ensure the allocation of value to all members of the polity. Welfare recipients and others disadvantageously situated to participate in the global economy are increasingly left to fend for themselves. A rising influx of poor immigrants only intensifies the confusion between the impoverished among the citizenry and the noncitizens among the impoverished.[91] In a global political economy where state affiliation matters less than it did before, the poor citizenry and illegal immigrants are both disenfranchised.[92]

A politics dedicated to the transformation of welfare ought to recognize that changing the "keywords" of poverty discourse, although important, is in and of itself insufficient to make political change happen.[93] Renamings get interpreted within prevailing structural contexts, such as the suburban consumer corporate culture of the late-modern United States. Although multiple interpretations remain possible, the powerful can use categories in a variety of ways to reinforce prevailing contexts and thereby discourage many possible alternative interpretations.[94] If such moves are to be effective, discursive politics must be part of displacing the power plays that reinforce prevailing structures. Discursive revision will be most effective when it is framed in the context of the specific needs of ongoing social movements dedicated to achieving institutional change.

This means that specific renamings will best serve political action to the extent that they can mobilize people and build coalitions that work toward revising dominant structural contexts that impart meanings, allocate value, and fix identities. As discursive moves in service of coalitional politics, renamings must necessarily be open, porous, and transitory, allowing for different interpretations from various constituencies and deployed with humility about their implications for change.[95] Renamings that are connected to a coalitional politics dedicated to structural change also recognize that a politics of transformation may start with but involve more than renamings. John Fiske writes:

> The point is that politics is social, not textual, and if a text is made political, its politicization is effected at its point of entry into the social.
>   This does not mean that all texts are equally political (even potentially), or that all politicized meanings are equally available in any one of them. Politics is always a process of struggle between opposing forces, always a matter of forging alliances and of defining and redefining the opposition. If the political potential of a text is to be mobilized, the text must reproduce among the discourses that comprise it a struggle equivalent to that experienced socially by its readers. And just as power is not distributed equally in society, so potential meanings are not distributed equally in texts.... We must recognize, too, that any progressive meanings that are made are never experienced freely, but always in conflicting relationships with the forces of the power-bloc that oppose them.[96]

Interrogation of ascendant categories is an important initial step in any politics seeking to displace how powerful actors deploy prevailing structures and create possibilities for making social relations more inclusive, equitable, and just. Yet isolated acts of renaming disconnected from attempts to contest those prevailing structures will prove insufficient. Inserting new names in old stories will not make a difference politically. Euphemisms that seek to affirm what they describe in terms of those prevailing structures will prove even more questionable.

CHAPTER THREE

Inverting Political Economy

Perspective, Position, and Discourse in the Analysis of Welfare

We can talk about poverty, the millions of working poor, and the viability
of the welfare system, but only by understanding how these abstract
notions play out in the lives of hardworking Americans can we cut through
the numbing statistics and conflicting arguments.
John E. Schwarz and Thomas J. Volgy, *The Forgotten Americans*

We are bound to seek perspective from those points of view, which
can never be known in advance, which promise something quite
extraordinary, that is, knowledge potent for constructing worlds less
organized by axes by domination.
Donna J. Haraway, *Simians, Cyborgs, and Women*

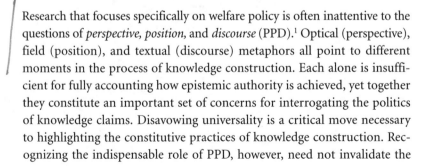

Research that focuses specifically on welfare policy is often inattentive to the
questions of *perspective, position,* and *discourse* (PPD).[1] Optical (perspective),
field (position), and textual (discourse) metaphors all point to different
moments in the process of knowledge construction. Each alone is insufficient for fully accounting how epistemic authority is achieved, yet together
they constitute an important set of concerns for interrogating the politics
of knowledge claims. Disavowing universality is a critical move necessary
to highlighting the constitutive practices of knowledge construction. Recognizing the indispensable role of PPD, however, need not invalidate the

work in question; instead, it can enhance the critical distance needed to justify the study of political economy from selected perspectives, certain positions, and particular discourses.[2]

Making *perspective* explicit involves confronting the possibility that much of welfare policy research is written from a top-down *position* and in a managerial *discourse* that assumes a particular point of view: an imagined policy maker/manager charged with the responsibility of containing the problems of welfare so that they do not become serious impediments to the smooth functioning of the overall system or society.[3] Interrogating the PPD in welfare policy research from alternative perspectives/positions/discourses opens up the possibility for research that accounts for the indignities of those who must experience the welfare system as it is currently constituted. Neglected topics, alternative interpretations, and revisionist assessments emerge once the dominant PPD and its alternatives are articulated.

It is important to stress that although the PPD of welfare policy research is most often expressed in statistical terms, providing an alternative political economy for welfare does not necessarily imply the need to limit research to qualitative narratives that relate the subjectivity of those on the bottom.[4] Nor does it necessarily suggest that the goal of such ethnographic work should be the reporting of the unadulterated experiences of individuals in some allegedly pure form that can claim the "authority of experience."[5] Interrogating PPD in any political-economic analysis is no less necessary for qualitative than for quantitative research. Research that critiques PPD grounds itself not in what is most objectively factual or what is most subjectively authentic, but in what is most informative in addressing the impediments to achieving political change. I want to suggest that interrogating the dominant PPD allows for what I call "inverting political economy" so as to narrate alternative understandings of political-economic arrangements.

An Analytic Matrix for Welfare Policy Research

It may be that policy analysts have overdone their commitment to "speak truth to power."[6] As Charles Lindblom has suggested, policy analysts operating in the dominant mode have seen fit to take policy functionaries as their primary clients.[7] Most policy analytic work is done for those in power and involved in the managing of public problems rather than for those challenging power and confronting these problems in their everyday lives. This sort of top-down perspective induces what Lindblom calls a "professional impairment" that prevents social scientists from being able to probe social problems and ameliorate them to the satisfaction of ordinary citizens.

The need for a bottom-up perspective for analyzing social problems usually implies two other moves.[8] First, the bottom-up approach is usually meant to imply an attempt to understand the subject matter in terms of the subjective experience of those being studied. This move suggests the need to articulate a particular point of view while rejecting the top-down pretense of achieving objective understanding. The bottom-up perspective suggests the situatedness of all knowledge. Second, the bottom-up approach registers the need to get at the qualitative dimensions of the subject matter. Experience, not easily reducible to statistical representation, needs to be narrated, and often in the vocabulary of those being studied, if it is to be captured more faithfully. Yet, as the typology illustrated in Figure 3.1 suggests, it is possible to imagine at least four variants of research: top-down-quantitative and bottom-up-qualitative as the more common pair and top-down-qualitative and bottom-up-quantitative as the less frequently invoked strategies. All four are logical possibilities that encourage the rethinking of issues of PPD.

Most quantitative work tends to be done from the imagined olympian, objectivist point of view of a manager responsible for overseeing the totality of welfare practices. Yet quantitative work need not be limited to the necessity of representing an alleged objective position or confined to serving managerial needs of human engineering. Conversely, whereas it is also the case that most bottom-up work tends to take the form of qualitative ethnographic narratives, work that is strategically positioned to view its subject matter from a bottom-up perspective can just as easily take the form of quantitative analysis.

A less pious reading of ethnographic narrative suggests that it, too, just as much as statistical research, represents a rereading of experience that does not do it complete justice. Privileging allegedly pure, unadulterated experience, ethnographic narrative fails to interrogate its own inability to achieve critical distance while simultaneously neglecting its own discursive practices that mediate representations of experience. In both quantitative and qualitative work, questions arise concerning who is constructing the representation and for what purposes. In both cases, attention to the constitutive practices of narrating the subject in question is necessary and creates the possibility that statistical work can play as great a role in bottom-up analysis as qualitative research does. All research is a form of narrative that involves questions of narrativity.[9] Rather than choosing qualitative research

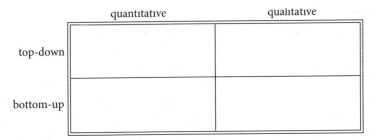

Figure 3.1. Possible variants of research.

on grounds that it will more faithfully represent experience, the researcher makes a choice based on how to narrate the subject matter. Both quantitative and qualitative work should be seen as less-than-definitive depictions, and each should be understood in terms of the perspective/position/discourse involved in its construction.[10] Yet, given attention to their PPD, they can contribute to descriptive material for making the experiences of those on the bottom comprehensible to others, such as policy makers, whose actions affect such persons.[11]

Ethnography as Publicity Stunt

The four categories of welfare policy research oversimplify. Each can itself take several forms. For instance, it is possible to imagine a variety of types of top-down ethnography, even if the idea of anything other than bottom-up ethnography may strike most ethnographers as odd. Some ethnographies may reflect a managerial orientation and serve managerial interests. Yet there remains the possibility that top-down ethnography might serve to contest managerial power. Barbara Sabol's excursion from publicly recognized New York City commissioner of human resources administration to covert impostor as welfare recipient is instructive.[12]

As the head of a welfare agency that served more than a million people and had an annual budget in 1992 of more than $6 billion, Barbara Sabol was an important, powerful, and highly visible participant in the New York City welfare policy-making system. She felt isolated from the human consequences of that system, however, and so she adopted another persona in order to see firsthand how the system affects the people who seek its assistance. From late April through October 1992, with the approval of Mayor David Dinkins, she periodically became a welfare recipient. Wearing disguises that included a sweatshirt, jeans, scarf, and wig, she applied for and eventually received food stamps and cash assistance, and "even showed up for three days for a mandatory work assignment" in another city office. It took her numerous appearances and six to eight weeks to get on the public assistance rolls: she was told repeatedly that she had not provided enough documentation; she found herself shunted from one office to another (more than once to the wrong one); she waited in long lines in dreary waiting rooms; she was treated rudely and dismissively by her own employees. She found that she was deprived of her privacy by a system that asked the most sensitive questions regarding her personal circumstances. Posing as one welfare recipient produced enough information for Sabol to suggest numerous changes in policy on concerns that policy makers usually do not include in their deliberations.

Sabol said that she went public with her forays into the bureaucracy when she did because the new administration in Washington was gearing up for welfare reform. Some suggested that the timing might have been tied to her own job prospects with that administration. In any case, Sabol's efforts are instructive, not so much for Washington policy makers as for what they say about how even a top-down exercise in participant observation may have its place in work designed to inform welfare discourse of an alternative point of view.

Sabol's research will probably not figure in any Washington welfare policy deliberations, and this is itself instructive. Policy makers tend to focus on the welfare system in terms of managerial concerns. They focus on total costs, eligibility requirements, mechanisms for reducing prolonged reliance on public assistance, elaborate reporting requirements, procedures for rooting out fraud, and so on. Sabol's work could inform policy makers if welfare policy discourse was predisposed to hear what she has to say. Its categories for welfare, however, make the problems she found secondary.

These categories do include the ostensible purpose of welfare — that is, to provide cash assistance to those who are deemed to be in need of it, and to do so in a timely way. They include at some level, usually the state government, consideration of the economic value of such benefits for recipients, although states have proven less and less interested in this question (this issue is discussed more fully in chapters 5 and 9). Yet these categories are unlikely to provide much space for considering how even services ostensibly provided to make life better for welfare recipients are structured in ways that actually are insensitive to recipients and their needs.[13] Managerial discourse emphasizes management of the welfare system even at the expense of meeting recipient needs. Given the ascendancy of managerial categories,

even programs designed to provide child care, work training and placement, and other additional supportive services are unlikely to meet the
needs of program participants. Benefit increases themselves often lead to
reduced buying power.[14]

Sabol believes that her efforts show that the system needs to be made
more responsive to recipients. In particular, it needs to be much more expeditious in supplying jobs for recipients, processing applications, providing privacy, and making the entire system more supportive and less intru-
sive. She found the system to be a serious impediment to people who are
busy trying to get their lives back on track. Time-consuming procedures
and long delays suggest a system that is deeply suspicious of recipients.
Moreover, it is a system less interested in enabling the eligible to receive
aid than in preventing the ineligible from getting assistance.

The existing categories of welfare discourse discourage managers from
considering any information other than what is relevant to the managerial
needs of the existing system. Sabol's efforts, however, show that even ethnographic work done from a managerial perspective might be of some value
in challenging those categories. Her work underscores how welfare policy
discourse is a "politics of need interpretation."[15] Nancy Fraser suggests that
"needs talk" has become a critical site for struggle among contending groups
as late capitalist society confronts the shifting boundaries separating "political," "economic," and "domestic" dimensions of life.[16] As these boundaries
blur, especially with the struggles of women, they become politicized and
subject to contestation. Expert and bureaucratic discourses operate within
more circumscribed settings in ways consonant with the broader hegemonic categories as to what is political, economic, and domestic.[17] Strug-
gles over needs in bureaucratic settings often involve the extent to which
hegemonic understandings and connected bureaucratic categories will serve
as the basis for defining people's needs, interests, and identities in terms of
whether they will receive service and under what conditions. Welfare recipients marked as deficient in self-sufficiency will experience bureaucratic
practices that treat them suspiciously and as people in need of regulation.
Any predisposition to have welfare operate in more supportive ways will
recede into the background. Like ethnographies that articulate alternative
understandings of recipients and their needs, Sabol's work provides a basis
for contesting the way in which the existing bureaucratic discourse imputes
identities and needs to persons seeking assistance.[18]

With alternative categories for constituting recipients' needs, it might
be possible to envision a welfare system that works for rather than against

recipients. To choose just one example: even when job placements and child care are provided, they often fail to account for the special difficulties that single parents confront in trying to juggle paid employment and work at home. Reconstituting the need for work in terms of the realities of single parenting would probably lead to (1) greater convenience in terms of location of both the site for paid employment and child care, (2) greater flexibility in work hours, (3) greater remuneration for the paid employment going to a single parent, and (4) less time spent reporting to the welfare bureaucracy. Reconstituting needs in managerial discourse in such ways become the promise of work like Sabol's.

The Rorschach of Ethnography/The Mystification of Statistics

Sabol's field research can even be described as bottom-up ethnography done with an eye toward promoting alternative top-down understandings. The matrix for welfare policy research can take many forms. This fact suggests the need to be attentive to who is doing ethnography and why. These issues are highlighted in attempts to reintroduce ethnography as an important form of welfare policy research.[19]

Growing dissatisfaction with the dominance of economists in conducting welfare policy research achieved an arched and pointed expression in a 1986 commentary by Nathan Glazer in *Focus,* the newsletter of the Institute for Research on Poverty (IRP).[20] Since its founding in 1966 under authorization from the Economic Opportunity Act of 1964, IRP had become one of the nation's premier research centers for studying poverty. In a commentary on the first twenty years of the institute, Glazer relayed how he understood but disagreed with the institute's penchant for promoting largely economic analysis of poverty and welfare. Like other research centers and the emerging field of welfare policy research more generally, the institute stressed economic analysis of these issues conducted by economists. Glazer did recognize the power of statistical analysis:

> The IRP was from the beginning cast in the mold of econometric and public policy research. This was the research the IRP was prepared to undertake, and that it did undertake, as in its major series of volumes on income maintenance experiments. This work has played a major role in the policies that are proposed and adopted to deal with poverty. No other line of research could have been as productive.[21]

There was a problem, however. Glazer asserted that econometric analysis left out the depth of understanding that comes from "intuitively comprehensible models of behavior based on detailed and sustained observation of and interaction with the subjects of research."[22] Glazer therefore persisted in his call for more ethnographic research of poverty, if for no other reason than to provide the necessary context for nurturing theoretical perspectives that could be invoked to interpret econometric data. Glazer argued that the problems of persistent poverty and welfare dependency were now forcing researchers to confront questions of culture and values. Researchers would increasingly have to confront why it is that some people are poor and others are not. Why do some people engage in self-defeating behavior that mires them in poverty and others seek to "pull themselves up by their own bootstraps"? In particular, ethnic diversity was going to show how some groups encourage the development of what Thomas Sowell calls "human capital"—the set of personal practices and habits of mind that allow them to be valued in labor markets—and others do not.[23] Ethnographic research is ideally suited, Glazer suggested, to providing answers, in ways that econometric work cannot, on the role of these increasingly crucial factors of character and culture.

> We are entering a period—we are in it now—when, I believe, these kinds of differences are going to play a larger and larger role in poverty and poverty research. We will be forced to confront them as a new age of mass immigration brings into the United States new groups that will demonstrate they can make economic progress even in times of adversity, as well as other groups who will apparently be incapable of emerging from poverty even in times of prosperity. Whatever our success in macroeconomics, for which I earnestly hope, we will have to work directly on human motivation operating in ways that we do not fully understand. That is what we are doing now, after all, with teenage pregnancy.... teenage pregnancy has become one of the major factors in poverty, and neither the availability of jobs or of welfare ... seems to have had much to do with it.... what could it have been, aside from a change in what was valued and approved behavior? Weak as this explanation appears before the power of economic reasoning, it is all that is available for those who are now trying to deal with this disastrous development. And if the largest single change in the character of American poverty escapes economic analysis and large-scale correlations and regressions in our efforts to understand it, we have a good argument for other kinds of research on poverty.[24]

Although his comments were grounded in legitimate frustrations with the abstract and reductionist quality of econometric work on poverty and welfare, Glazer elided the fallacy of representation implicit in the ideal of ethnography. For Mark Seltzer, the fallacy of representation in ethnography replicates the representational fallacies implicit in statistical social science.

Seltzer suggests that the realist narrativity of ethnography, with its emphasis on the uniqueness of cases, reinforces a "bourgeois individualism" that parallels what he calls "statistical personation." Statistical social science produces "regularities irreducible to individual intentions"; such studies "provide models of individualization: models for the generic, typical or average man — what we might describe as the production of individuals as statistical persons."[25] Therefore, ethnography, like statistical research, could promote a reifying individualism that served insufficiently to articulate the context, often political and economic as well as cultural and social, that animated people to act as they did.

In fact, Glazer seriously misread econometric research. Writing in 1986, he failed to anticipate the burgeoning of statistical, as well as ethnographic, studies that would highlight value and culture factors.[26] Both representational forms were ideally suited for narratives alleging how the culture factor operated in individuated ways. Both provided a substantial body of empirical work to suggest that there was a "culture of poverty." Both could provide evidence that was sufficiently congenial to the prevailing biases about how poverty was attributable to personal practices. Both types of work could be done by bracketing contextual factors and insinuating individualist explanations into the discourse of welfare policy research.

According to Michel Foucault, most social statistics operate as the science of the state, aggregating social practices into reified populations, whose mean and range serve to define, rather than reflect, norms and margins.[27] Statistical work most often is used then to identify repetitions that can be used to suggest ways for regulating individuated behavior to conform to such norms. Yet ethnography also risks replicating the myth of individuation that underlies social statistics. Glazer was hoping for a more up-close and personal representation that would allow him to capture the "culture of poverty."[28] The researcher, like the tourist or the fieldworker in an exotic land, would get to know the "alien other" so as to see how they were and were not like "us." Yet the "us/them" divide implicit in such a formulation reencodes the opportunity to read "the poor" as the negative referent they have been historically, especially for liberal, individualist, capitalist modernity, with its insistence on achieving through the market the identity of a self-sufficient autonomous self. Reading the poor in this way revisits the opportunity to say good things about "us" by contrast with "them." Ethnography of the poor, in Glazer's hands, would risk becoming a reassuring tale of how the "not poor" are to be understood.[29]

Patricia Clough's critique of ethnography underscores how it glosses over its own animating impulses to make sense of the viewing subject by interpreting the viewed object.[30] Ethnography's realism backgrounds the psychoanalytic subtext that helps construct the narrative used to depict those who are viewed. Ethnography's narrative subtext can be read to be about the ethnographer's attempt to break with tradition, authority, established knowledge, or ascendant empirical understandings by showing how his or her ethnography makes an authoritative, original, genuinely new contribution. This "oedipal" struggle invites the reader to identify with the narrative's subtextual insistence to make empirical claims that suggest that the viewed object can be best understood in coherent terms as an "other" from the particular viewpoint of the viewing subject.

> It is for this reason that realist narrativity can be said to function ideologically. Realist narrativity is ideological for making invisible the relays it produces between the terms it opposes. Especially important are the relays it produces between those oppositions upon which bourgeois individualism depends, such as self and society, nature and environment, sexuality and economy, private and public....
>
> If, then, it is to be concluded that ethnography is informed with an oedipal logic of realist narrativity, developed through the eighteenth and early nineteenth centuries, it is because ethnography treats the subject's struggle for self-knowledge as a struggle to obtain factual representations of empirical knowledge.[31]

The riddle of how knowledge is constructed is not solved by trying to make the false choice between allegedly factually objective statistics and authentically pure experience. Interrogating perspective must be matched by accounting for position, and both must appreciate the political implications of how discourse narrates what is represented.[32] If ethnography reenacts the psychoanalytic subtext of realist narratives, including other forms of empirical science, it also must address the positional issue of who gets to do ethnography on whom. In particular, to choose just one case of particular relevance for studying welfare, what is at work when white, male, middle-class social scientists are trying through ethnography to make sense of poor women of color?

Ethnography as Voyeurism

Glazer was right that ethnographic work would follow in his wake; however, he hardly could predict that this genre would gain as much popularity as it has. In just the past few years, there have been numerous works using ethnographic depictions of the poor, including, to name just a few, Leslie Dunbar's *The Common Interest*, Susan Sheehan's *Life for Me Ain't Been No Crystal Stair*, John Schwarz and Thomas Volgy's *The Forgotten Americans*, Mark Rank's *Living on the Edge*, Mitchell Duneier's *Slim's Table*, Nicholas Lemann's *The Promised Land*, Alex Kotlowitz's *There Are No Children Here*, and William Julius Wilson's work on inner-city African American poor families in Chicago.[33] The last three of these in particular highlight the limitations of such work.

Nicholas Lemann, born and raised in New Orleans, offers a book that moves back and forth between policy machinations in Washington, D.C., and the changing fortunes of black families moving from Clarksdale, Mississippi, to Chicago, Illinois. Revised after earlier articles received criticism, the book jettisons an explicit "culture of poverty" argument.[34] Instead, by tracing migration from Clarksdale to Chicago and back, Lemann makes a more understated argument (about two-thirds of the way through the text) and implies that the legacy of the sharecropping system broke the African American family and set it on the road to ruin.[35] This cultural explanation is almost smothered by rich narratives of the families he studied. Their lives are hard. Only some of those who return South seem to get a reprieve. How this narrative underwrites the sharecropping thesis anymore than the bad statistical work of previous studies is left unexplained. Racism, economic dislocation, and political marginalization are mentioned, but the narrative continues to suggest that sharecropping and migration from the rural South to the urban North were critical factors in making poor, inner-city African American neighborhoods unlivable. Instead, Lemann remains intent on telling a tale of migration about southern sharecroppers, all the while backgrounding his own southern roots, which may very well drive his insistence to tell a tale of how the South shaped the lives of those who left and those who returned.[36]

Alex Kotlowitz's ethnography of two young boys, Lafayette and Pharoah Rivers, from the Henry Horner Homes in Chicago is a withering tale of childhood hardship in one of the poorest neighborhoods in the United States. Kotlowitz stresses the psychic cost of growing up amid consistent violence, crime, drug abuse and drug trafficking, clashes with the police, and grinding poverty. In a moving narrative, Kotlowitz's preoccupation with the physical violence of the immediate neighborhood de-emphasizes the structural violence the broader society has inflicted on such neighborhoods. Racism, economic dislocation, and even bureaucratic insensitivity are mentioned, but the violent nature of community life is the story line. Kotlowitz cares for the boys he studied; he continues to visit them and pays for their private schooling. In the book's preface, Kotlowitz notes that the children's mother, LaJoe, had a hope, which Kotlowitz shared, that a "book about the children would make us all hear, that it would make us all stop and listen."[37] His work therefore represents an attempt to overcome the silences that surround the deterioration of poor inner-city neighborhoods. Yet Kotlowitz's uncontextualized and close reading of the psychic costs of growing up in a violent neighborhood allows his work to be appropriated by white readers to tell other stories. They are free to use it for self-rationalizations that reinforce stereotypical notions about poor inner-city African Americans. Kotlowitz's narrative tells white audiences what they are already predisposed to hear — depravity persists in the inner city.[38] The white outside observer chronicles the inside of the alien black culture without suggesting how the outside is implicated in constructing the inside. bell hooks provides an important point about the need of even the progressive, antiracist white documentarian to identity himself and the position he adopts: "As critical intervention it allows for the recognition that progressive white people who are anti-racist might be able to understand the way in which their cultural practice reinscribes white supremacy without promoting paralyzing guilt or denial."[39]

William Julius Wilson's most recent work builds on his earlier *The Truly Disadvantaged*.[40] This time, Wilson uses survey data and in-depth ethnographic studies of families in Chicago to make the case that racism and economic dislocation have contributed to the persistence of inner-city poverty. Yet a culture of resignation and resistance among some poor persons, particularly some young African American males, prevents them from making the most of the few opportunities that are available.[41] The connection between the story and the conclusion is not obvious. The telling of the tale is taken by itself as justifying the conclusion. The lure of ethnography is the power of its narrative. To narrate lives is the privilege to say what they mean. Narrative becomes self-legitimating, especially through retelling. Wilson's often-repeated narrative is about how the loss of middle-class role models has allowed many poor inner-city African American youths to forgo committing themselves to the world of work and achievement. Yet it is surely possible to tell other stories about these same individuals — stories that stress even the persistence of role models in the face of grinding poverty.[42]

In all three cases, the story exists for the point, and not the other way around. This problem, however, does not so much invalidate ethnographic narrative as highlight the dangers involved. Not all ethnographies of poor women with children, for instance, read the poor as an alien "other" who serves to reinforce ascendant notions of "us" versus "them." Carol Stack's work on the coping practices among poor African American families is a case in point.[43] Attention to who is writing ethnography and how is critical, however.[44] Ethnography must become a form of self-reflective criticism attentive to its own constitutive practices. Ethnography becomes social criticism directed against the discursive practices at how viewing subjects make sense of what is being viewed. Donna Haraway has written:

> There is a premium on establishing the capacity to see from the peripheries and the depths. But here lies a serious danger of romanticizing and/or appropriating the vision of the less powerful while claiming to see from their positions. To see from below is neither easily learned nor unproblematic, even if "we" "naturally" inhabit the great underground terrain of subjugated knowledge.... The standpoints of the subjugated are not "innocent" positions. On the contrary, they are preferred because in principle they are least likely to allow denial of the critical and interpretative core of all knowledge. They are savvy to modes of denial through repression, forgetting, and disappearing acts — ways of being nowhere while claiming to see comprehensively.... "Subjugated" standpoints are preferred because they seem to promise more adequate, sustained, objective, transforming accounts of the world. But *how* to see from below is a problem requiring at least as much skill with bodies and language, with the mediations of vision, as the "highest" techno-scientific visualizations.[45]

Confessional Character of Welfare Ethnography: Inverting Political Economy

The question of how one sees leads to the question of who is seeing and what discourse that person uses to represent what he or she has seen. Therefore, at some point, the psychoanalytic subtext of any political economy must be interrogated if we are to make intelligible the basis for a strategically chosen political economy. I must recognize, then, that my efforts on public assistance are affected by my self-identity, my personal preoccupations, and my political interests. Some form of confessional, therefore, is in order. This is not a confessional in the sense that Foucault has identified as a critical technique for expanding the disciplinary practices of subordination that invalidate my perspective as something I must strive to control.[46] Instead, this is a confessional that seeks to highlight the constitutive practices that make a political economy of welfare possible.

For too long a time, I have studied welfare politics while periodically suffering from self-inflicted wounds of guilt and shame unique to academic preoccupations. My self-doubt was that of a student of political economy who felt that he was not studying what was central to real political economy. Political economy in a variety of idioms told me that studying the poor was not sufficiently connected to the life forces that make society function, not focusing on the central issues of production and consumption in the "civilization of productivity" in a consumerist society.[47] Welfare and poverty dealt with the "underclass" — that is, those below the class structure of society — marginal people not central to the mainstream of American life. People on the margins, families on the bottom, practices outside the primary institutions were not critical.

I feared that my preoccupation with welfare as centered in the state led me to study things that were peripheral to what was at the heart of the political economy of market-centered societies. Real political economy was centered in the activities of production, emerged out of the relations of production, and was reflected in the political conflicts emanating from tensions between people involved in production — the owners of capital and the providers of labor. Yet I eventually began to appreciate that this inferiority complex was in good part a product of my unreflectively accepting the dominant economistic biases of a market-centered society.

I also feared that my preoccupation with welfare led me away from the central issues of political economy, because welfare was largely about reproduction as opposed to production. Welfare was largely concerned with the secondary, marginal, residual activities associated with the private realm of family relations. But after a while I started to realize that my self-doubts were in part attributable to my unreflectively buying into dominant patriarchical biases in our society that emphasized production over reproduction when in practice the allegedly private activities of reproduction are as central to society as those associated with the supposedly public realm of production.

Third, my self-doubt was compounded by the fact that I concentrated on activities that were salient primarily for marginal people of color in our society, whereas the real political economy was largely about the activities of white males who were at the center of political and economic decision making. Yet, again, I slowly started to realize that my doubts emanated largely from my thoughtless acceptance of the dominant race biases about who and what are important in our political economy. I came to realize that welfare is at the heart of the political economy and that it was only my unreflective acceptance of economic, gender, and race biases concerning what was commonly taken as central to our political economy that reinforced the idea that welfare was somehow marginal.

What passes for common sense, in other words, is not always so sensible. As Antonio Gramsci reminds us, it is often just like academic philosophy—a subordinate meaning system that, while reflecting a struggle to achieve reflectiveness, still remains tied to the dominant ideology.[48] The prevailing common sense of contemporary capitalist political economy minimizes how the modern welfare state is critical to politics in advanced capitalist societies such as the United States. Scholars in international affairs have become preoccupied with the tumultuous changes in Eastern Europe, the Middle East, and Africa. World politics has become increasingly about how nation-states everywhere seek to find how they can survive in an increasingly global economic order. Domestic political conflict in the United States, however, is increasingly grounded in and emerges out of the social welfare state.[49] Whether it is child care for working parents, prenatal care for pregnant women, catastrophic health insurance for the old, basic health care for the nearly 39 million Americans who as late as 1994 had no health insurance at all, wage equity, welfare, housing, jobs, or even such issues as worker safety, consumer protection, and clean air and water, our domestic politics is centrally shaped by division over the social welfare state. Whereas once divisions in the market were the basis for most political conflict, it is now more the case that divisions emerging out of the welfare state are the basis for domestic politics. The politics of market relations is being replaced by the politics of welfare state relations.[50] The debates about the Clinton administration's "public investment" strategy, health care proposal, and welfare reforms are but the latest installment in the ways in which the political economy of the welfare state has become the ascendant political economic discourse of even the United States and its market-centered understanding of these problems.

The prevailing common sense in political economy could therefore prove to be woefully ignorant. The line of vision it suggests could be blinding as well as distorting. Welfare and poverty, as allegedly marginal matters, are actually sites for ongoing political contestation where persons in need resist the structures of power in their daily lives. What is at the margin, offstage, and not part of the public transcript may in fact prove to be critical to understanding how the institutional practices of society play out in the lives of real people.[51] Although often considered marginal, these arenas of social exchange between those who have and those who do not may leave a

telling trace as to the real implications of the exercise of power and the allocation of resources. Examining the margin may be critical for understanding the "actually existing political economy."[52]

Every once in a while, something would happen, almost by accident, to
remind me that dominant modes for conceptualizing political economy
were askew. At one point, it was the Hill-Thomas hearings over Clarence
Thomas's alleged sexual harassment.[53] At another, it was a "nannygate" that
chased not just Zoë Baird but also Kimba Wood from the nomination for
the office of U.S. attorney general.[54] Whatever it was, there were events, in
the recent and not so recent past, that could remind me that what was
marginal was really central and that dominant modes of political economy,
Marxist as well as liberal, Keynesian as well as supply-side, served to marginalize social problems.

Therefore, even when the dominant modes of political economy did account for what is at the margin, they often did so in ways that trivialized
the significance of those practices. What was the problem of sexual harassment in the Hill-Thomas hearings was strictly a "women's issue," and not
the problem of reencoding African Americans as the alien "other."[55] What
was "nannygate" was a problem of child care, and not the problem of exploitation of low-wage labor.[56] What was called "welfare fraud" was often
not recognized as an honest attempt to make ends meet in the face of hor-
rendous bureaucratic obstacles. What was called "lack of work effort" was
often not seen as an expression of commitment to family and children.
What was called "welfare dependency" was often not appreciated as an attempt to escape difficult circumstances, leave an abusive spouse, take control of one's own life, and protect one's children.[57] A political economy
that marginalized welfare and poverty could also trivialize them.

The Political Economy of the Bottom-Up Perspective

What is marginal within any political economy is, therefore, critical to understanding the processes of marginalization implicit in any "actually existing political economy." With Foucault, we might want to suggest that what
is marginal is arguably crucial for viewing the exclusionary practices at work
in any political economy.[58] What is on the bottom is arguably what we need
to understand if we are to see how such political economies create hierar-
chies of power, privilege, and purpose. Knowing how it is that some come
to be seen as being on the margin or on the bottom can tell us much about
how the discursive constitution of social relations contributes to deciding

meaning and value, identity and the other, inclusion and exclusion, "us" and "them." The outside is inside; the marginal, central; the bottom, the top for providing the strategic view that allows for understanding the systemic forces at work in getting people to help reproduce life the way it is through their daily actions and exchanges.

Therefore, the problem of political economy is not just one of perspective or position; it is also one of discourse. Foucault asserts that political economies are to be understood as discourses of classification that allow for the creation and allocation of value in a variety of forms and venues — from construction of normality/madness to the imputation of self-sufficiency/dependency. My concern, however, is not with political economy in this generic sense, as implied rules of exclusion within discourses writ large. Instead, my concern here is with political economy in its common, if banal, sense — the realm of production and consumption of material goods. Mine is then a "political economy of political economy": a political economy of political economy written from the strategic position of those marginalized and excluded by that discourse. Writing about welfare in a way that attends to the consequences of that system for those on the bottom is therefore arguably an admittedly partial political economy that has special political merit. An alternative narrative that resists marginalizing the problems of welfare and poverty makes a major contribution to reducing the poverty of social science and enhancing the social science of poverty. Such a situated narrative can help articulate what is silenced by dominant discourses. Understanding welfare or any social phenomenon may be contingent on insisting on inventing an imagined position that has strategic advantage for articulating the perspective that needs expression. As Donna Haraway writes: "We are bound to seek perspective from those points of view, which can never be known in advance, which promise something quite extraordinary, that is, knowledge potent for constructing worlds less organized by axes by domination."[59]

Conclusion

Attention to perspective, position, and discourse suggests that political-economic narratives can be justified on grounds other than factually objective truth or authentically pure experience. In such narratives, quantitative work is no longer tied to the mystifying practices of social statistics that simultaneously individuate and aggregate people into reified groupings. Qualitative work forgoes the insistence that it capture authentic experience in some unmediated fashion. Instead, both qualitative work and quantitative work are limited to providing descriptive material within the terms of strategically positioned narratives that are attentive to their own knowledge construction practices.

One such narrative is the attempt to invert political economy in a way that accounts for how political-economic practices affect those on the bottom or margin. In the chapter that follows, I provide the first of several demonstrations with a bottom-up narrative of what I call the growing "privatization of public assistance" of recent years and its consequences for those on the bottom of the prevailing social structure.

~

Demonstrations

CHAPTER FOUR

Bottom-Up Discourse

Narrating the Privatization of
Public Assistance

> I myself would ask, isn't the emergence of new types of political struggle
> linked to the birth of new subjectivities that require more strategically
> located forms of critical analysis? There are not only multiple truths but
> multiple ways of articulating them.
> Lawrence Kritzman, *Michel Foucault: Politics, Philosophy, Culture*

If a political economy written in terms of consequences for welfare recipients is a political economy of the bottom, then a political economy of welfare written in terms of consequences for the growing numbers of people who are forced to rely on the increasingly privatized system of food assistance is a political economy of the margin of the bottom. "Inverting political economy" in this way to examine the welfare system in terms of the consequences posed for people by what can be termed the "privatization of public assistance" is a strategic choice justified by how it brings into view what is submerged in other discourses. In what follows, I provide a narration of the proliferation of food banks, food shelves, and privatized feeding programs in recent years as an example of the benefits of inverting political economy and examining the political-economic system in terms of its consequences for those on the bottom.[1]

The Privatization of Public Assistance

The continuing decline of welfare benefits has been extensively documented; however, the consequences of this decline for the poor are most often left undiscussed as attention continues to focus narrowly on attempts to reduce welfare dependency.[2] From 1960 to 1988 the real value of Aid to Families with Dependent Children (AFDC) had decreased 32 percent in the average state; from 1974 to 1988 the combined value of AFDC and food stamps had declined 18 percent in the average state.[3] One unavoidable consequence of the continuing retrenchment of public assistance has been the elaboration of a network of public and private emergency food and shelter programs. Added pressure for the growth of this network has been fueled by sharp cutbacks in food stamp allocations.

> First, in 1981, the Reagan Administration ceased funding for outreach. Then, between 1982 and 1986, it cut $6.8 billion from the budget. These cuts pushed 1 million recipients out of the program and reduced benefits for the remaining 20 million. By the time Reagan left office in 1988, the 18.7 million people still receiving food stamps reflected a decline in the participation rate (recipients as a proportion of poor people) from 65.6 percent to 58.9 percent. This figure was the lowest ever since the elimination, in 1977, of the requirement that the stamps be purchased. In effect it meant that another 12 million individuals were eligible for food stamps that they were not receiving.[4]

Nonetheless, by 1992, one in ten Americans was receiving food stamps, even if many more were eligible to receive and did not. Cutbacks in housing assistance have been even more dramatic.[5]

Over the past decade, soup kitchens, food shelves, and food banks have grown on a scale unparalleled since the Great Depression.[6] In Minneapolis, for instance, the Salvation Army's two food shelves were serving in 1990 about one hundred people a day for emergency food assistance, whereas ten years prior to that they served about one hundred people a month.[7] This eruption of food shelf users at these two centers occurred during a period when the total number of food shelves in the Greater Minneapolis area jumped from an isolated few to nearly thirty. By 1990, about fifty of the total 260 or so food shelves in the state had organized themselves into several networks— including, most significantly, the Emergency Food Shelf Network (EFSN) based in Minneapolis—and sought to pool resources, coordinate food drives, solicit contributions, and lobby government officials. All of this activity took place within the context of an emerging national food bank network called Second Harvest, which serves as the main supplier to food shelves for many canned and packaged goods, especially cereals and soups. Corporate donations, local food drives, and other contributions have helped fund this increasingly complex and increasingly bureaucratized emergency food network.

This emerging private food network suggests that the provision of aid for the poor has undergone substantial changes in the past two decades. Quietly, subtly, and almost entirely without explicit public policy, there has been an ongoing "privatization of public assistance"—a retrenchment of public welfare programs and the corresponding elaboration of a network of substitute services, often in the form of private aid. This shift in public assistance has included, most significantly, a decline in emphasis on income maintenance programs and a growing reliance on services, such as emergency food assistance, temporary shelter arrangements, and a variety of forms of treatment and supportive programs. These services often are in good part publicly financed even while they are often provided privately. They also often are only supplementary to cash assistance, which remains the major form of aid for many poor persons.[8]

Regardless of the funding sources and the extent to which the poor rely on these services, the shift, in both venue and type of assistance, is noteworthy. By moving to a greater reliance on services that are often provided privately, the country is developing forms of assistance that are more fragmented, less accessible, less visible, and less likely to offer the poor resources that can effectively address the problems they confront.[9]

This privatization of public assistance seems to be a resounding affirmation of the Bush administration's rhetoric calling for "a thousand points of light." The reality is more what Robert Kuttner has called "a thousand pints of Lite."[10] The privatization of public assistance is a pale, inadequate substitute for the economic resources that welfare previously provided. Private contributions have never matched the lost public funding. They tend to decline during economic slowdowns, just when the poor's needs increase. Charity drives are strongest when contributors feel like giving (around the winter holidays), not when the poor most need help buying things like food (in the summer when children are out of school and without hot-lunch programs). The shelter and food provided are inferior to what welfare benefits could buy previously. The system of private charity is extremely demeaning, reducing people to begging instead of allowing them to exercise their rights to public benefits.

Welfare by the Bag: The Political Economy of Food Shelves

Food shelf practices themselves represent the marginalized and submerged dimension of the increasingly privatized system of public assistance in the United States in the current period. Yet an examinination of this sort of "shadow work" may tell us much about what practices are really necessary if we are to address the needs of persons in poverty.[11] By making visible the practices of food shelves, we can "publicize" how the privatized system of public assistance is subjugating understandings of the poor's real needs. Making food shelf practices a recognized part of the privatized system of public assistance makes more visible the extent to which the existing system of public assistance is inadequate for meeting the needs of poor people. What is on "the margin of the bottom of the political economy" becomes critical for understanding the consequences of a deindustrializing postindustrial America for poor persons today.

The privatization of public assistance forces people to go hat in hand from agency to agency, never getting quite enough of what they need. The system of private charity makes a mockery of the social safety net — everyone falls through. The social safety net becomes an infinite regress. It is a multilayered patchwork of different agencies, all of which fail to appreciate adequately what the others have done. No single agency is prepared to take responsibility for the hunger problem in the United States today. Each poor person then falls from layer to layer, never sufficiently saved by the supposed safety net. The provision of emergency food services in the Twin Cities is a good example.[12] First, as many hardworking, dedicated workers in area agencies will agree, "emergency" is a misnomer. Most of the people coming to these agencies for help are from consistently hungry families who run out of food most months of the year. If they lose work or income, they often apply for welfare benefits, but food stamps rarely last more than three weeks into the month. They then often go to a food shelf. Most food shelves, as a rule, will provide each family with only one bag of food a month, enough to last three to five days. When that "emergency" allotment runs out, families have to rely on other food shelves, some of which will provide only one bag of food per family every six months, the Salvation Army, Catholic Charities, or some other generalized helping program. For the hungry, this usually means another emergency food bag. Still failing to get all that they need, some families then go to cooperative buying programs, such as Fare SHARE. Using these programs takes time; the food usually arrives one month later. Most poor families cannot wait. Next, adult family members skip meals; then everyone goes hungry.

In recent years the food shelves have become even more restrictive, given the demand for their services. Many shelves will take clients only by appointment. Those in need must now schedule their emergencies. The only food that will be dispensed without appointment in these shelves is baby food.[13] Hard-pressed to supply food to all who request it, the shelves are tightening access to include only those who successfully complete a scheduled intake interview. Under the press of too many clients and not enough food, the informal emergency food network becomes more formalized and begins to approximate the bureaucratic maze of the public assistance system. Consistent with Michael Lipsky's theory of "street-level bureaucracy," even these informal, charitable, emergency food shelves fall back on standardization, routinization, and other distancing and alienating case-processing practices in order to cope with the disjuncture between the demand for service and their ability to provide it.[14] Consistent with Foucault's writings on the disciplinary character of discourses of the self in modernity, food shelf discourse reconstitutes people who are coping with hunger as the "other" who lacks those qualities needed to be seen as a self-sufficient autonomous self.[15]

The food shelf as a site for disciplinary practices raises the question of just how far such practices reach into the institutional matrix of contemporary society. That prisons and mental institutions are sites for disciplinary practices invites very little surprise. Hospitals and schools are more challenging in terms of prevailing popular understandings. The welfare office is probably more often than not situated somewhere between these two sets in the popular imagination today. Work on the "soft coercion" of therapeutic practices has helped to highlight how such forms of "helping" can involve disciplinary practices that impute to clients needs, interests, and identities that reencode their deficiencies according to prevailing clinical, professional, bureaucratic, and social standards of autonomous, self-sufficient persons.[16] Food shelves provide an even more troubling site for disciplinary practices. As private, nonprofit centers of charity, often located in churches and community centers, food shelves are neither state-bureaucratic nor professional-clinical settings for regulation of the poor. They are private sites for the dispensing of voluntarily provided charity. Yet, as ostensible havens from the disciplinary practices of professional and clinical settings, food shelves provide especially insidious sites for such practices. Their private, voluntary character can serve to mask the reach of their disciplinary practices. That this occurs, even if only implicitly and in spite of all the goodwill of volunteers and dedication of staff, is what is most troubling.[17]

There is an almost inevitable reencoding of the prevailing discourse of dependency operating in food shelves.[18] Given their inability to handle the flood of people coming to them for food, those who staff food shelves ineluctably must adopt a discourse consonant with prevailing attitudes about the poor. Food shelf personnel must invoke discursive practices that enable them to shift responsibility for hunger back onto the poor themselves. Imputing deficiencies to the poor allows food shelf staff the room to justify the regulation of clients' behavior and the rationing of food and to maintain a sense of control over their own operations. Through these discursive practices, food shelves mete out discipline, regiment their clientele, and create the conditions for making their operations consonant with other efforts to rationalize the inadequacies of the actually existing political economy.

Food shelf discourse gets assimilated into the dominant discourse of "blaming the victim" — this time with the twist that, even if it is simply out of necessity, food shelves must insist that their "clients" learn to change their food-related behavior. Irrespective of their dire circumstances, persons in need are instructed to reconsider old truisms — this time for maximum effect while living on the edge. "Waste not, want not"; "Buy smart, eat wise"; "Look for nutrition, not enjoyment"; and even "Cooking is the fastest way to a man's heart" — these old saws circulate in food shelves, where recipients are regimented into the discourse of making do with less. The insistence that they act out such old homilies would seem trivial and banal were it not for the cruelty inherent in insisting that it is they who must change when they already have so little margin for error. Given the desperateness of their situation, clients must accept the insistence on increased discipline on their part. They have no choice but to allow themselves to be reconstructed as to their identities and practices. In order to receive food, they must allow themselves to be characterized implicitly as bad shoppers, poor cooks, ignorant dieticians, and thoughtless eaters. In order to achieve the means to continue to cope toward self-sufficiency, they must accept their participation in a food shelf discourse that marks them as dependent.

The discursive food economy of shelves is overly tied to food discourse in the broader society, especially as it relates to fulfilling "basic needs." Food, like clothing, and both more so than shelter, is considered such a fundamental basic need that it can be given away, if only in limited amounts.[19] Food here is associated more with necessity than with freedom, tied more to what is needed to be a productive member of society than to being a pleased consumer. Food then is a basic need that society must ensure is available to all its members if they are to be expected to make a productive contribution to the society. Even children's hunger is often addressed as needing rectification so that children can be healthy, alert, and attentive students.[20] The emphasis is therefore necessarily on meeting basic nutritional needs — food as necessity, not as a source of pleasure. Shelves therefore try to stock what people "need," not what they "want." Yet, as charity, food operates as a gift, and the gift givers determine what is given.[21] Ironically, they provide food that they themselves, whether they are individuals or corporations, do not need or want. To receive food, however, is to receive an excess in more ways than simply in getting surplus food. Accepting food from shelves also involves accepting the surplus meaning associated with that food. Such food is invested with notions of dependence and failure to achieve basic standards necessary for being a productive member of the social order. In addition to the nutritional value of donated surplus food, the symbolic value of the food exchange reinvests dependency in its recipients.[22]

Much of the discipline insisted upon by the food shelves emerges from their need to fit into the institutional matrix in which they find themselves.[23] Dependence on food banks, food drives, contributors, the state, and even volunteers necessitates practices that prove the shelves to be acting responsibly. The food shelves are dependent on others for obtaining the food they supply to the needy. In turn, they prove their reliability by organizing the way they dispense food so as to reassure those on whom they are dependent that they can be trusted to distribute food in ways that do not threaten vested interests.

First, most food shelves have limited paid staff and need volunteers from the neighborhood to serve clients. Volunteerism has its virtues, but it also creates an opening for parochial community standards to dominate understandings of what assistance can be provided, who qualifies to receive it, and under what conditions.[24] Just as food shelves reencode dependence in their recipients, the same happens to them when they accept the charity of the surrounding community, whether in the form of donated food or volunteered time. The charitable value of volunteerism necessitates rituals of food distribution. Volunteers, like good will and donated food, are in short supply. Shelves must try to limit client use if for no other reason than that they cannot be staffed sufficiently to meet demand. Shelves are often open only for selected hours on certain days. The net result is that a 1989 count of 1,184,425 individual visits representing 386,906 households in the state of Minnesota indicated that they visited food shelves on average approximately five times a year, even though more than one-fourth of these households reported that they had been chronically hungry and using shelves for more than two years.[25] By 1993, in Hennepin County alone, the home of Minneapolis and approximately one-fourth of the state's population, there were 622,683 visits to shelves by approximately 117,000 families, indicating a probable increase not just in the number of families using shelves but in the frequency with which each family relied on the shelves for assistance.[26]

Second, food shelves are heavily dependent on food banks, food drives, and donations. Most of the food they receive through these sources comes in the form of boxed and canned goods. Additional perishable foods, such as meats, are purchased on a lesser scale with cash contributions. The dependence on food donors means that shelves must necessarily tailor their operations to fit the food available. One immediate problem is availability itself. Dependence on local food drives means that food supplies have to be rationed in the hopes that they last until the next drive. Reliance on charitable campaigns makes it extremely difficult to plan how much food can be dispensed at any one time. Therefore, variation of client needs becomes secondary to the need to regulate the outflow of food.

Food drives also have other problems. Although they reflect the charitable efforts of members of the community, charity comes in many forms. People often donate leftover canned goods and other items that they themselves find to be of lesser quality and nutritional value than what they keep. Such foods are often high in salt and fat content. Some drive organizers and shelves have responded to this problem by publicizing the need for certain types of foods, and this has done much to improve the quality of the food donated.[27] Yet the bulk of food donated during drives remains canned goods. Drives pose the problem of generating food of a limited type and value. Shelves are then put in the position of having to dispense food that may not be best for recipients. Additional efforts in the immediate community to raise food donations are not enough to ensure that shelves can ensure both the quality and quantity of food needed. Cash contributions can provide even greater flexibility and help food shelves to procure high-protein items, such as meat, but money donations remain the smallest source for food shelf supplies.[28]

Food banks play a distinctive and particularly troubling role in the dependent context of food shelves. Food banks remain the most consistent source of food for the shelves; however, because of the way the structure of food banking in this country has been institutionalized, food banks are less-than-ideal sources. A food bank is a regional warehouse that accepts food donations, usually from corporate donors, to distribute to local food shelves, which in turn distribute the food to individuals and families who need it. The main food bank in Minneapolis, like more and more food banks around the country, is part of the Second Harvest nationwide network of affiliated food banks. In Minneapolis, food shelves buy food from the food bank at a bookkeeping charge of $.12 a pound.

Second Harvest is a growing national organization serving food shelves across the country. Food banking began at a St. Vincent de Paul soup kitchen in Phoenix, Arizona, in 1960. Second Harvest was founded there in 1979. It is now located in Chicago, Illinois, and comprises a nationwide network of more than two hundred food banks around the country.[29] As of 1990, it distributed more than 475 million pounds of food valued at more than $750 million.[30] Although much of its food goes to food shelves, Second Harvest also serves soup kitchens and various other feeding programs (see Figure 4.1).

The institutionalization of Second Harvest in less than a decade suggests the extent of the privatization of food assistance as an important part of the growing system of the privatization of public assistance writ large. Second Harvest reflects a recognition by the private sector that increased charitable assistance to the poor is needed in an age of reduced public assistance. Yet the particulars of Second Harvest pose new concerns about such alternative forms of assistance. Second Harvest is a nonprofit agency that is inextricably tied to the corporate food industry. In 1990, the chair of its board of directors was Carl Curry, vice president for logistics at Quaker Oats. Representatives of other food-related corporations and lobbies predominated on the board, including such brand names as Beatrice, Procter & Gamble, Stop & Shop, J. M. Smucker, Kings Super Markets, and the Grocery Manufacturers of America. The rest of the board was made up of representatives of participating food banks. A lone representative of any advocacy groups for the poor had just been appointed that spring.[31] Second Harvest is so entwined with the corporate food industry that there is good reason to suspect that its operations are designed to serve the interests of that industry. Corporations receive tax deductions for their food contributions to Second Harvest. Simply to keep its donors satisfied and willing to donate food again in the future, Second Harvest therefore specializes in distributing these corporate donations, and until recently did not solicit other types of donations, except money contributions to help fund its campaigns to solicit donations from corporate donors. In 1993, Second Harvest began

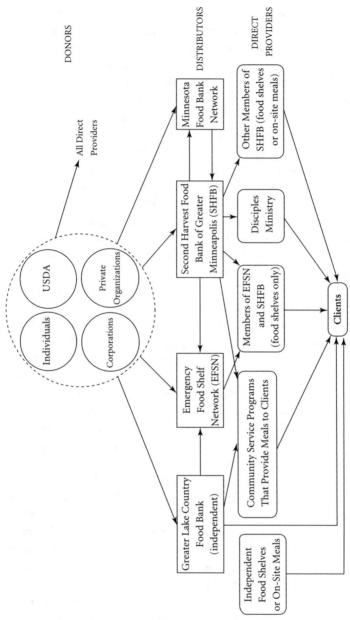

Figure 4.1. The flow of commodoties.

Source: Hennepin County Office of Planning and Development, *Description and Evaluation of the Emergency Food Distribution System in Hennepin County* (Minneapolis: Hennepin County Office of Planning and Development, March 1994), 4.

to solicit funds for "Value Added Processing" projects, where it took money contributions for the purpose of buying bulk foods, such as "rice, cereal and seafood," to distribute to food banks.[32]

Second Harvest's preoccupation with moving its corporate donors' particular contributions would not be such a problem were it not that much of their food is of limited variety—mostly cereals and grain-related products and canned goods. As Table 4.1 shows, Second Harvest reported in its 1990 *Annual Report* possessing 4.233 million pounds of meat, fish, poultry, and protein in addition to 10.304 million pounds of fruits and vegetables, compared with 36.476 million pounds of cereals and grains, 26.334 million pounds of snack foods and cookies, and 18.187 million pounds of household products. In fact, Second Harvest food banks possess so much unwanted and unsalable "product" that there is evidence that in some communities a substantial amount (as high as 60 percent) gets dumped as garbage.[33] Much of the meat and vegetables that Second Harvest distributes goes to hot meal programs and never makes it to food shelves. In 1990, food shelves in Minneapolis received no meat distributed from the food bank and had to seek other ways to ensure that foods rich in protein were in the bags of food they distributed.[34] As a major supplier of foodstuffs for shelves, the

Table 4.1. Second harvest product category summary of donations for 1990

Category	Millions of pounds
Assorted nonfood items	1.318
Beverages	11.088
Cakes, pies, puddings	2.600
Cereals and grains	36.476
Complete meals, entrées, soups	6.398
Dairy products	8.490
Dough products	11.400
Fruits and vegetables	10.304
Household products	18.187
Juices	9.613
Meat, fish, poultry, protein	4.233
Mixed assorted food items	16.843
Paper products	1.083
Pasta	3.093
Personal, health, beauty care	3.723
Snack foods, cookies	26.334
Spices, condiments, sauces	10.563

Source: Second Harvest, Second Harvest Annual Report: 1990 (Chicago: Second Harvest, 1990), 12.

Second Harvest food banks therefore create a serious constraint. They force shelves into trying to garner food from other sources, providing clients with a limited variety of foods, or placing limitations on client visits. Food shelves have responded by pursuing all three of these options.

Given these circumstances, the food shelves themselves are forever running out of food. As the economy turns down, so do private contributions. Food shelves have necessarily turned to the government for their own survival. Yet a proposal put forward first in 1991 and then again in 1992 to allow state taxpayers to earmark income taxes for food shelves was defeated in the Minnesota legislature. Some key players in the politics around the legislation emphasized that a tax checkoff would set a bad precedent, because it would institutionalize the food shelves when what is needed is more government commitment to guaranteeing adequate income assistance and jobs. For now, the shelves have had to content themselves with temporary appropriations from the legislature, first being funneled through the food banks and more recently directly to the shelves themselves.

It is clear that other concerns were also at work in the resistance to this legislation. Perhaps most vexing was the reluctance of food banks to support it. The Second Harvest food banks have preferred that the shelves be required to work through them. At best, then, the food shelves in Minneapolis, working with those in St. Paul and around the state, have been able to get appropriations put in the state budget for them to be able to make purchases from the food banks. This of course continues their dependence on the food banks and their supplies donated by corporate contributors. By 1993, the food shelves in Hennepin County were also receiving funding from the county, with $199,884 in 1993 going to the twenty-six food shelves organized in the EFSN (constituting 15 percent of EFSN's total funds) and an additional $485,360 going to other agencies offering food shelf services.[35] These appropriations provided opportunities for the shelves to acquire food from vendors other than the food banks, yet EFSN shelves on average in 1993 still acquired 22 percent of their total incoming pounds from the Second Harvest Food Bank of Greater Minneapolis. The county was also providing $46,819 to that Second Harvest bank, an amount equal to 9 percent of that bank's $507,730 1993 budget. Also, the county provided $234,788 in 1993 to an independent food bank named Greater Lake Country.[36] In addition, the county's Office of Planning and Development issued a report recommending that "the County should redirect funding from individual food shelves to the food banks and networks."[37]

Thus, government funding has not supplanted the rapidly institutionalized system of the privatization of public assistance, but instead is being used to further that institutionalization on terms favorable to the corporate interests promoting it. In turn, shelves necessarily continue to be forced to rely on the limited types of foods that the institutional donors supply, such as and in particular cereals, other grain-related products, and various canned goods. With an overreliance on these items, food shelves continue to have to work to get clients to tailor their cooking and eating habits to what donors want to give away and not to what is most nourishing. They must enforce disciplinary practices aimed at getting clients to cook and eat in certain ways not so much to get clients to "eat right" in the nutritional sense as to get them to "eat smart" in the sense of planning meals in terms of what is made available. Food shelves consequently feel an obligation even to draw on the assistance of nutritionists to run clients through workshops on buying food, planning meals, and "making meals from what's on hand"—as the helpful hints from a brochure given to food shelf users indicates (see Figure 4.2).

Food shelf workers stress that their efforts are only part of a broad mosaic of sources for meeting people's needs for food in the increasingly privatized system of public assistance. The food they supply is only part of the solution to hunger in their communities. Wages, cash assistance, and food stamps also contribute. Food shelves are, strictly speaking, providing emergency food assistance. Their food should not be understood to constitute the entire diets of recipients. Food shelf supplies are only "emergency" provisions designed to fill in the gaps in the food system. Yet that is the rub—food shelves are becoming a source of food for people who are chronically hungry. Although many food shelf users may be well served, others rely on "emergency" aid to address a chronic problem. Under such circumstances, food shelves are increasingly pressured to get recipients to make their chronic needs conform to the offerings designed to serve "emergency" purposes.

This is not to say that food shelves out of necessity must in all instances respond as they have. It is entirely possible that shelves could organize themselves in ways more attentive to client needs. This is especially the case when people in need in a community organize to provide food for themselves. Then it is likely that there will be fewer bureaucratic procedures and fewer restrictions on who gets food when, what food is available, and so on. In Minneapolis one such alternative food shelf organized by needy people themselves has emerged in the Powderhorn Park neighborhood. In addition, nothing currently prevents shelves or other providers from removing all

EFNEP Lessons may include the following:

- Making Meals from What's on Hand
- Planning Makes the Difference
- Let's Make Something Simple
- Home Invaders
- Shopping Basics
- Nutrients We Need
- Fruits
- Vegetables
- Milk and Cheese
- Bread, Cereal, and Pasta
- Meat, Poultry, Fish, and Eggs
- Dried Beans and Peas
- Protein Pairs
- Putting It All Together
- Eating Right . . . for Two
- Feeding Your Infant
- Feeding Baby Solid Food
- Feeding Your Preschool Child
- Gardening Basics
- Food Preservation
- Eating Right and Light

Figure 4.2. Brochure listing of nutrition workshop lessons.

Source: Brochure from the Expanded Food and Nutrition Education Program (Minneapolis: University of Minnesota, Minnesota Extension Service, 1990).

constraints and eliminating all overhead, as well as avoiding substandard food, by taking the funds used to create and maintain shelves and giving them directly to the people in need.

Nonetheless, a 1990 survey of Minnesota food shelf users underscores the difficult situation of food shelves in trying to meet the needs of people who come to them for assistance (see Table 4.2). Using shelves about five times a year, about one-quarter of the users surveyed had been using shelves for at least two years; about 60 percent were receiving food stamps, although almost all seemed eligible; and about one-half of households eligible for the federally funded and state supplemented Women, Infants and Children (WIC) food program were receiving WIC assistance. About 52 percent of eligible families had school-age children receiving assistance through the federal school breakfast program, and 78 percent had children receiving assistance through the National School Lunch Program. Nearly two-thirds of the households surveyed had children under 18 years of age. Fully 87 percent of those surveyed had household incomes below the government's official estimated poverty level; in households with one or more persons the average wage of the highest-paid worker was $5.82 an hour. Half of the households using shelves spent half or more of their income on housing, and children lacked health insurance in one-third of the households.[38]

In Minnesota in 1993, the number of food shelves had reached approximately 350. In all likelihood, developmemts in this area in Minnesota are indicative of developments around the country. Food shelves are becoming more commonplace. From the vantage point of food shelf users, the privatization of public assistance has elaborated a nationwide pattern: reduced public assistance for the poor means more and more families being shunted into the growing system of private emergency assistance. The paternalism of the system of public assistance intensifies as it moves from cash assistance to food stamps to food shelves. The growing reliance on in-kind benefits provided privately through such entities as food shelves suggests a turning away from the provision of publicly funded cash assistance. Like the poorhouse of old, this development represents a way of instituting discipline and enforcing the concept of "less eligibility": the idea that assistance to the needy should be as much as possible less than what wage work provides, so that the poor will be willing to take whatever meager means of support the labor market will provide them. This age-old disciplinary logic gets insinuated into food shelf practices even as food shelves strive to be sources of compassion. The institutional matrix in which food shelves

Table 4.2. Minnesota food shelf users

Total respondents	January 1990 13,085		July 1990 12,882	
	Number	Percentage	Number	Percentage
When was the first time household used a food shelf?				
Today	1,408	11.3	1,509	12.1
1–6 months ago	3,452	27.6	3,231	26.0
7–12 months ago	1,950	15.6	1,884	15.2
1–2 years ago	2,479	19.9	2,492	20.0
More than 2 years ago	3,199	25.6	3,315	26.7
Total	12,488		12,431	
Does anyone in the household receive food stamps?				
Yes	7,066	55.8	7,565	60.6
No	5,592	44.2	4,928	39.4
Total	12,658		12,493	
Does the household participate in the WIC program?[a]				
Yes	2,420	47.5	2,086	49.5
No	2,671	52.5	2,125	50.5
Total	5,091		4,211	
Do children participate in the free/reduced-price school breakfast program?[b]				
Yes	2,101	46.8	1,946	51.6
No	2,393	53.2	1,824	48.4
Total	4,494		3,770	
Do children participate in the free/reduced-price school lunch program?[c]				
Yes	3,512	78.8	2,886	77.7
No	946	21.2	828	22.3
Total	4,458		3,714	
Households with one or more children under 18				
Children under 18	8,141	64.2	7,968	64.7
No children under 18	4,545	35.8	4,341	35.3
Total	12,686		12,309	
Household income below the poverty line				
Below the poverty line	9,161	87.3	8,945	87.1
Above the poverty line	1,331	12.7	1,328	12.9
Total	10,492		10,273	
Current hourly wage of highest-paid worker in the household[d]				
		$5.63		$5.82
Percentage of income devoted to rent or mortgage				
30 or less	2,645	28.1	2,761	29.3
30–50	1,980	21.0	1,933	20.5
50–75	2,541	27.0	2,572	27.3
75 or more	2,251	23.9	2,168	23.0
Total	9,417		9,434	

Table 4.2. (continued)

	Number	Percentage	Number	Percentage
Are children covered by health insurance?				
Yes	5,011	64.6	5,120	67.1
No	2,741	35.4	2,514	32.9
Total	7,752		7,634	

Note: Data are from surveys conducted with as many food shelf users as possible who went to food shelves in January and/or July 1990.
[a]Asked only of households including a pregnant woman or a child under 6 years old.
[b]Asked only of households with children 6–17 years of age.
[c]Asked only of households with children 6–17 years of age.
[d]Average for those workers who indicated hourly wage.
Source: Anne Hamre and Peter Rode, *Hunger Hurts: How Government and the Economy Are Failing Minnesota Families* (Minneapolis: Urban Coalition and the Minnesota Food Bank Network, February 1991), 29–32, app. A.

operate creates insistences that disseminate disciplinary practices. The old is new. Just like the poorhouse that sought to reform and correct the poor, the food shelf becomes a site for helping poor people learn to be "self-sufficient" according to the insidious logic that excludes consideration of the political-economic context in which they must struggle for survival. And food shelves are but one element of the rapidly growing system of privatization of public assistance and its reliance on in-kind services provided privately through charitable organizations. With the institutionalization of the food shelf, the soup kitchen, and the homeless shelter, postindustrial North America lives to witness the figurative return of the poorhouse.[39]

Conclusion

Narrating political economy in terms of a discourse that accounts for the consequences of those on the bottom can help produce situated knowledges resistant to the homogenizing and marginalizing practices of top-down discourses. Inverted political economy can make central what is taken to be marginal. Without claiming a monopoly on the capture of authentic or geniune experiences of those on the bottom, bottom-up discourse can help offer alternative understandings that are attentive to how those on the bottom are denied voice, identity, and agency. The needs of those on the bottom can be rearticulated in terms that account for how prevailing structures work to marginalize them. Such a political economy can, for instance, help highlight the not usually visible workings of the increasingly privatized system of public assistance. Such a situated knowledge can provide a counterpoint for welfare policy research that continues to insist on its often implicit presumption that it explains the political economy of welfare from some imagined objective olympian perspective, outside the system, and is ready to offer those in positions of responsibility the managerial advice they need to reform the relationships of welfare and poverty.

CHAPTER FIVE

Home Economists as the Real Economists

For the purposes of government policy, poverty is not deprivation; it is a
bureaucratic category to facilitate the routine collection of statistics and the
determination of eligibility for public assistance. It is also a political
category, for if nothing else the history of the poverty line illustrates the
politics of numbers. Federal administrators have waged a quiet but
persistent campaign against increased standards and, at every juncture,
have both checked the expansion of benefits and minimized the problem of
poverty in America.
Michael B. Katz, *The Undeserving Poor*

In what follows, I examine how a top-down managerial discourse constructs
poverty and welfare statistics in ways that emphasize the state's managerial
concerns at the expense of the concerns of the poor. "Poor" statistical accounting is shown to be a product of a top-down, managerial perspective
that reinforces the logic of a market-centered society. I argue that the power
relations embedded in prevailing political-economic structures serve to
promote an interest in top-down statistics for the purposes of managing
the poor and welfare.[1] Interrogating the managerial character of these statistics can create leverage for making welfare policy more attentive to the
needs of the disadvantaged even within existing institutional arrangements.
Rather than seeking to replace managerial discourse with the allegedly more

genuine "authority of experience" of the poor, I suggest how questioning the biases of managerial discourse can open the possibility of replacing it with statistical narrations that are more attuned to the daily coping practices of the poor. In other words, the political efficacy of statistical work might begin when we start to appreciate that "home" economists have more to offer rather than "real" economists for understanding the political economy of welfare and poverty.[2] The poverty line, welfare needs standards, and error rates in the administration of public assistance provide three examples.

A Real "Home Economist"

Although most quantitative policy research related to poverty issues is inattentive to the question of perspective, there are selected instances of self-conscious attempts to ground statistical analysis in a perspective that emphasizes the effects of policy on poor people. For instance, many real, flesh-and-blood "home economists" have produced such statistical work. One is Mollie Orshansky, the author of what thirty years ago was to become the government's official poverty line.[3] Orshansky struggled valiantly but unsuccessfully to ensure that her eloquent articulation of poverty was not appropriated by other sorts of economists and policy makers, who eventually succeeded in transforming her work into a measure that is no longer tied to her original perspective.[4]

Mollie Orshansky's story is a paradigmatic example of how powerful men at times appropriate the skilled work of women and put it to use for their own purposes. As one of many bright, capable women who went into government service in order to help make a difference in the lives of those who were less fortunate, she worked for years in the shadows — in what she herself has called the "women's research ghetto."[5] One prominent policy analyst has referred to those women as the "ladies who studied poverty."[6] Their work may have been appreciated, but in a very patronizing way. More important, given their subordination in the public policy-making process, the work of "home economists" such as Mollie Orshansky was always at risk of being appropriated by public policy makers with a managerial orientation.[7] Orshansky's story is therefore also one of what happens when work that reflects the situated perspective of the home is taken over by analysts and policy makers who use that work according to the managerial orientation of a top down perspective. The moral of the stories that follow, therefore, may just be that until the alternative perspectives of the "home economists" are kept in the foreground during the making of public policy, there is little reason to expect any social policy to help the people who are ostensibly served by it.[8]

Poverty Redefined from the Bottom Up

One would not know it from the social science of poverty, with its pragmatic willingness to read its research agenda uncritically off the prevailing preoccupation with reducing welfare dependency, but the deteriorating value of the welfare grant is part of the current welfare dilemma. The median state monthly AFDC benefit for a family of four fell 42 percent in real dollars from 1970 to 1990. When combined with food stamps, the decline was 27 percent between 1972 and 1990.[9] Although states do not determine the size of their welfare grants according to the official poverty level, the national government's method for estimating the size of the poverty population is seriously implicated in the decline of benefits and is a factor in determining eligibility for such programs as food stamps and Medicaid.[10] For instance, if the poverty line is drawn so as to underestimate the poverty population, then the poor are likely to be seen as a marginal group with distinctive problems, and efforts to help the poor are likely to concentrate on narrow issues, such as the reduction of "welfare dependency," to the neglect of broader ones, such as the inability of a deindustrializing economy to create enough decent-paying jobs for a growing number of citizens. Interrogating the way the government has defined the poverty level from a managerial perspective can shed light on how the official poverty level is constructed in ways that fail to account for the basic needs of people living in the United States today. The value of questioning perspective in the construction of the poverty line is ever present, if only more so now given that in early 1992 the Committee on National Statistics of the National Academy of Sciences began a thirty-month study requested by Congress that includes an examination of the statistical issues involved in measuring poverty.[11]

The government's official poverty line was originally developed in 1963 by Orshansky, who, although not formally trained as a home economist, had surely become one of the government's best by the time she arrived at the Social Security Administration in 1958. Her formula for determining the poverty line, with estimates grounded in the realities of family practices for buying necessities, was far more sophisticated than previous ones. In particular, her work recognized that the cost of necessities would vary with family structure and composition.[12] The previous estimate had come from the Council of Economic Advisors (CEA). The CEA developed its own poverty threshold in May 1963, relying on the work of staff member Robert Lampman, and arrived at a $3,000 poverty threshold for all families regardless of size. This CEA threshold was hardly as sophisticated as the work being done by Orshansky at the time and that would appear in published form a short time later in July 1963. Orshansky's work relied on the "low-cost" and "economy" food plans for 1961 prepared by the Department of Agriculture to suggest how to achieve a nutritious diet in terms of common American food preferences at given levels of expenditure.[13] The "economy" food plan was an "emergency" plan "designed to provide a poor family with the minimum diet required to avoid basic nutritional deficiencies" as defined by the National Academy of Sciences, National Research Council's Recommended Dietary Allowances (RDA).[14] The "low-cost" food plan was designed to suggest how much a family with low income would have to spend on what foods in order to provide its members RDA on a regular basis.[15] On the basis of a 1955 Department of Agriculture study, Orshansky calculated that the average family, for all income levels, spent about one-third of family income on food. Thus, Orshansky multiplied the "low-cost" and "economy" food plans by three to arrive at poverty threshold.[16] Using the "low-cost" plan produced a poverty threshold for a nonfarm family of four of $3,955 a year, whereas the "economy" plan yielded a threshold of $3,165.

In January 1965, Orshansky published an analysis in which she revised her own work so as to indicate explicitly the poverty thresholds adjusted for family size on the basis of the number of children present, whether the family was headed by a man or a woman, and whether or not the family lived on a farm.[17] According to these calculations, in 1965 there were 31.9 million poor, or 12.7 percent of the population, down from 38.9 million or 22.1 percent in 1959.[18] In May 1965, the Office of Economic Opportunity (OEO) adopted the lower estimates for a working definition of poverty and as a basis for establishing eligibility levels for participation in the Johnson administration's Community Action programs, including Head Start. Orshansky was less happy about the use of her poverty thresholds to determine eligibility than about the fact that OEO chose her lower estimates.[19]

In 1969, the Bureau of the Budget adopted Orshansky's lower "economy" standard as the basis for establishing the government's official poverty thresholds for each year. The bureau had shortly before rejected the Social Security Administration's efforts to institutionalize continual updating of the poverty standard according to changing consumption patterns. Instead, the bureau accepted the recommendations of a federal interagency policy committee it had headed to review the poverty level and decided that the poverty line was no longer to be adjusted for the rise in the per capita cost of the economy food plan; after that it was corrected each year according to changes in the Consumer Price Index (CPI). Orshansky and others at the Social Security Administration had wanted the poverty thresholds to be adjusted periodically, yearly if possible, according to the best available information as to the costs of buying necessities and the proportion of those necessities constituted by food. The 1965 household food consumption survey provided such information and indicated that the low-cost plan should be 4 percent higher and the economy plan should be 8 percent higher than the current estimates. The new data also suggested a new multiplier as well. Yet both the Johnson administration in 1968 and the Nixon administration in 1969 rejected the idea of updating the poverty thresholds in this way. The net result was the compromise of adjusting the existing thresholds with their established patterns of consumption each year by the CPI.[20] Orshansky took solace in this move on the grounds that the CPI was moving up faster than the cost of food in the low-cost and economy plans. By the early 1970s, however, the reverse was to be the case.[21]

The decision to adjust the poverty line by changes in the CPI was, therefore, a compromise of sorts that over time would disconnect the poverty standard from the original concept that animated Orshansky.[22] By then, the other kinds of economists (i.e., mostly male macroeconomists) had taken over, and they relied on one of their most significant achievements—the measurement of price increases (i.e., the CPI)—to tell them how to adjust the poverty level each year.[23] This meant that in time the poverty level came to be less and less tied to the original concept of poverty that informed Orshansky's "bottom-up" home economist's perspective. The problem was deeper than the fact that the CPI does not measure the changing cost of living but only changes in prices of commodities or that it does so imperfectly.[24] For Orshansky, the shift to the CPI reflected the tendency of macroeconomists to want to think about poverty in terms of aggregates, such as the overall change in prices, rather than the specifics of day-to-day coping practices that would be better captured in a budget that would be adjusted periodically according to the most recent information available about changes in the cost of budgeted items, changes in the patterns of consumption, and related changes reflecting what people actually have to do in order to get by.

The poverty level came to be a reified entity disengaged from the realities of buying the necessities needed to achieve the generally accepted minimally adequate standard of living.[25]

Given its political construction, the poverty level in its transformed state was bound to receive much criticism. Liberals faulted the inadequacy of the "economy" food plan, the inappropriateness of the multiplier, and what was seen as the misleading use of the CPI.[26] Rather than focusing on the construction of the poverty line, conservatives focused more on how families were determined to be below the line. In particular, they stressed the failure to account for unreported income and noncash benefits.[27] Just about everyone complained about the failure to account for regional variations.

Examining the poverty line from the perspective of people who have to eat from the food budget used in its calculation provides a way to see how the current poverty line reflects managerial concerns about tracking changes in the poverty population, as opposed to trying to ground estimates of the poverty population according to the daily practices of people who have to try to get by on low incomes. Patricia Ruggles, in *Drawing the Line,* and John Schwarz and Thomas Volgy, in *The Forgotten Americans,* make the important point that times have changed, and where food may have once been one-third of a family's budget it now most often is a much smaller proportion, largely because of the growing costs of other necessities, especially housing.[28] By 1980, food for basic nutrition had fallen to one-fifth of a family's budget, and by 1990 its proportion was one-sixth. Using a multiplier of five, the 1990 poverty line for a family of four would have been $22,300 rather than the official standard of $13,360.[29]

In addition, as Harrell Rodgers and others have noted for years, the "economy" food budget was known from the outset to be simply too spartan to support people for any length of time beyond an emergency. In 1963, the Department of Agriculture found that those who were spending at the dollar cost level of the economy food plan had a one in two chance of achieving a "fair" diet and a one in ten chance of achieving a "good" diet, where a "fair" diet met two-thirds of the recommended minimum nutritional daily allowance and a "good" diet met 100 percent of that minimum.[30] What is more troubling is that the federal government has had alternative standards available for years. The Department of Labor's Bureau of Labor Statistics had until 1981 estimated a lower living standard that reflected a more realistic market basket of goods on which a family could be expected to get by. Using the last lower budget in 1981 would have put the poverty line 65 percent above where the official line was drawn, but only 10 percent above where it would have been drawn had the government revised the multiplier to adjust to the rising cost of nonfood necessities.[31]

Using Ruggles's and others' work, Schwarz and Volgy developed their own "threshold of self-sufficiency" to establish a more reasonable economy budget.[32] This is a budget more tied to the original relational and normative concepts of poverty behind the Orshansky formula. Gordon Fisher has noted that the Orshansky methodology was very much designed to reflect a relational concept of poverty:

> Orshansky made use of the economic principle known as Engel's Law, which states that the proportion of income allocated to "necessaries," and in particular to food, is an indicator of economic well-being.... It is important to note that Orshansky's "multiplier" methodology for deriving the thresholds was normative, not empirical—that is, it was based on a normative assumption involving (1955) consumption patterns of the population as a whole, and not on the empirical consumption behavior of lower-income groups.[33]

The original Orshansky poverty standard was therefore also normative in the sense that it was related to the normative practices of all families in allocating about one-third of their disposable income for necessities to their food budgets.[34] The Orshansky formula was not designed to measure economic destitution, but how much money an *average* family would need to achieve the lowest healthful level of the prevailing standard of living.[35] As that standard and the cost of necessities on which it was based changed, it would be necessary for the poverty standard to change. Adjusting the poverty standard only for price levels would not capture how the standard of living was changing, especially if those price levels were like the CPI and not limited to the necessities people needed to achieve a minimum adequate standard of living.[36] Schwarz and Volgy's budget is therefore more like Orshansky's "home economist's" budget, for it is more thoroughly grounded in the home budgets of people today and what they have to spend in order to get the basic necessities of food, housing, transportation, medical care, clothing, and related items. In fact, their work is even more directly grounded in the costs of necessities because theirs is a standard budget that costs out all items, whereas Orshansky's arrived at a total cost indirectly by costing out food and then using a multiplier. Theirs is a complete "standard budget" or "market basket" approach.[37]

Tied to the material costs of living in this country today, Schwarz and Volgy's budget produces a threshold of self-sufficiency of $20,658 for a four-person family in 1990. This is actually below what the official poverty line would produce if it were simply updated by the CPI and the more appropriate one-fifth multiplier. Nonetheless, using this standard, Schwarz and Volgy find that in 1989 about 56 million Americans, or 22.8 percent of the population, were below their threshold of self-sufficiency. Using Orshansky's original poverty concept that led to the official measure and multiplying the "economy" food plan (after 1975 that plan was replaced by the "thrifty" food plan) by its inverse proportion of the average family's budget, we find that 63 million, or about 26 percent of all Americans, lived in families with incomes below that threshold in 1989.[38] The conservative complaint that other uncounted resources, especially in the form of non-cash benefits, inflate the poverty population are not relevant, because their cash value would not likely bring families over this "new" line.

Schwarz and Volgy have also added the important point that the radical changes in the composition of the poverty population that conservatives like to stress are in good part caused by the way the poverty level has distorted estimates of the prevalence of poverty over time.[39] Once corrections are made, not only do we find that there are approximately 62.8 million poor people (26 percent of the nation's population), or twice the number of poor estimated by to the government, we also find that the poverty population is *not* composed of nonworking, welfare-receiving, or female-headed families to anywhere near the extent those conservatives would suggest. Only an increasingly irrelevant official poverty measure has led us to that conclusion; the alleged "feminization of poverty" (i.e., the increase in the proportion of poor in female-headed families) is in good part an artifact of the government's "poor" statistical accounting. The poverty of many poor female-headed families may be real, but it is not new or something that is crowding out other types of poverty. Also, welfare dependency is not the problem it is often made out to be. Only about one-fifth of Schwarz and Volgy's poor are on welfare, rather than the 40 percent the government estimates. In addition, contrary to the emphasis of many policy makers, work is not the solution; there are 7 million rather than 2 million full-time, year-round workers living in poverty. A poverty line drawn from the perspective of a "home economist" and estimated on the basis of what it takes to achieve what Schwarz calls "the lowest healthful level of the prevailing standard of living" provides a very different view of "reality."[40] Whether the National Academy of Sciences will take the perspective of "home economists" remains to be seen.[41]

Looking at the Welfare Grant from the Bottom Up

Interrogating the managerial biases implicit in the official poverty line helps to show how the current poverty standard insufficiently accounts for the daily realities of coping with poverty. It also helps us to understand how underestimating the poverty population contributes to an antiwelfare climate that encourages the erosion of welfare benefits. Drawing the poverty line from a discourse that gives weight to the coping practices of the poor can help to begin to redress this state of affairs. In fact, there is much to be gained by looking at the welfare grant itself from a perspective that resists managerial biases and narrates statistical analysis of the welfare grant according to how it is used by recipients in their daily lives.[42]

Examining the welfare grant in terms of the extent to which it helps meet the daily needs of welfare recipients is something that is too often neglected by elected officials, administrators, and taxpayers who prefer to rely on a vocabulary that stresses the costs of "welfare dependency" rather than the capacity of the welfare guarantee to ensure well-being.[43] New York, as one of the states that has suffered sharp declines in the value of welfare benefits over the past two decades, offers an excellent example. New York has the second-largest welfare population in the United States. It is also a traditionally liberal state and therefore can perhaps serve as a litmus test. If New York's grant is deficient in various ways, it is likely that the grants of less liberal states are as well. The New York welfare grant provides a glimpse of the convolutions inherent in many states' current welfare grant systems and their effects on the ability of recipients to maximize their potential.

Today, New York has a partially consolidated AFDC grant. It is one of ten states that does not provide its AFDC benefits in one allowance.[44] Nonetheless, the current system is more consolidated than what came before. This system can be traced to the late 1960s, when the state moved away from multiple "special needs grants" to a consolidated grant for special needs before eventually instituting the current system for AFDC. At that time, the state established separate grants for "basic" needs and "shelter." (Since 1981, the state has added a third grant — a "home energy" allowance.) This grant system therefore actually represented a consolidation. Before 1970, welfare recipients in New York could receive a series of special needs grants, such as a furniture allowance every two years, in addition to a recurring monthly grant. The "flat grant" was initiated in 1970 both to save money, by consolidating all special needs grants into one $100 grant, and to counter organized efforts by welfare rights groups to leverage special grants for all their recipient members.[45] The flat grant also facilitated a shift to a more routinized system by automatically providing basically the same benefit to each household (adjusted for family size). In short, the flat grant offered standardization and cost savings.[46]

New York then replaced the flat grant system with a "basic" grant and a "shelter" grant. The basic allowance is based on a "standard of need." The development of the standard was precipitated by the decision in *Rosado v. Wyman* (1970), in which the U.S. Supreme Court ruled that each state must specify a "standard of need" as the basis of its AFDC payments. The Court, however, made allowances for a state "to accommodate budgetary realities" and pay recipients less than the standard of need. The Court stated that while this system "leaves the states free to effect downward adjustments in the level of benefits paid, it accomplishes within that framework the goal, however modest, of forcing a State to accept the political consequence of such a cutback and brings to light the true extent to which actual assistance falls short of the minimum acceptable."[47] In other words, states were obligated to set a need standard based on real costs, but they were not obligated to pay it. The difference between what the state paid and what was "needed" constituted the basis for future political discourse. What the Court overlooked was that a state could underestimate need when setting its standard and then pay recipients the "full amount." In this way, a state could shortchange recipients and save money without paying a political price for the hidden shortfall. This is exactly what New York did.

The basic grant was based on a modified version of the U.S. Bureau of Labor Statistics Lower Living Standard (LLS). The LLS was the lowest of three budgets developed by the federal government for a four-person family. It was the sum of costs of a specified list of goods and services deemed necessary for a "minimum standard of adequacy." New York's modifications consisted of making various downward adjustments to the LLS. Logically, certain categories of goods and services included in the federal LLS budget were eliminated because they were met by other grants or programs. For example, the shelter category was eliminated because it would be covered by the "shelter allowance." Other LLS categories were eliminated because they were determined to be nonessential or inappropriate items of consumption for families in need of public assistance. Consequently, the need standard contained no allocation for such items as reading materials, recreation, nonpublic transportation, tobacco, alcohol, gifts, contributions, and food away from home. When New York eliminated the LLS allocation for "food away from home," it did not compensate by adding to the allocation for food at home. Apparently a welfare family was expected not only *not* to eat in restaurants, but to do completely without food when the LLS family dined out. Other downward modifications also took place, the most dramatic of which was a final 12 percent reduction of the remaining total based on the composition of the average welfare family and its alleged lesser needs.[48]

The net result of these modifications was a welfare grant that amounted to 42 percent of the total LLS budget and only about two-thirds of the cost of comparable categories of the LLS (in other words, excluding shelter costs, occupational expenses, medical expenses, tax payments, social security and disability payments, gifts, contributions, and insurance, as well as the items mentioned earlier).[49] Worse, although the newly devised grant was issued effective July 1, 1970, it was based on May 1969 prices. A family of four received a maximum of $231 per month in 1970 in the basic, or nonshelter, portion of the grant. The first and only actual net increase in the basic grant per se occurred in 1974, when benefits were brought up to the costs of the same goods and services for January 1972. Other than utilities—which, like shelter, have come to be treated separately—all items in the basic allowance were still pegged to the cost of living in January 1972 by as late as 1990. Excluding utilities, in July 1987 it cost $589 to purchase the same quantity of goods and services that the welfare grant provided only $243 to cover (compare the second and third columns in Table 5.1). Thus, welfare recipients in the compassionate "family of New York" received in 1987 an average of $1.96 per person per day to cover about half their food (food stamps added a modest amount), some of their medical expenses (Medicaid is often erroneously assumed to cover all health care needs), and all of their clothing, furniture, transportation, baby bottles, soap, school supplies, toothpaste, toilet paper, kitchen utensils, and so on. If a welfare mother takes one round-trip ride on the subway in search of an elusive job, she is already dipping into her children's benefit share. Or just consider the cost of baby shoes for feet that change size every three months.

The inadequate nature of New York's "basic" grant cannot be made more painfully obvious than through a consideration of its effects on the food budget of recipients. Even when food stamps are added to the allocation for food at home, New York's "food package" falls short of need. In fact, the combined total for food is estimated to be less than the food package available in most other states—including Mississippi, the poorest of the fifty states. In 1979, the food stamp allotment for a four-person family receiving maximum AFDC benefits in New York was $83 per month. The

Table 5.1. Monthly basic allowance in New York State for a four-person family, compared with real costs as of July 1987

Categories of goods and services included in the basic allowance (utilities excluded)[a]	Original basic allowance set at May 1969 prices (in dollars)	Adjusted allowance of 1974 set at January 1972 prices (in dollars)	Cost of items in allowance at July 1987 prices[b] (in dollars)
Food at home	121	137	357
Household furnishings	24	26	54
Public transportation	7	9	35
Clothing	47	50	85
Personal care	13	14	39
Education and miscellaneous	6	7	19
Total	218	243	589

[a]Utilities were included in the original calculation of the basic allowance; however, separate "home energy allowance" grant increases in 1981 and 1985 based on energy-related inflation have changed the technical construction of the total welfare grant. Originally, utilities were budgeted in the basic allowance at $13 per month and then adjusted upward to $15 per month in 1974. This $15 was still in the basic allowance in July 1987, but it would be misleading to compare it with 1987 energy costs because 1981 and 1985 "home energy allowance" grants had by 1987 added $68.70 to the total monthly grant for a four-person family. The "home energy allowance" is now a separate grant alongside the basic and shelter allowances, therefore all utilites are excluded from the comparisons in this table.
[b]Actual costs for food, furnishings, clothing, and personal care are according to corresponding items in the Bureau of Labor Statistics' Consumer Price Index. "Education and miscellaneous" was by 1987 no longer used as a category in the CPI, so the 1987 actual costs shown here were calculated according to the cost of the CPI's "other goods and services" category. Actual costs for transportation are calculated from the rate of change in the actual cost of public transportation in New York City.
Source: The data in this table appeared originally in Theresa Funiciello and Sanford F. Schram, "Post-mortem on the Deterioration of the Welfare Grant," in *The Reconstruction of Family Policy*, ed. Elaine A. Anderson and Richard C. Hula (Westport, Conn.: Greenwood, 1991), 158. Reprinted with permission of Greenwood Publishing Group, Inc.

state assumed that $137 (29 percent) of the $476 total monthly AFDC grant was to be spent on food. The total food package for these New York families therefore was $220 a month. In Mississippi for that year, a four-person family receiving maximum AFDC benefits was eligible for $189 a month in food stamps. Mississippi's welfare grant, which in 1979 was a maximum of $120 per month for a family of four, was designed to include 42 percent, or $50, for food. Adding the food portion of the welfare grant ($50) to the food stamp allotment ($189) brought the Mississippi total monthly food package to $239, or $19 more than was made available for food in New York State.[50] Using the same methodology for 1987, the gap widens to $28, with Mississippi's total food package at $331 and New York's at $303.[51]

New York recipients had, of course, more money in the rest of their AFDC budget than recipients in Mississippi and could, theoretically at least, shift funds to cover their food costs. But New Yorkers would be doing this at the expense of other basic needs, which have been underbudgeted from the very beginning of the state's need standard and have fallen increasingly short of actual costs. In addition, by 1988 the position of New York's food budget vis-à-vis other states had not improved, and if anything had gotten worse, as changes in New York State shelter benefits resulted in decreases in the food stamp allotments for the state's AFDC recipients. In spite of automatic cost-of-living increases in food stamp allotments, on two occasions between 1980 and 1988 significant downward shifts in food stamps took place for New Yorkers as shelter allowances were increased — an ironic and troubling circumstance explained below.

The fact that the New York grant is compartmentalized into different allowances serves to limit recipients' access to all of the grant and to constrain the extent to which they can juggle it. In New York, as in nine other states, benefits for "shelter" are determined separate from other benefits and are specifically allocated for housing. In some cases the "shelter" check is a two-party check that is cosigned by the landlord. In most cases only the recipient's signature is needed to use the check, but flexibility in using it for needs other than housing remains limited. This benefit is paid out according to the individual's or family's actual rent payment, up to a specified maximum. If a recipient's rent is lower than the maximum (or "shelter ceiling"), his or her grant is lowered accordingly. On the other hand, if the amount needed for rent is higher than the ceiling, the "excess" must be taken from some other portion of the total grant — that is, from some part that is technically allocated for some other item of need. Relatively high shelter grants may make the total New York grant seem high, but they often merely pay high rents for the inadequate housing the poor normally get. In addition, because "shelter" benefits are supposed to be used only for housing, the "basic" grant is left to cover other needs — a job that, as we have already seen, it does not do well.

The problem, however, is more serious and more ironic. To be sure, some income increases have accrued to New York's welfare budget in forms other than the "basic" grant. For instance, the shelter allowance had been raised twice during the Cuomo administration, for a total average increase of 51 percent. This sounds like a major benefit increase, and it is, but the actual beneficiaries are not the poor, whose food stamp allotments decrease by one dollar for every three-dollar increase they receive in rent allotments.

The real beneficiaries are landlords, who raise rents in direct response to each shelter allowance increase. In New York City, for instance, median gross monthly rents had risen by only 6.8 percent during the three-year stretch prior to the first shelter allowance raise implemented in 1984. Researchers who examined the low rent patterns concluded that the ceiling for welfare rents was acting like informal rent control.[52] They were right: in the very first year subsequent to the shelter grant increase, the median gross monthly rent was up 7 percent; by 1986 it had swelled 19.7 percent.[53] The second of these shelter grant increases was implemented in January 1988. For the most part, recipients are likely to be living still in the same quality (usually dilapidated) housing, paying more for it, and eating less. Because more dollars passed through their hands on the way to landlords, fewer dollars were available for the purchase of food when their food stamps were automatically reduced. For nonwelfare poor families who share approximately the same low-rent market, the effects were likely even worse. That is, general housing market increases would not have been met by automatic wage increases on the job.

There has been one portion of the welfare grant in which purchasing power has actually increased: energy—heating and other utility costs included. In view of severe oil price inflation, the federal government in 1979 exempted energy-related public assistance grant increases from consideration in the calculation of food stamp budgets if states could prove the need for such increases based on actual costs. Because New York had severely underbudgeted utilities in the first place, and given the impact of inflation, the state was able to take advantage of this provision in 1981 and 1985, instituting and increasing a "home energy" allowance. (Several other northern states with cold winters and high heating and other utility costs did likewise.) The first and larger of these was enacted in the Hugh Carey administration following a two-year organizing drive for basic grant increases led by welfare recipients themselves. The second was initiated by Governor Mario Cuomo, largely to offset the reduction in food stamps allotments precipitated by the first of his two shelter grant increases. Together, these home energy supplements have added a monthly total of $68.70 for a four-person family. As such, energy is the only item of need for which welfare in New York maintains a resemblance to real costs.

The "basic" grant, the shelter allowance, and now the home energy allowance constitute New York State's "standard of need" for welfare recipients. In 1975, New York State's standard of need for New York City for a three-person family was 110.1 percent of the poverty line. By 1987, this figure had dropped to 62.9 percent of the poverty level.[54] Even when food stamps were added in, recipients generally still fell below 75 percent of the poverty line. In 1990, New York State finally increased the basic allowance, but only by 15 percent, hardly enough to compensate for the ongoing deterioration in the real value of the welfare grant. This increase, of course, resulted in another drop in food stamps for New York State welfare recipients, thereby perhaps promoting the Cuomo administration's political popularity among liberals more so than the interests of poor families. In 1981, the Bureau of Labor Statistics stopped producing estimates for the LLS, making further comparisons between changes in the rising cost of the standard and stagnant welfare grants extremely difficult. Even without such comparisons, given that there have been no actions to reverse the trend, it is surely still one of a widening gap between what people needed and what the state was willing to provide.

Yet, viewed from the perspective of purchasing power, the New York State welfare grant looks even worse than the numbers can show. For instance, the shelter allowance has increased 51 percent since the ceilings were first established in 1975, but the housing available to poor people in New York City, where two-thirds of the state's welfare recipients live, has never been more scarce or in worse condition. It also costs far more than it ever did. That is, recipients must pay more and get less. Purchasing power has therefore decreased even in the part of the grant that has seen the biggest increase over time. Also, shelter grants cover only shelter costs and do nothing to compensate for shortfalls in the rest of the welfare grant. What is true for New York is also true for the rest of the country, at least in terms of the purchasing power the welfare grant affords recipients: by 1992, state cutbacks in public assistance were intensifying, and after two decades of declines in the real value of welfare grants, AFDC benefits were far below the poverty level throughout the country. As of 1992, the combined benefit from AFDC and food stamps together was above 80 percent of the poverty line in only seven states; thirty-six states had benefits below what the states themselves had determined to be needed for subsistence, according to their own needs standards.[55]

Churning: Welfare Fraud from the Bottom Up

Even if welfare recipients get all the income to which they are entitled, they remain among the poorest of the poor. However, securing all they are entitled to continues be a major undertaking. In other words, the problem of

AFDC in New York State is not just with what is given out but also with what should be given out and is not. For instance, one-fourth of all active public assistance recipients outside of New York City were not receiving their food stamps in the late 1980s.[56] In addition, in New York City more than 44,000 people were getting cut off welfare each month for reasons unrelated to financial eligibility. More than two-thirds of these cases returned to the rolls within six months—a clear indication of continued need.[57]

The practice of cutting people off and putting them back on the rolls later has been called "churning."[58] For weeks or even months, families churned from the rolls are left without public assistance. This practice has been linked to increased homelessness and hunger.[59] Yet, given the prevalence of a "top-down" managerial perspective, much of social science has ignored this phenomenon.[60] Piven and Cloward note: "One searches in vain in the hundreds of social science research reports on AFDC that were published in this period for an examination of the regulatory and administrative changes that were used to drive the rolls down. Instead, evidence of changes in actual welfare practices was produced mainly by the anti-poverty legal services community."[61] Statistical accounting of churning is not a major concern for those with a managerial orientation. States and the federal government continue to resist pressure by welfare rights advocates to measure the phenomenon. If concern registers, it is more likely to be chalked up as part of the administrative effort to reduce fraud and abuse. The story of why churning remains part of the invisible netherworld of welfare administration tells us much about the managerial myopia that afflicts "poor" statistical accounting.

How does churning occur? There are many ways, but one of the most common is usually termed "noncompliance" by welfare departments. From a welfare department's point of view, noncompliance occurs when a client is cut off welfare for failing to meet some obligation. One frequent cause of the accusation of noncompliance is the failure of a client to return a "letter recertification." Welfare departments mail questionnaires to the homes of recipients; the recipients must fill out and return the questionnaires by specified return dates in order to be recertified as eligible to receive benefits. Thousands of people are cut off every time recertification letters go out, because they never receive their letters, the letters are not in a language they can read, they fail to return them, or a variety of other reasons. It is difficult to imagine that any recipient would willfully disregard such a "mailout," given that the result of such disregard most often is termination of welfare benefits. In fact, it has been shown that many cases of "noncompliance" are the result of mailouts never being received by clients; returned, completed questionnaires never being recorded properly by the department; and questionnaires in English being mailed to non-English-speaking clients, who treat the mailouts like junk mail. In the late 1980s, more than 44,000 people in the Big Apple were losing benefits each month for reasons unrelated to financial eligibility. More than two-thirds of these cases returned to the rolls within six months.[62] The local welfare offices have argued that such terminations are "correct" in that, irrespective of cause, the recipients did not return the required paperwork. This is taken de facto as noncompliance.

The New York State Department of Social Services (DSS) responded to charges of churning in 1984 by performing an internal audit of case closings and reopenings.[63] The department reported that the problem of churning was not confined to New York City, but was a statewide practice. Although DSS officials did not dispute the two-thirds figure for cases returned to the rolls within six months, they maintained that "only" 54 percent of the cutoffs could be categorized as inappropriate. (The department decided that only those cases returned to the rolls within sixty days, not six months, should be considered inappropriate closings.)[64] Of this 54 percent, about half were the result of "technical errors" and the other half were classified as "worker errors." For example, some recipients who had clearly notified their workers of address changes were cut off and designated "whereabouts unknown." This occurred because the information on address changes stored in the workers' case files was never entered into the computer that generated the mailing labels. When recipients in these cases "did not comply," they were removed from the rolls. These and similar terminations were classified as "worker errors."

Despite a commitment to reduce the frequency of these "administrative closings" (as officials preferred to call them), very little progress was made by the end of the 1980s. Instead, the practice increased. According to Anna Lou Dehavenon, an anthropologist working primarily in this field, more than 400,000 people, at least half of whom were children, were removed from the welfare rolls in New York City alone each year in the late 1980s.[65] Doug Lasden and his colleagues reported in 1987 that 64 percent of those interviewed at New York City soup kitchens were eligible for welfare but were not getting it.[66] In some cases, applicants had been incorrectly rejected at intake; in others, recipients had been cut off for "administrative reasons." In an era of retreat from social responsibility, the callous admin-istration of welfare — even to the extent of denying essential legal entitle-ments to poor people — has become acceptable.[67]

Churning is also not just a New York problem, nor is it a relic of the 1980s. A study by Timothy Casey and Mary Mannix for the Center on So-cial Welfare Policy and Law indicates that it is a nationwide phenomenon, and that in 1984 alone more than two million *eligible* children and one million *eligible* adult caretakers were denied AFDC simply because they failed to comply with procedural verification requirements.[68] An estimated "two-thirds of procedural denials (which represented about one-third of all denials) were to eligible families."[69] Evidence continues to appear that churning is still occurring throughout the country, and that it is working to reduce people's access to assistance.[70] There is also evidence that churn-ing increases the administrative burden and costs associated with an in-creased number of appeals and fair hearings.[71]

During the past two decades, churning has been exacerbated by states' attempts to reduce their error rates in overpayments to recipients and pay-ments to ineligibles in order to avoid penalties in lost funds that the federal government has threatened to impose under its quality control procedures.[72] After being phased in during the 1970s by the retrenchment-oriented Nixon administration, the procedures required states to reduce errors in pay-ments and eligibility determination. From the one-sided managerial per-spective that emphasizes reducing costs and controlling the size of the wel-fare rolls, the federal government decided to count errors only in granting aid, not in denying it. This built-in bias, in effect, encouraged states to deny aid to many who are eligible. Failure to reduce errors in overpayments to 3 percent, as defined by federal quality control audits, would lead a state to lose the federal share of the total overpayments that exceeded the 3 per-cent cutoff. Responding to complaints by states, Congress imposed a mora-torium on the imposition of federal penalties.[73]

Legislation in 1986 removed the moratorium while reducing the extent to which states were at risk of penalty.[74] The Omnibus Budget Reconcilia-tion Act of 1989 authorized a new AFDC quality control system beginning in fiscal year 1991 that pegged penalties for *over*payments to whether they were above the national average and for the first time gave states credit if their error rates in making *under*payments were below the national aver-age.[75] Yet states are still not penalized for *under*payments. Error rates also are still considered, potentially encouraging denial to people who actually are eligible as part of efforts to avoid *over*payments and keep costs down. Churning has continued, and evidence indicates that probably more than a million cases a year are still being churned from the rolls.[76]

A congressionally commissioned National Academy of Science study in 1988 was extremely critical of the quality control system and its effects on people's ability to get and maintain public assistance.[77] In spite of the 1989 changes, the quality control system still creates greater incentive to reduce overpayments as opposed to underpayments.[78] Meanwhile, for active and potential recipients, getting and keeping benefits have remained arduous tasks.[79]

Overcoming Managerial Myopia in the Welfare Grant

As the one-sided nature of the government's definition of *errors* illustrates, the solution to the problems of the welfare grant are not easily visible from the managerial perspective, with its preoccupations of reducing recipient fraud, minimizing dependency, saving money, and placating landlords. The managerial perspective highlights recipient fraud and deemphasizes the fraudulent nature of its own practices. In the case of New York, it leads to some simple responses. Increase the basic allowance and reduce draconian administrative practices. An increase in the basic allowance would generalize to an overall increase in purchasing power, because the market for items covered by the basic allowance is not sensitive to welfare benefit increases. The price of the public transportation system, for instance, is not sensitive to welfare grant levels in any discernible way. Therefore, an increase in the allocation for public transportation should not have any effect on its cost. The result would be an increase, then, in the purchasing power of recipients. A substantial increase is particularly critical for the basic allowance, which has declined greatly in real value because of inflation. Consolidating the grant and reducing the heavy hand of the bureaucracy would also allow needy people to receive aid in ways that would free them to cope with their circumstances and not waste time playing serious games just to keep the benefits to which they are entitled.

Even for states that do not have partitioned grants, rethinking grant levels in terms of what they afford recipients would be a refreshing change from the ongoing slide in welfare benefits. The federal call to reexamine state needs standards provides an opportunity. That the federal government has made this a perfunctory exercise should not stop states from trying to set grants at levels commensurate with need. The logic of the bottom-up perspective is clear, but it is yet to be followed in New York or elsewhere to any great extent. Although the federal government's Family Support Act of 1988 requires that states review their needs standards with an eye to determining what their welfare grants ought to be, the U.S. Department of Health and Human Resources has written rules that make this review a pro forma exercise.[80] The net effect is that most states are currently contributing nothing to the overall purchasing power of welfare recipients, while continuing declines in the real value of benefits sink people ever deeper into poverty.[81] These developments suggest once again that when managers call for bottom-up analysis it is most often a halfhearted request doomed to fall outside the established managerial categories for thinking about welfare. Until the issue of perspective is taken seriously among analysts and policy makers who still find comfort in the pieties of allegedly neutral social science, how government constructs statistics about welfare and poverty will continue to be part of the problem and not part of the solution.

Conclusion

Narrating welfare statistics in terms of the effects on persons living in poverty provides a basis for understanding the meaning of welfare in the current period. We live in a time when the issue of poverty has been supplanted by the issue of "welfare dependency." Welfare is now seen as part of the problem rather than as part of the solution. Increased welfare benefits and liberalized policies that started in the 1960s have been alleged to encourage irresponsibility among the poor, but the foregoing narration of the welfare grant raises questions about this perspective.

Drawing a poverty line risks marginalizing those whose incomes place them below it. There are good reasons to count the poor, but underestimating what people need in order to get by, and correspondingly underestimating the number of poor, only marginalizes the poor further and reduces the already slim prospects for universal social welfare programs. There are good reasons to believe that there are many more poor people than official estimates indicate. Many more of the poor are working full-time and year-round, and a smaller proportion are welfare dependent, than government figures show. The poverty population today is probably not very different in demographic composition from the poverty population of thirty years ago. The managerial orientation of many who study, influence, and make welfare policy has de-emphasized this reality, concentrating instead on the issue of welfare dependency. This perspective has contributed to the prevailing notion, insufficiently grounded in the realities of poverty, that poverty is primarily a problem of a distinctly marginal group. The climate in which this notion persists has in turn allowed a serious erosion of the real value of welfare benefits.

CHAPTER SIX

Rewriting Social Policy History

Our knowledge will take its revenge on us, just as ignorance exacted its
revenge during the Middle Ages.
Friedrich Nietzsche

The fact is that every writer creates his own precursors. His work modifies
our conception of the past, as it will modify the future.
Jorge Luis Borges

Once human enactments are banished from the value- and meaning-
creation process, the effect is depoliticizing, for the assumption that a
discursive mode delivers truth, rather than being one practice among other
possibilities, discourages contention.
Michael J. Shapiro, *The Politics of Representation*

To the New Right, the most shocking and pernicious example of the
permissiveness that gripped American society was located in the public
sector, in the form of government programs to aid the poor. The New
Right's analysis of poverty and welfare became for a time, the conventional
wisdom. By the mid-eighties, liberalism appeared, for all practical purposes,
to be dead.
Barbara Ehrenreich, *The Fear of Falling*

During the 1980s, conservatives initiated an active rewriting of social policy history. The sixties came to be seen as an era of irrational profligacy and the Johnson administration's War on Poverty as a misguided attempt to blame society for the problems of poverty.[1] The alleged excesses of the sixties were accused of helping promote abuse of the welfare system that led to "welfare dependency" replacing poverty as the preeminent problem for social policy. By discouraging attempts to achieve "self-sufficiency," growing welfare spending was increasing poverty, not decreasing it.[2] Yet, a discursive sleight of hand may have been at work. What once was called "use" now was "abuse." Where welfare benefits were once contingent upon how long one needed them, now any extended spell of welfare taking was seen ipso facto as exploitation of the system. Given the persistence of this perspective, it should be no surprise that the Clinton administration has continued the line of welfare reform that started in the 1980s by trying to bring about "the end of welfare as we know it" by attaching a two-year limit to the receipt of public assistance.[3]

What follows is a case study that illustrates how narrative, especially historical narrative, is profoundly political.[4] It is a case with a particular point. The 1980s rewriting of social policy history exemplifies how social science statistical work is often implicated in the construction of historical narrative and simultaneously comes to be constructed out of such narratives.[5] I want to suggest that even though conservative commentators were at the forefront of the 1980s transformation of use into abuse, social scientists helped underwrite this rewriting and in turn came to be influenced by it. I want to suggest how this rewriting of social policy history has proven critical for producing statistical interpretations that have in turn reinforced that interpretive context. This reciprocal relationship between social context and social science has one redeeming feature — it invalidates the myth of autonomous social science and highlights the extent to which such work is implicated in politics.[6] Less hearteningly, the dialogic relationship between the broader social context and social scientific research has helped rationalize the draconian welfare policies of the past decade. The analysis that follows shows how this context persists in the current period in spite of the availability of data that suggest other possible interpretations.

Rewriting the Past/Present

The 1980s rewriting of social policy history reencoded the old distinction between the "worthy" and the "nonworthy" poor, this time with extended welfare use as a sign of unworthiness. A person's worth in the past was derived from his or her being able to exhibit practices that pass for self-sufficiency—practices that are increasingly unavailable for growing numbers of people who confront a lack of decent-paying jobs in a declining, deindustrializing economy.[7] Rewriting social policy history to stress welfare dependency makes it possible to deny the significance of the economic changes overtaking the United States and instead to locate the site of the problem in welfare and the poor's dependence on it.[8] Rewriting social policy history has made plausible the counterintuitive idea that less welfare spending will produce less poverty.[9]

The 1980s conservative rewriting of social policy history can therefore be seen as a socially significant instance of how narrative operates to legitimate historical understandings, which in turn act as controlling metaphors for structuring contemporary practice.[10] What William Connolly calls "critical histories of the present," or what Michel Foucault calls "genealogy" or "eventualization," reveals the reversibility of this process.[11] Such analytic exercises show how narratives are politically potent, especially to the extent that they get to be seen as constituting the definitive story of how that past informs the present.[12]

Hayden White suggests that narrative is a problem only when we try to give "*real* events the *form* of a story."[13] Yet, as Michael Shapiro suggests, narrativity is ever present, irrespective of the genre of writing, history and policy included, for there are never any real events as we know them until there are narratives. Jean-François Lyotard suggests that pretensions toward objective historical scholarship are no solution to this dilemma, whether the perspective is for moving from the present to the past or the past to the present.

> We habitually pose the following sequence: there is the fact, then the account of the witness that is to say a narrative activity transforming the fact into a narrative.... This position on the problem of history poses a theatrical model: outside, is the fact, external to the theatrical space; on stage the dramatic narrative unfolds; hidden in the wings ... is the director, the narrator with all his machinery, the fabricator of narration. The historian is supposed to undo all the machinery and machination and to restore the excluded, having beaten down the walls of the theater.... But it is obvious that the historian is himself only another director, his narrative another product, his work another narration.[14]

Rather than trying to search out which are the "real events" and which are the narratives, Shapiro emphasizes that what is worthy of analysis is the type of narrativity and the consequences for historical understandings of the past and regulative ideas of the present.

Recognizing the narrative dimension of history is particularly important. History, especially in the form of stories of origins, beginnings, sources, or other instances of genesis, has political purposes in bestowing lineage and the power of continuity on present-day practices. The present comes to be seen as consonant with that from which it allegedly derives.[15] Given the ascendance of temporality as an authorizing dimension, Foucault, Edward Soja, and others have stressed the political potency of historical narrative, even while searching for ways to displace its supremacy.[16] For Jacques Derrida, historical narrative sets the terms for deciding what is "historic" in a profoundly doubled sense: what is historic is that which represents a break or rupture or discontinuity; however, it is also something that has the salience to endure becoming that which animates, activates, or catalyzes continuity.[17] The historical emerges out of narrative practices that decide what is to be the same or different. From a psychoanalytic perspective, the historian who constructs such binaries repeats an already repetitive process reenacted in everyday life each time in order to achieve stabilization within his or her own identity and in relation to the historicized world. For Jacques Lacan, the historian trades on the trope of metonymy (i.e., renaming by association) and is animated by desire (as a compulsive but unsatisfiable need) that motivates yearning for full narrative closure and the stabilization it affords.[18] At a basic level, historical narrative responds to the impulse to evaluate the different in terms of the familiar so as to enable the past to inform the present and the present to be a(n) (ad)vantage point for understanding the past.

Historical rewritings are therefore politically potent. In the case of the 1980s conservative rewriting of social policy history, that potency was realized in ways that have had probably more effect on contemporary policy than on understandings of the past. For more than a decade now, "welfare dependency" has replaced poverty as the main object of social policy. Correspondingly, welfare reform has stressed welfare-to-work programs designed to get recipients to take whatever jobs are available. The workfare orientation of the new welfare approaches is rooted in the old ways. It is based on the historical and invidious distinction that rewards the poor who earn paychecks while denigrating those poor who do not have wage-earning jobs.[19] It is rooted in the history of public assistance in the United States and has taken many forms over the years, from the "worthy" versus the "nonworthy" poor of colonial nomenclature to the "truly needy" versus "welfare chiselers" of the Reagan years.[20] Yet the concern about "welfare dependency" was not just business as usual. Focusing on welfare dependency to the neglect of burgeoning poverty became credible in no small part because of the success of the historical narratives that circulated in the 1980s. The Reaganite variation on the old theme helped inspire a concerted effort by many on the right to rewrite the history of public assistance so as to suggest that in the current period welfare has been overused and abused according to historical standards.[21] This rewriting of social policy history has helped insinuate old distinctions into the current postindustrial context in a way that has helped forge a "new consensus" to fight welfare dependency as the key problem of public assistance today. A "new consensus" on welfare among conservatives and liberals in Congress reflects this rewriting in that it stresses that welfare dependency rather than poverty is now the major problem confronting public policy makers.[22]

The Conservative Rewriting of Social Policy History

The major theme of the rewriting of social policy history that took place in the 1980s emphasized that public assistance programs of the contemporary welfare state, beginning with the Social Security Act of 1935, were invariably intended to be temporary forms of assistance. This perspective has appeared again and again in recent years in discussions regarding social programs, from welfare to food stamps to housing assistance and others. What has been lost in this rewriting is that most, if not all, of the programs under discussion never included any time-specific limits on how long people could receive these benefits, whether they were housing placements, food stamps, or cash assistance.[23] The skirmishes in the policy-making process over limits on the receipt of benefits never resulted in such limits being specified. The past decade's new orientation on social policy was, therefore, another instance in the long historical battle over just how long people should be expected to rely on social assistance. It reflected a growing desire on the part of conservative political leaders in particular to emphasize that social programs in general and welfare in particular are forms of temporary, short-term "relief." The conservative rewriting of social policy history, therefore, reflected an attempt to win the battle over how long people should receive benefits by suggesting the matter had already been determined.

The extent of this rewriting of social policy history is reflected in the case of housing policy. From the first major piece of housing legislation to the onset of massive cutbacks in federal housing assistance in the 1980s, no act of Congress or any administrative regulation ever suggested that residents of public or publicly assisted housing were eligible to reside for only a limited or fixed time period. There was never any suggestion that extended residence was an abuse of this form of public assistance. The Housing Act of 1937 defined eligibility for residence largely in terms of low income.[24] Subsequent legislation continued to refine these guidelines. Initial eligibility eventually was tied to percentages of median income. Rent was also scaled to income. Residence could be for an indefinite period of time. That never changed.

What did change over time was the availability of these units for those who needed them. Federal housing legislation was given to setting construction goals that housing programs never met. The Housing Act of 1937 promised to build one unit for every substandard unit destroyed, for no net increase.[25] Urban redevelopment and then urban renewal became the emphasis starting in 1949, with the intent to clear away dilapidated housing and improve the inner city with business development and housing projects constructed by private developers. The 1949 legislation promised 822,000 new units but funded only 322,000. Yet, between 1950 and 1980 some 735,000 families were displaced, and between 1948 and 1969 approximately 425,000 units, almost all of them occupied by the poor, were demolished and only 125,000 new units were constructed. The 1980s brought massive reductions in housing assistance, from $32.1 billion in 1978 to $9.8 billion in 1988, a decline of 80 percent in real dollars. Whereas on average 377,000 new households received housing assistance annually from 1977 to 1980, only 82,000 new households on average were assisted annually from 1981 to 1988, a decline of nearly three-quarters.[26]

Throughout this time it was not eligibility according to length of residence that changed, but waiting lists for public housing in many cities; these lists grew ever longer, with thousands languishing on them for years. "In 1987, 13,000 families were signed up for vacancies in one of Baltimore's 17,000 units of public housing. Similarly, in Chicago, 49,000 units of public housing had a waiting list of 44,000 people; in Sacramento, almost the entire public housing stock of 2,800 units would have to turn over in order to make room for the 2,700 families who were awaiting vacancy."[27] By the end of 1992 the waiting list for Housing Authority apartments in New York City had reached its highest level ever at 240,000, nearly equaling "the total number of units in all of the city's public housing projects and subsidized apartments."[28] And with longer waiting lists came rising homelessness.[29]

Such developments might be expected to spur new construction, but by the 1980s blame-the-victim attitudes were even stronger than they had been in the past. By 1992, they turned even to housing — the bedrock of the American Dream. Rather than confront the failure of federal housing policy, the Bush administration began to complain that resident use was really abuse.[30] Extended use of public housing was a sign of welfare dependency. As with workfare and other new requirements for welfare, the administration announced the Family Self-Sufficiency Program, which was designed to promote self-sufficiency of tenants by getting them to complete their education, take training, or fill job placements. People on waiting lists could leapfrog over others if they agreed to participate. The underlying assumption behind the program was that it would "restore public housing to its original purpose of serving as a way station for the upwardly mobile."[31] The phrase "way station" was used to suggest a temporary resting place. Now public housing had been integrated into the "welfare dependency" mentality. Legitimation for such a move required rewriting of social policy history to suggest that public housing had strayed from its original purposes. Yet this was not the case. Only from the vantage point of the contemporary obsession with welfare dependency could such a suggestion be made. Historically, public housing was about replenishing and expanding the availability of affordable housing. Whether people lived there for extended periods was not an issue, at least not until it became part of the discussions on how to retrench the welfare state. By then, discussion pushed on to increasing evictions, enhancing management prerogatives, and, finally, privatizing housing.[32]

The rewriting of social policy history had come to suggest that the shortfall of federal housing construction was really the abuse of extended residency. Similar arguments were made about food stamps and income assistance. Given this reorientation, policy makers were encouraged to focus on what was wrong with welfare and welfare recipients rather than on what was wrong with the economy and society at large. In perhaps the most astonishingly unabashed version of this rewriting of social policy history, Lawrence Mead has suggested that this reorientation is of such profound proportions that it has restructured the political agenda writ large:

> The problem of entrenched poverty in the United States has caused a sea change in American politics. Since poverty first became a leading issue thirty years ago, the questions that most bitterly divide Americans have shifted from how to secure working Americans more of the good things of life to how to cope with the problems of seriously poor and dependent

Americans, most of whom do not work. Once the most divisive demands on government were inspired by the working class; they now arise from the nonworking underclass.... My main point is to define the essence of the new dependency politics and contrast it with the progressive past.[33]

Mead assumes that this new orientation in policy reflected a qualitatively distinctive set of problems concentrated in the people dependent on welfare that made them different from the poor who preceded them. These differences lay, for Mead, in the psychological attitudes of the "nonworking" poor.[34] Yet it does not take too much familiarity with the history of welfare policy discourse in the United States to appreciate the banal familiarity of the "worthy" versus the "unworthy" poor. Mead knows he is often focusing on poor African Americans and single mothers, but he seems blithely unaware of how his insistence that the poor are "different" reinforces standards biased in favor of white males. For Mead, "the poor" really are different in moral standards and social practices. Mead's insistence that "psychology is the last frontier in the search for causes of low work effort" verges on returning welfare policy discourse to the realm of sociobiology. Like the colonists in the writings of Frantz Fanon, Mead needs to naturalize the differences of his "other" to reinforce the standards he sets for himself.[35]

Like so many other apologists for a market society, Mead wants to stress the personal traits of "the poor" over the inability of the economy to provide opportunities. But what Mead takes to be a change in attitude may in fact be a result of a change in economics. In other words, even if we accept the debatable idea that there is a pervasive attitude problem among the poor, it is distinctly possible that after long bouts of un- and underemployment many people do lose a commitment to work.[36] These attitudes are often a manifestation of the extent to which a postindustrial economy has left many people without much reason to be hopeful that work will provide the means for escaping poverty.[37] Rather than a new class of poor with qualitatively different attitudes, instead there is a new political economy less prepared to create opportunities for a growing number of people.

The Politics of Autonomous Social Science

The 1980s rewriting of social policy history has affected public policymaking perhaps most dramatically by reinforcing the context for interpreting policy-relevant social science data. This rewrite helped reinforce statistical interpretation in counterintuitive ways: more welfare spending will create more poverty; less spending, less poverty. Ostensibly neutral data open to multiple interpretations have been read to validate welfare as the cause of persistent poverty (see the discussion on this point in chapter 1). Major social science investigations of welfare dependency, formation of female-headed families, and related topics were read in the 1980s by conservative analysts, commentators, and policy makers as legitimating their draconian reforms even when the research in question was open to other interpretations less supportive of these reforms. In turn, social scientists then responded by taking this interpretive context as given and allowed it to cycle back and frame their own investigations such that more and more work has been done about "the underclass," "unstable families," and other coded characterizations of those marginalized by the class, race, and gender barriers operating in this society.[38]

The relationship to popular biases underscores a double bind for contemporary social science. Social science proves to be at its most policy efficacious when it is helping to reinforce the dominant biases that serve as the backdrop for its own statistical interpretations.[39] Feminist scholars have helped show how the work of natural scientists systematically works to deny the extent to which their efforts are framed in terms of the broader social, cultural, political, and economic context that their writings in turn help reinforce.[40] Helen Longino has stressed that the objectivity of scientific inquiry will be achieved only when scientists recognize the socially constructed character of such inquiry; that is, "contextual" values in the broader society, along with "constitutive" values in scientific practice itself, influence scientific interpretation.[41] And what is true for natural sciences is no less true (indeed, is probably more true) for social scientific investigations dedicated to understanding the social order. Just as Darwin's theory of evolution was immediately recognized for its troubling parallels to political economy,[42] so too should the ideas of a passive and dependent welfare population be seen in terms of the troubling subtext of race and gender relations in the United States today.

The writings of conservatives, such as Charles Murray and Lawrence Mead, did not by themselves provide the social science that reinforced common biases about welfare. More authoritative sources, presenting original analyses using large-scale data sets and sophisticated statistical treatments, were necessary to lend the legitimacy of allegedly autonomous social science to the rewriting of social policy history. Ostensibly neutral research on such matters as the length of stay on welfare, the effects of welfare on family structure, and the work disincentives of welfare has helped to reinforce the dominant perspective, if often in ways unintended by the researchers.[43]

This literature offered evidence that became "facts with a life of their own" that could provide ammunition on the alleged deleterious effects of welfare on the behavior of poor families.[44] The conclusion offered was that welfare breeds dependency and therefore more poverty. Less, rather than more, welfare spending must therefore be the cure for the ills of poverty.

Social Science in the Conservative Rewriting of History

Conservative social scientific work has had a more explicit role in helping to reinforce the interpretive context for suggesting the counterintuitive relationship between welfare and poverty. The "new consensus" on welfare reform has been helped along by a growing body of conservative social science literature.[45] Most of the frequently cited conservative tracts, however, have relied on reinterpretations of the statistical works of others. Mead, for instance, has contented himself with grinding through large numbers of statistical studies to twist findings out of context so as to reinforce his persistent belief that the poor ought to work more.[46] For instance, he uses data on all minimum-wage workers that show most of them to be in families with other sources of income to suggest that taking minimum-wage jobs does not lock most family heads into poverty. Only after working through numerous statistics does he note in passing something that undercuts the entire argument: most minimum-wage workers are teenagers living at home with their parents.[47]

Mead also attacks the spatial mismatch hypothesis, which suggests that rising unemployment among the inner-city poor may be attributable to the flight of jobs to the suburbs, suggesting that equivocal findings of others are not enough to convince him. He then proceeds to minimize the costs of transportation, assuming that everyone has access to buses that will get them to where the jobs are.[48] He never discusses the Gattreaux program in Chicago, which suggests that when poor minorities are located in the suburbs, closer to where many jobs have moved, they are more likely to find work.[49] He claims without evidence that the growth of part-time work in recent years is largely voluntary.[50] He dismisses the widening gap in wages between black and white males as not relevant to the issue, except to imply that black males are reducing their work effort.[51] He dismisses data on declining wages, only to point out that aggregate family incomes rose from 1970 to 1986, overlooking that the gap in family incomes has widened.[52] He overlooks that single mothers worked as much in 1984 as they did in 1959, even while the proportion receiving welfare fell from 63 percent in

1972 to 45 percent in 1988.[53] He discounts the lack of availability of child care as a reason for nonwork among single mothers; however, he hangs his case on two isolated 1979 studies that projected at best a 10 percent rise in work effort by these women given the availability of child care.[54] He also dismisses low wages as an obstacle to work for these families, arguing that the frequent unavailability of medical insurance is not a serious impediment.[55] Mead's work is at least instructive in that it highlights the practice of making much of statistical studies that did not necessarily imply the conservative policy prescriptions that commentators insinuated.[56]

Original statistical work conducted by conservatives actually has been rare. Much of it has been in the form of trend-line analysis on welfare and poverty data.[57] Explicit conservative interpretations of these data became the preferred way to galvanize the opinions of conservatives on this topic, to get them to take an interest in welfare reform. Spokespersons for a "New War on Poverty," which has concentrated its attention on attacking welfare, have often relied on Charles Murray's *Losing Ground* and its trend-line data to make the case that welfare has been producing poverty since the War on Poverty.[58] Murray and his followers suggested that something happened during the Great Society years of the mid- to late-1960s that started to promote welfare dependency. The trend-line data indicate that over time poverty has not evaporated in the face of increases in social welfare spending. Indeed, increased social welfare spending has at best only papered over how much poverty there really is and has obscured our ability to see the persistence of what Charles Murray has called "latent" or "dependent" poverty—that is, the level of poverty that would exist if people did not receive (or if no one had ever received) welfare payments from the government.[59] A more pointed version of this argument is that increases in cash public assistance payments to poor persons have since the 1960s not only obscured the persistence of "latent" poverty but have in fact been one of its contributing causes.[60]

The "latent" poverty measure was actually a relabeling of a statistical construct, "prewelfare" poverty, originally designed by other poverty analysts. Their purpose was to show how much poverty existed before government provided assistance, to provide a baseline for assessing the relative antipoverty effectiveness of welfare expenditures in recent years.[61] This statistical hypothetical also took on a life of its own and came to be used by Murray and the others to show how the growth in "latent" poverty and a continuing gap between the official poverty rate and "latent" poverty meant that government assistance was promoting "welfare dependency." The official government poverty rate included only those who were poor after receiving government assistance. The "prewelfare" poverty rate included the "latent" or "dependent" poor who subsisted on government aid. Increases in "latent" poverty and the gap with "official poverty" implied that more people were dependent on government assistance. For Murray in particular, "latent" poverty was not a baseline for assessing the antipoverty effectiveness of government expenditures, but a measure of growing "welfare dependency" (see Figure 6.1).

Murray's transformation of the "prewelfare" poor into the "latent" poor was tendentious. The "latent" poor include people who are made not poor after receiving government assistance. Why this is necessarily a bad thing is something Theodore Marmor, Jerry Mashaw, and Philip Harvey asked Charles Murray:

> To put the point slightly differently, Murray's idea of increasing "latent poverty" or "dependency" suffers from a seriously misleading lack of focus. "Dependency" sounds like a bad thing, but that is because we tend to associate it with particular sub-groups of the "latent poor," those whom we believe should be supporting themselves. Does Murray really think, for example, that the very substantial reduction of poverty among the aged over the past twenty-five years has been a bad thing? Would he argue that Social Security pensions should be viewed as having created a group of "dependents" who represent a serious social policy failure? Again, clearly not. He has simply used a technical term, "latent poverty," interchangeably with a pejorative label, "dependency," to justify a massive and unnecessary sense of disquiet about our social welfare arrangements.[62]

Murray's data were quickly seen by many as bad social science — simplistic and misleading.[63] However, this did not stop these data from being used to reinforce popular biases that then cycled back to serve as the interpretive context for social science work. Much the same thing had happened two decades earlier, when Daniel Patrick Moynihan offered impressionistic interpretations of trend-line data on welfare cases and black male unemployment rates. "Moynihan's scissors," as Moynihan himself likes to call it,[64] showed how welfare rolls continued to rise even as nonwhite male unemployment rates declined (see Figure 6.2). These data could mean many things, especially because only troubling assumptions could uncritically pair welfare cases regardless of race with nonwhite male unemployment rates, but to Moynihan they came to mean, in the infamous phraseology of his 1965 government report, *The Negro Family*, that the African American family was wrapped in a "the tangle of pathology" from which it could not extricate itself even with improvements in employment rates for African American males.[65]

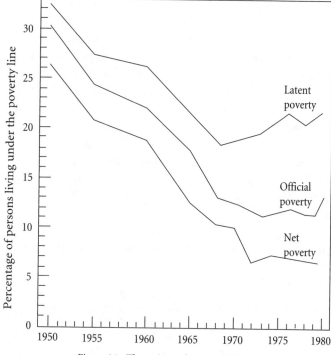

Figure 6.1. Three views of poverty, 1950–80.

Source: Charles Murray, *Losing Ground: American Social Policy 1950–1980* (New York: Basic Books, 1984), 65. Copyright 1984 by Charles Murray. Reprinted by permission of Basic Books, a divison of HarperCollins Publishers, Inc. All figures are based on the March Current Population Survey conducted by the Bureau of the Census. "Official poverty" is the standard statistic published by the Bureau of the Census. "Latent poverty" figures for 1965–78 were taken from Sheldon Danziger and Robert Plotnick, "The War on Income Poverty," in *Welfare Reform in America,* ed. Paul M. Sommers (Boston: Kluwer-Nijhoff, 1982), Table 3.1, p. 40. Latent poverty for 1980 was computed using the same procedures and a comparable database, as reported in *Focus: Newsletter of the Institute for Research on Poverty* 7 (Winter 1984): 2. Figures for "net poverty" are taken from Timothy M. Smeeding, "Recent Increase in Poverty in the U.S.: What the Official Estimates Fail to Show," testimony prepared for the U.S. House of Representatives, Committee on Ways and Means, Subcommittee on Oversight and Subcommittee on Public Assistance and Unemployment Compensation, October 18, 1983, Table 4, p. 17. Figures for latent poverty and net poverty in 1950, 1955, and 1960 are estimated.

Moynihan drew this conclusion from the change in the pattern in welfare rolls and nonwhite male unemployment rates shown in the shaded area of Figure 6.2 (the data available at the time). The "scissors" would open wider in the years that followed. How Moynihan could conclude so much on the basis of so little might seem prophetic on his part; however, closer

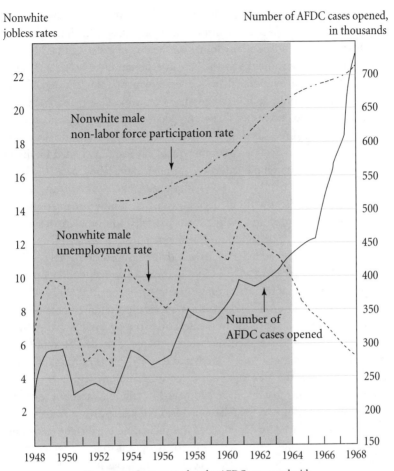

Nonwhite
jobless rates

Number of AFDC cases opened,
in thousands

Figure 6.2. Cases opened under AFDC compared with
jobless rates for nonwhite males, 1948–68.

Sources: Figures on the nonwhite male unemployment rate and number of AFDC cases opened appeared originally in Daniel Patrick Moynihan, *The Negro Family: The Case for National Action* (Washington, D.C.: U.S. Department of Labor, 1965). Figures on the nonwhite male non-labor force participation rate appeared originally in William Julius Wilson and Katherine M. Neckerman, "Poverty and Family Structure: The Widening Gap between Evidence and Public Policy Issues," conference paper, Institute for Research on Poverty, Madison, Wis., December 1984, 72.

scrutiny suggests that his inference was more likely social science's most egregious policy analysis crime until Murray interpreted his inkblots.[66]

Moynihan overlooked many things on the way to insisting that his "culture of poverty" argument was the best interpretation of his data. In particular, Moynihan overlooked how unemployment rates among African American males could decline not because job prospects were increasing but because they were decreasing.[67] Discouraged unemployed workers dropped out of the labor force, allowing the unemployment rate among those still in the workforce to decline. Unemployment rates are calculated by dividing the number of unemployed by the number in the labor force (the labor force consists of all employed and unemployed). Therefore, the unemployment rate could drop without decreases in the number of unemployed, simply because of declining labor force participation or increases in the non-labor force participation rate (see Figure 6.2).

Michael Katz has added the insight that the upsurge in new welfare cases that began around 1962 was in good part attributable to increases in the welfare participation rate among African Americans.[68] Whereas a "welfare stigma" and onerous and arbitrary application requirements had for many years kept the participation rate down among the eligible population, that situation began to change when welfare rights advocates started to make inroads into the welfare system and the civil rights movement began to help legitimate the idea that poor persons of color are legally entitled to exercise their rights to assistance.[69] Moynihan's failure to account for these developments led him to the false conclusion that for African Americans a proclivity toward welfare dependency was increasing even in the face of increased economic opportunities. It is not my point to argue which came first — the declines in the labor force or the increases in welfare cases. In neither case is there support for Moynihan's claim that increased welfare taking accompanied improved job prospects for African American males. The evidence for those improved job prospects is not there. Rather, my point is that Moynihan did not get this far. He simply allowed prevailing biases to do his interpreting for him, and the rest is history — the "Moynihan Report," as it came to be known by the time the Johnson administration released it in 1965, was on its way to becoming another milestone in the questionable history of social science and welfare policy.

These "bookends" to exercises in "poor" statistical accounting reveal how social biases can be easily insinuated into the interpretation of data in ways that resist challenge and reinforce the dominant biases of welfare policy discourse. A popular refrain had become ascendant by the time Murray's

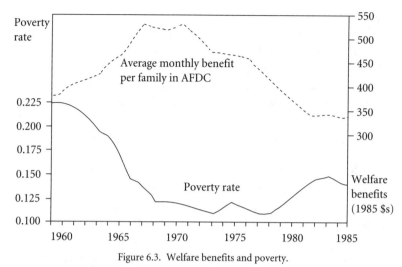

Figure 6.3. Welfare benefits and poverty.

Sources: Data on the official poverty rate are from U.S. Bureau of the Census, *Characteristics of the Population below the Poverty Level*, Current Population Reports, P-60 series (Washington, D.C.: U.S. Government Printing Office, various years). Data on AFDC benefits are from U.S. Bureau of the Census, *Statistical Abstract of the United States* (Washington, D.C.: U.S. Government Printing Office, various years).

"findings" had gained notoriety: the 1960s War on Poverty had led to a welfare state that encouraged welfare dependency. But compounding confusion about the recent history of antipoverty policy is no way to create an informed basis for discussing what to do about poverty today.

There are better explanations for the growth in the "dependent" poor. By the early 1970s, the following elements were in play: (1) a decline in relatively good-paying low-skill jobs had begun, especially in manufacturing (i.e., "deindustrialization"), and a corresponding decline was beginning in real wages, especially among lower-income groups; (2) the bulk of the remaining poor were the "very poor," and the greater expenditures needed to help them out of poverty were not forthcoming; (3) female-headed families became a growing proportion of the poor (i.e., the "feminization of poverty"), and the additional services they needed to escape poverty (e.g., child care) did not develop as quickly as needed; and (4) benefits in AFDC began decreasing (see Figure 6.3).[70]

The average size of families on public assistance did decline gradually in the 1970s and 1980s, which accounts for some of the decline in benefits. Also, counting food stamps and other benefits lessens the decrease. Yet taking these factors into account still leaves the downward trend in welfare benefits intact, and the real value of such benefits is now further below the poverty level than at any time since that level was set.[71] Since the mid-1970s, most states have allowed AFDC benefits to decline in real value simply by not increasing them to keep pace with the rising cost of living. In all states, the declines have been so substantial that welfare benefits are far less likely than in the 1970s to raise poor families above the poverty level.

Rereading Data on Welfare Spending and Poverty

The uninitiated, like the proverbial stranger in a strange town, might want to assume that more poverty leads to more welfare spending and leave it at that. Yet, as we have witnessed for over a decade now, there has been a penchant for lining up these data to suggest that since the 1960s welfare causes poverty, and not the other way around. Like inkblots, these policy-relevant data are interpreted within a context. That context of late has been the counterintuitive one that assuages the consciences of those who feel welfare spending is not worth the commitment it once received. Yet there is more than one way to read these data, especially as time marches on. While they may have served in the 1980s to create the statistical basis for affirming popular bias, in the 1990s they may prove less useful for that exercise.

Figure 6.4 illustrates trends in poverty from 1959 to 1985. The secular decline in the official poverty rate from the 1950s until the early 1970s was replaced by first stagnation and then increases in the rate until 1985. In addition to the official poverty rate, Figure 6.4 reports the "prewelfare" and "pretransfer" poverty rates. The official poverty rate is calculated on the basis of all income that individuals and families receive, including welfare benefits. In order to distinguish it from the other measures, it can also be referred to as the "postwelfare" poverty rate — that is, the level of poverty *after* government income transfers, including welfare benefits, are taken into account. The prewelfare rate indicates the proportion of the population with incomes below the poverty line, disregarding any income people may have received from government welfare payments. The pretransfer rate is based on discounting any and all income people may have received from the government and takes into account only income from private sources. The pretransfer rate therefore excludes all government payments, including social insurance benefits such as social security and public assistance benefits such as AFDC. Thus, the prewelfare measure disregards government welfare payments and the pretransfer measure does not count any government benefits at all.[72]

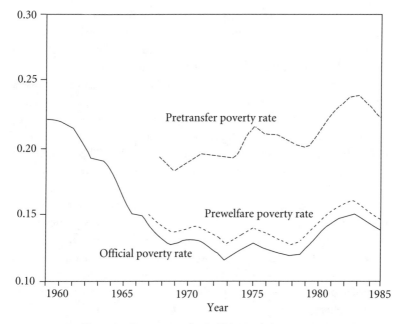

Figure 6.4. Poverty rates for the U.S. population, 1959–85.

Sources: Data on the official poverty rate are from U.S. Bureau of the Census, *Characteristics of the Population below the Poverty Level*, Current Population Reports, P-60 series (Washington, D.C.: U.S. Government Printing Office, various years). Data on prewelfare and pretransfer poverty rates are based on an analysis of the annual Current Population Survey taken from George Slotsve and Thomas Donley, "A Supplement to the Trend in Poverty, 1967–1987: Tables from the Current Population Survey," unpublished manuscript, Institute for Research on Poverty, Madison, Wis., 1988.

There is a trick to these data. Because these measures provide an indication of the level of poverty independent of income from government sources, they can be used to assess how government benefits affect preexisting poverty levels, positively or negatively, depending upon the interpretive context used. For instance, should the prewelfare poverty rate vary positively with welfare spending, it could, on the one hand, indicate that welfare grows in response to the failure of the market economy and other government transfers to lift people out of poverty, or it could, on the other hand, indicate that people are less likely to rely on the market and other transfers the more welfare is available. Liberals stress the former interpretation, and conservatives the latter. The same goes for changes in the *gap* between the prewelfare and official poverty rates. If it grows, for liberals this means greater antipoverty effectiveness in welfare spending. For conservatives, it means growing welfare dependency.[73]

The following analysis suggests that there is more than one way to read these data. The prewelfare and pretransfer measures are available in consecutive series only from 1967. In Figure 6.4, the measures show fluctuation in an upward direction, particularly in the 1980s. If anything, there is something to the idea that "latent" poverty has persisted and in recent years has increased. But to what extent, if any, have the government's cash welfare payments since the 1960s played a role in the persistence and increases in poverty, latent or otherwise? Figure 6.5 shows cash public assistance payments per poor person and the prewelfare poverty rate from 1967 to 1985. This comparison has an advantage over using the official or posttransfer poverty rate. The official poverty rate takes into account income from the government, and therefore we would logically expect that when cash assistance to the poor declined the poverty rate would mirror that with an increase. Conversely, increases in payments are mirrored by declines in the poverty rates.

The data in Figure 6.5 show, however, a similar relationship between welfare spending and the prewelfare poverty rate. Available data for the pretransfer poverty rate also show the same pattern. These measures do not take welfare payments into account; however, they both indicate decreases in poverty when spending grew in the late 1960s and increases in poverty when welfare payments decreased in the late 1970s and early 1980s. Figure 6.5 does not show the perfect mirrorlike effect that one gets when comparing welfare expenditures and the official poverty rate; however, the data suggest an inverse relationship between welfare spending and "dependent" poverty in recent years. Declines in spending per person adjusted to constant 1985 dollars are matched with increases in the prewelfare poverty rate. This is the antithesis of what conservatives argue when they suggest that increases in welfare spending lead to increases in "latent" or "dependent" poverty. Whereas conservatives would predict a decline in the "dependent" poor with decreased welfare spending, there was instead an increase. Whereas conservatives were looking for decreases in welfare dependency to lead to increased work effort and less poverty, it could be that decreases in welfare spending reduced resources going into poor communities and poor families, making it harder for them to get by and driving up the poverty rate, even when public assistance is not figured in the calculation of the number of poor people. More important, I am not suggesting that these data constitute evidence that welfare expenditures in various ways, such as by serving as an economic stimulus, produce less rather than more "latent" poverty, though that may indeed be the case. Rather, my point is that these data do not consti-

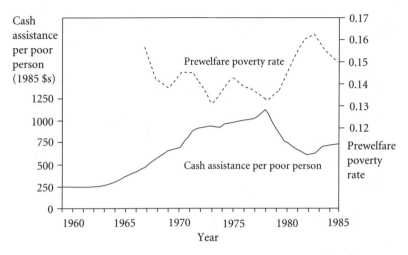

Figure 6.5. Prewelfare poverty rate and cash assistance per poor person (1985 $s).

Sources: Data on the number of poor persons are from U.S. Bureau of the Census, *Characteristics of the Population below the Poverty Level,* Current Population Reports, P-60 series (Washington, D.C.: U.S. Government Printing Office, various years). Data on cash assistance are from U.S. Bureau of the Census, *Statistical Abstract of the United States* (Washington, D.C.: U.S. Government Printing Office, various years). Data on the prewelfare poverty rate are based on an analysis of the annual Current Population Survey taken from George Slotsve and Thomas Donley, "A Supplement to the Trend in Poverty, 1976–1987: Tables from the Current Population Survey," unpublished manuscript, Institute for Research on Poverty, Madison, Wis., 1988.

tute evidence that decreases in welfare spending produce less "latent" poverty.

More Is Less

Figures 6.6 and 6.7 provide some insight into the inverse relationship between welfare spending and poverty rates. One reason poverty rates have increased even as welfare spending has remained at high levels is the decline in the real value of public assistance expenditures in the late 1970s and early 1980s. Another possible reason is that welfare expenditures have not kept pace with the needs of the poor. Therefore, although expenditures may seem high, they may actually have declined relative to need. Figures 6.6 and 6.7 suggest that this may in fact have been the case.

Figures 6.6 and 6.7 present trend lines for the poverty rate, cash public assistance payments, and the prewelfare poverty "gap" or "deficit." The

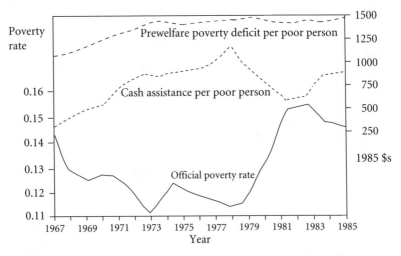

Figure 6.6. Official poverty rate, cash assistance per poor person, and prewelfare poverty deficit per poor person (1985 $s), 1967–85.

Sources: Data on the prewelfare poverty deficit are based on an analysis of the annual Current Population Survey taken from George Slotsve and Thomas Donley, "A Supplement to the Trend in Poverty, 1967–1987: Tables from the Current Population Survey," unpublished manuscript, Institute for Research on Poverty, Madison, Wis., 1988. Data on cash assistance are from U.S. Bureau of the Census, *Statistical Abstract of the United States* (Washington, D.C.: U.S. Government Printing Office, various years). Data on the official poverty rate are from U.S. Bureau of the Census, *Characteristics of the Population below the Poverty Level,* Current Population Reports, P-60 series (Washington D.C.: U.S. Government Printing Office, various years).

poverty gap or poverty deficit is the total amount of money needed to lift the poor up to the poverty line. The prewelfare poverty gap is the total amount needed to raise the prewelfare poor up to the poverty line. It is the amount needed before people receive welfare benefits. It is therefore an excellent indicator of how much additional income the poor need in order to escape poverty.[74] Figures on the prewelfare poverty deficit are available from 1967.

Figure 6.6 shows that in the late 1970s and early 1980s, when total cash assistance expenditures declined relative to the prewelfare poverty gap, the official or postwelfare poverty rate soared. The official poverty rate, however, is in part based on cash assistance, and we should therefore expect, to some extent, corresponding increases in the official poverty rate with decreases in government welfare expenditures relative to need. Figure 6.7 shows, however, that the prewelfare poverty rate also increases in similar

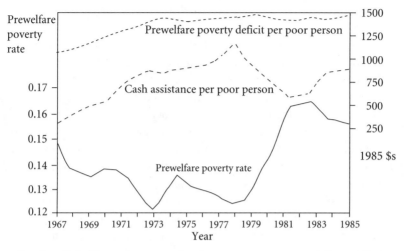

Figure 6.7. Prewelfare poverty rate, cash assistance per poor person, and the prewelfare poverty deficit per poor person (1985 $s), 1967–85.

Sources: Data on the number of poor persons are from U.S. Bureau of the Census, *Characteristics of the Population below the Poverty Level,* Current Population Reports, P-60 series (Washington, D.C.: U.S. Government Printing Office, various years). Data on cash assistance are from U.S. Bureau of the Census, *Statistical Abstract of the United States* (Washington, D.C.: U.S. Government Printing Office, various years). Data on the prewelfare poverty deficit and the prewelfare poverty rate are based on analyses of the annual Current Population Survey taken from George Slotsve and Thomas Donley, "A Supplement to the Trend in Poverty, 1967–1987: Tables from the Current Population Survey," unpublished manuscript, Institute for Research on Poverty, Madison, Wis., 1988.

fashion when government welfare expenditures are scaled back relative to need. For Figure 6.7 to offer support for dependency theorists, it would have to show that when either cash assistance expenditures increased or the gap between cash assistance and the poverty deficit lessened (i.e., when expenditures began to approximate need), the prewelfare poverty rate would go up. Instead, the data can be read to show exactly the opposite: when expenditures in the late 1970s and early 1980s declined, especially relative to need, the prewelfare or "latent" or "dependent" poverty rate increased markedly. In fact, the prewelfare poverty rate shadows the official poverty rate. "Dependent" poverty increased when expenditures fell relative to need.[75] Although these figures are hardly definitive, they show that the trend-line data used by conservatives to rewrite social policy history can be read to undermine that rewriting.

Conclusion

An active rewriting of social policy history has helped create an alternative basis for reading trend-line data. Declines in the availability of work, decreases in the real value of wages, the deterioration of inner-city education to prepare students for available jobs, and a host of related economic factors are pushed to the background when social policy history gets rewritten to stress welfare dependency as the root cause of poverty. To the foreground come not economic but cultural arguments suggesting that the flight of the black middle class, the absence of fathers as role models, the loss of moral standards, the overall deterioration of culture, and the ready availability of welfare are the culprits in a new plot regarding causes of poverty. Symptoms become causes; coping practices become a "culture of poverty" and justifications arise for not directly confronting how an emerging postindustrial economy disadvantages the poor in general and poor minorities in particular (see chapter 9 for more on this subject). Rather than rewriting social policy history so that old distinctions can be made relevant to the current postindustrial context, there is a real need to consider a "postindustrial system of allocation" geared to changes in the job and wage structures of society. Rather than rewriting social policy history to fit the new context, perhaps it is better to rethink old ideas about guaranteeing income in an economy that cannot guarantee decent jobs for all who need them.[76]

It is important to account for context in the interpretation of policy-relevant data. The case discussed in this chapter suggests that the insistence on rereading social policy history as a problem of dependency produces data analysis of questionable value. And questionable data analysis helps reinforce questionable historical narratives. Recognizing the narrativity of data on welfare and poverty involves questioning the extent to which historical narrative and data reinforce each other in politically significant ways. Such analysis gains in importance as policy makers find the rewriting of social policy history a convenient way to deny the need to confront the economic realities that are emerging. The will to rewrite history to reinforce political intransigence and to rationalize the systematic denial of the economic character of poverty persists into the current period. Until that context is challenged, all sorts of data will be interpreted in all sorts of politically convenient ways. As part of that challenge, social scientists need to give up the idea of the autonomy of academic work and begin to question the extent to which their own work helps to reinforce and is simultaneously informed by the prevailing biases of the social order.

Applications

CHAPTER SEVEN

The Real Uses of a False Dichotomy

Symbols at the Expense of
Substance in Welfare Reform

Social welfare policy cannot be fully understood without recognizing that it
is fundamentally a set of symbols that try to differentiate between the
deserving and undeserving poor in order to uphold such dominant values
as the work ethic and family, gender, race, and ethnic relations. In this
sense welfare policy is targeted not only at the poor, but equally at the
nonpoor, through the symbols it conveys about what behaviors are deemed
virtuous or deviant.
Joel F. Handler and Yeheskel Hasenfeld, *The Moral Construction of Poverty*

In a time when welfare dependency is seen as a greater problem than poverty,
the Family Support Act of 1988 has been heralded as a milestone in welfare reform.[1] The act offers supportive services and requires participation
in "workfare"-related education, training, and placement programs that
will reduce "welfare dependency" and increase "self-sufficiency." Much has
been made of how the act is grounded in research that indicates what it
will take to reduce welfare dependency.[2] Yet close examination of the 1988
legislation suggests that this research has performed largely a symbolic role
of legitimating welfare policy that has itself been dedicated primarily to reinforcing the idea that the poor are deficient according to ascendant notions
of self in contemporary society.

Symbolic Policy

The distinction between symbolic and substantive dimensions of policy is itself somewhat artificial; however, its usefulness has been demonstrated in policy analysis for some time. Murray Edelman's work on symbolic politics effectively underscores the need to consider the symbolic roles most policies play.[3] Edelman's writings on welfare reinforce the idea that welfare is a contested terrain that, to a large degree, serves symbolic purposes at the expense of substantive benefits. The provision of welfare is constituted in a language, a set of professionally and scientifically sanctified objectives, and a constellation of bureaucratic requirements all designed to reinforce the idea that poverty and welfare dependency are chronic but treatable problems within the confines of existing policies.[4]

The symbolic significance of welfare lies in no small part in its role as a reminder that, although poverty and dependency are problems, the state has them under control and can manage them. Welfare is part of the state, and state leaders have an obvious interest in being able to talk about the nature of welfare problems in ways that are politically advantageous. State leaders are interested in both the activation and the quiescence of relevant elite and mass publics, as they want their support for both change and continuity in the program.[5] State leaders, however, are also interested in reassuring the public that they have the information, resources, and plans of action necessary to handle the problem. The symbolic role of welfare policy, as with other policies, is to specify the origin and responsibility of the policy problem so that specific individuals, institutions, professional practices, and ideological perspectives are reinforced and authorized as appropriate for acting on the problem.[6] Welfare therefore serves symbolic purposes by re-creating the conditions of political legitimacy for a political order incapable of ensuring or unwilling to ensure all of its members the opportunity to live life at some agreed-upon level of subsistence on par with that of, say, persons in other nations.[7]

Deborah Stone emphasizes how public policies always unavoidably use narrative, rhetoric, metaphor, and other discursive practices to suggest implied understandings of the problems they purport to attack.[8] Conceptions of public problems are not given, nor do they predate policy solutions. Public policy debate rarely, if ever, goes forward with everyone agreeing as to the existence and definition of a particular problem. Instead, policy solutions are more likely to be the basis for discussion, with problems being defined in particular ways so as to justify treating them according to one or another policy approach. Rather than problem definition, it is more a process of problem selection, or even of "strategic representation" of policy problems.[9] In this sense, policies create problems: each policy creates its own understanding of the problem in a way that justifies a particular approach to attacking the problem. The discursive practices embedded in any particular policy work to prefigure our understandings of policy problems. The use of symbols, metaphors, and other figurative practices promotes the narrative implied by the policy. Symbols, metaphors, and so on narrate a particular understanding of a problem and reinforce the idea that it is an accurate depiction. They "naturalize" that depiction by making it seem to be the only "real" way to understand the problem, and not just one of many ways to understand it.[10]

A symbol, for instance, according to Stone, is anything that stands for something else. The symbolic practices implicit in any policy approach suggest that the problem under consideration should be understood *as if* it were *like* something else; once the parallel is established, the problem can be treated that way, even if the analogy is tenuous at best. Attempts to make our understandings of public problems concrete in the form of quantified measurements are a form of discursive practice. Stone considers numbers the most preferred form of metaphor when it comes to public policy making, because numbers are often thought to be the antithesis of symbols, in that they suggest a precise and accurate depiction of what is being examined. But numbers are metaphoric, for all attempts to quantify imply a "decision rule" as to what will count as something. Such a criterion determines when ostensibly different things (e.g., different jobs) will be treated and therefore counted as the same thing, and when ostensibly similar things (e.g., working inside or outside the home) will be counted as different. Numbers do not simply count up a preexisting reality. Instead, they metaphorically and symbolically imply what does or does not count as if it were like something else.[11]

The discursive dimension of welfare policy reinforces particular understandings of the problems of poverty and dependency. This includes the numbers on which policy makers and analysts often rely to assess the extent of these problems and measure the effectiveness of policies designed to attack them. A pertinent example is job training programs. By focusing largely on employment rates and earnings of program participants, without consideration of labor market conditions, the numbers produced in some evaluations of these programs reinforce the implied understanding that poverty is an individual problem best solved when the welfare-dependent person is counted as failing to take what employment the job market has to offer or whatever man the marriage market has made available. One major consequence of such a perspective is that the symbolic significance of these numbers operates to limit the benefits provided to poor people.

The Contradictory Character of Welfare Policy

Frances Fox Piven and Richard A. Cloward's theory of welfare change offers a useful explanation both for policy changes over time and for the contradictory purposes of welfare policy at any one point in time. Piven and Cloward see welfare as a secondary institution that must serve the needs of the primary institutions of both the polity and the economy.[12] It must promote political legitimacy as well as economic viability.[13] It must mollify the poor by providing assistance while doing so only in ways that are consistent with the market. Benefits must help the poor survive while not undermining the incentive for them to participate in the market and take whatever jobs are available. Welfare is both benefits for those who are not in the labor market and a set of rules to reinforce the work ethic and the norms of self-sufficiency. Welfare policy thus becomes something that both provides assistance and regulates the conditions under which assistance is to be denied. These competing purposes make for a contradictory welfare policy that serves both political and economic purposes in ways that are simultaneously substantive and symbolic.[14] This is especially the case for poor, able-bodied, single males who are expected to be self-sufficient without government assistance and therefore find it difficult to receive public benefits at all. They are ineligible for any federally subsidized form of public assistance, and must rely on state-funded general assistance programs.[15]

Some feminist theorists, such as Linda Gordon, Barbara Nelson, and Virginia Sapiro, have shown that welfare policy has historically also sought to reconcile the provision of benefits with ascendant notions of womanhood and motherhood.[16] "Most social policy aimed at women has been designed explicitly to benefit them in their capacity as wives and mothers and more particularly, to benefit those who depend upon them for nurturance and domestic service: husbands, children, and elderly relatives."[17] Welfare is a key part of what Nancy Fraser calls the "juridical-administrative-therapeutic state apparatus" (JAT), which imputes specific needs to clients and then requires them to satisfy those needs.[18] The JAT seeks to reinforce socially constructed identities on behalf of the existing order more than it tries to provide individuals the rights to the specific resources needed to address their problems. Ironically, it has distinctive programs geared largely for female-headed families that fail to meet the particular needs or recognize the special circumstances of these families.[19] Welfare policy in such a state constitutes women exclusively as "mothers" — a distinctive population with special needs. Yet being defined exclusively as a mother forecloses the possibility of a woman's being considered the family breadwinner, ensures the status of "dependent," and sets up the idea that a single woman and her children constitute a "broken family." The result is that "welfare mothers" are not seen as needing or deserving those supportive services, education, training, and other resources that will enable them to provide a "family wage" on their own.[20] In these terms, welfare is not something that promotes people's rights to self-sufficiency; instead, it focuses on meeting specified needs according to clients' predefined roles or positions in society. Welfare at best meets women's needs as mothers, while their dependence in the family and the economy goes unaddressed.

Other analysts have emphasized the need to consider also the racial dimension of welfare policy. In the early progressive period, Gwendolyn Mink argues, efforts on behalf of the American welfare state were done in good part in the name of "an idealized American citizenry" to counter racial diversity.[21] Welfare was rationalized, especially by white women reformers, as a socialization agent that promoted conformity with the norms of white motherhood. In the process, welfare perpetuated race as well as gender distinctions. Receipt of welfare was in large part premised on conformity that implicitly assumed white motherhood as the operative standard. Variations across ethnic and racial groups in family structure and the relationship to a wage-earning spouse were taken into account because the standard of white womanhood was implicit.[22] Welfare policy is in this sense very much dedicated to making "them" more like "us."[23]

Welfare therefore can be said to serve symbolic purposes by reinforcing dominant, if conflicting, notions of work, motherhood, and family. Receipt of welfare marks recipients as "dependent" by virtue of their failing to measure up to ascendant notions in society of the ethic of work, the ideal of the virtuous mother, and the norm of responsible parent. In this way, welfare serves to reinforce the symbolic order that constitutes the everyday lives of all of society's members, including the poor. Welfare policy is as much about reinforcing a grand story or narrative about what it takes to be seen as self-sufficient person, virtuous woman, and responsible parent as it is about supplying the benefits and supportive services that can help people achieve self-sufficiency, virtue, and parental responsibility. Welfare policy is then at least as much about regulating the conditions under which people count as being entitled to make claims against the state as it is about supplying benefits.[24] This means that welfare policy is dedicated at least as much to reducing welfare dependency as to providing resources to fight off the effects of poverty. As Joel Handler and Yeheskel Hasenfeld emphasize:

> Social welfare policy cannot be fully understood without recognizing that it is fundamentally a set of symbols that try to differentiate between the deserving and undeserving poor in order to uphold such dominant values as the work ethic and family, gender, race, and ethnic relations. In this sense welfare policy is targeted not only at the poor, but equally at the nonpoor, through the symbols it conveys about what behaviors are deemed virtuous or deviant.[25]

Welfare therefore arguably has both symbolic and substantive dimensions that coexist in contradictory fashion. The symbolic purposes of welfare often operate to limit the quality and quantity of substantive benefits provided under welfare.[26] The substantive benefits the state provides are in fact constituted within a symbolic context that goes a long way toward determining their significance and value to the poor. Alternatively, substantive benefits operate to undercut the effectiveness of welfare policy by reinforcing dominant norms about self-sufficiency, womanhood, and parental responsibility. Benefits that enable mothers with children to live on their own outside the traditional two-parent family and without working pose a potentially serious threat to societal standards.[27]

For poor, able-bodied, single males, this often means receiving very little, if anything, in the form of public benefits that might help them escape their dependency. For poor women with children, this often means receiving benefits that do not help them overcome their dependence in the family and the economy. It is entirely possible that the recent welfare changes brought about by the Family Support Act may perpetuate these contradictions, if in their own distinctive and contemporary way.

The Symbolic Significance of Welfare Policy Today

The contemporary discourse on welfare is very much a discourse of dependency. The poor and the welfare dependent have served historically as convenient, useful, and instructive mirror images for encoding the distinctions that set the standards for acceptable individual conduct in society.[28] Designating welfare taking as deviant, even criminalizing welfare dependency, has served the purposes of social control by negative example.[29] The standards for a self-sufficient, autonomous individual in society are encoded and defined in terms of what the welfare dependent, as the "other," is not. In recent years, the "feminization of poverty" and the growing identification of public assistance as programs for minorities have intensified the idea of the welfare dependent as the "other." The contemporary discourse on dependency suggests that the rich and poor really are different; where rich people may need tax incentives to be productive, poor people need welfare disincentives to encourage them to work. As the distinctions solidify, it is easier to argue that opposites have to be treated differently — rewards for some and punishments for others — in order to get the same result.[30]

This contemporary discourse of dependency is in no small part preoccupied with the issues of self-sufficiency, work, productivity, and related designations of self-worth.[31] Although these concerns have historically been present in welfare narratives,[32] they take on a heightened sense of urgency in an era in which the nature of work and its place in our lives has been subject to change and uncertainty. What is at issue is the ability of work to serve as a regulating norm for the social order. The concern about work is heightened when it takes on more abstract, intangible, and even ephemeral qualities as we move from an industrial to a postindustrial economy.[33] This is reinforced by an era in which the public space of wage earning is no longer reserved exclusively for men and the private space of home is no longer the only place for women, for the idea that work at home should be valued on par with wage labor further destabilizes our understanding of what constitutes work. In addition, questions about work are bound to increase in a time of growing concern about productivity and competitiveness, particularly of the manufacturing sector in the U.S. economy. At the same time, anxiety about work increases as restructuring of the industrial economy results in fewer manual jobs that pay a "family wage." Finally, the concern about work is heightened also by the growth of the welfare state itself and the increasing numbers of people who derive their means of support primarily from the state rather than from employment.

Although the availability of jobs, the level of wages, and people's standard of living generally are to a great extent contingent upon the actions of the state, the contemporary discourse reinforces the distinction between the independent and the dependent in terms of those who have jobs (or receive public benefits in some way tied to their previous employment) and those who do not. In this context, it becomes ever more apparent that the welfare dependent are deficient because they do not have "work." The contemporary welfare narrative becomes one that highlights this deficiency and proposes work programs as the cure for the ills of the poor, as exemplified by the Family Support Act of 1988.

The changing status of women in the contemporary order contributes to the anxiety about welfare. Notions of the "virtuous woman," "motherhood," and "family" are all subject to reconsideration as women become more likely to have children outside of marriage, to head families without a male present, and to work outside the home while raising even very young children. "At present," Nancy Fraser reports, "fewer than 15 percent of U.S. families conform to the normative ideal of a domicile shared by a husband who is the sole breadwinner, a wife who is a full-time homemaker, and their offspring."[34] The past three decades have witnessed a substantial increase in the proportion of working women with young children. More women are heading families on their own as well. None of this is to say that women always choose to combine wage earning and mothering; it is often a necessity. Nor are women any less vulnerable to the vagaries of the market economy. In fact, women's wages still lag behind men's, and female-headed family incomes are dropping even further behind those of male-headed families, contributing to the "feminization of poverty."[35] Concern about the economic status of female-headed families reinforces older concerns about shoring up the traditional two-parent family. This makes for a potent combination on behalf of tightening welfare requirements and encouraging welfare mothers to move off welfare, either into the workforce or into marriage. In the face of the changing status of women in society, workfare becomes a logical response that now possesses the legitimacy to require mothers to take jobs while acting in the name of the traditional two-parent family.

The growing problem of isolation in inner-city, particularly African American, neighborhoods is also embedded in the contemporary welfare discourse. In particular, the rise in black female-headed families has contributed greatly to interest in welfare reform. By the mid-1980s, about 45 percent of black families were headed by women, whereas that was true for only 12 percent of white families and 25 percent of Latino families.[36] The availability of welfare has often been suggested as a factor contributing to the rise in female-headed families among poor blacks.[37] The lack of employed and therefore "marriageable" males and the lack of jobs that pay a family wage are given less stress.[38] Increased restrictions on welfare become logical responses to reinforce dominant notions of work, motherhood, and parental responsibility.[39]

The New Consensus on Welfare

In Congress, debate over welfare intensified throughout the 1980s. By 1988, near unanimity had been achieved that welfare dependency was a significant problem and required dramatic change in welfare policy. The Family Support Act of 1988 reflected what some came to call the "new consensus" on welfare.[40] The legislation became possible because of both political compromise and ideological convergence between liberals and conservatives.[41]

Many conservatives found the legislation acceptable because it mandated work, training, and education in exchange for the receipt of welfare.[42] Welfare policy would thus reinforce both the work ethic and the traditional understanding of self-sufficiency, sexual propriety, and parental responsibility. Conservatives were concerned, however, that the work requirements might in the end be somewhat superficial. Many liberals supported the legislation because it provided more support services than had previous work schemes. They hoped it would be more than a symbolic exercise, and feared it might do more to discourage welfare taking than to help the poor to achieve self-sufficiency.[43] Liberals recognized that welfare reform had a symbolic dimension, however. Welfare reform that mandated work was needed to legitimate providing public assistance in an era when welfare dependency had become indefensible and working mothers had become commonplace. Welfare could be justified only when it provided ways to encourage poor families to be like others. In particular, if women with young children were increasingly entering the job market, it was no longer possible to justify the provision of public assistance to poor women with children unless the women were expected to work.[44] Liberals also sought to ensure that the provision of supportive services would not be illusory. Now, six years after the passage of the Family Support Act, Laurence E. Lynn Jr. doubts that this compromise was evenhanded:

> Conservatives have successfully revived nineteenth century fears of the low morality and antisocial behavior of the poor among economically insecure voters of the working and middle classes.... For liberals, however, this alliance is a Faustian bargain. In exchange for a promise to join the nominal welfare reform coalition and support some transitional "carrots" such as EITC [earned income tax credit] expansion, conservatives expect a set of budgetary and behavioral ground rules. They then pick and choose from among the elements of a balanced reform agenda those which resonate well with conservative voters and call the selection process "recognizing the political facts of life." Anxious to govern, liberals accept these "facts" as immutable, their role as creative intellectuals diminished while they accept assignment as technocrats and pore over census data.[45]

Given their differing concerns, conservatives and liberals had to compromise politically in order to produce the legislation, but ideological convergence also played a part. This convergence was forged in part on the basis of particular interpretations of relatively new research about the behavior of recipients of the main welfare program—Aid to Families with Dependent Children.[46] Perhaps crucial here were studies showing that a sizable proportion of welfare recipients at any one time were in the process of completing a long-term "spell" of welfare dependency.[47] The new perspective emphasized a relatively large dependent population: "At any one time, about two-thirds of the mothers on AFDC are either continuous or multiple users."[48] These recipients were more likely to have had their first children out of marriage in their teenage years, to have not completed high school, to have not married, and to be black. Although these findings eventually would receive scrutiny, they proved critical in helping to forge the "new consensus" and its focus on reducing welfare dependency. Not all the liberal and conservative proposals for attacking welfare dependency were included in the 1988 legislation; however, the "new consensus" survived the legislative process and was reflected in the final legislation.[49]

The Family Support Act of 1988

The title of the 1988 legislation misleads as to the policy it entails. The Family Support Act of 1988 is almost exclusively about welfare rather than families. The legislation has four major components, three of which concentrate largely on AFDC. The law is thus, for the most part, limited to revising AFDC and child support for either welfare families or other families. Family support in this context is primarily about reinforcing traditional norms of familial responsibility and only secondarily about public aid to support families. In particular, the legislation did nothing to stop the ongoing decline in the real value of the cash benefits recipients receive.[50]

The first of the four major components in the 1988 legislation is that by October 1, 1990, states had to start to phase in the Job Opportunities and Basic Skills (JOBS) program. JOBS requires most AFDC mothers with children over 3 years of age, as well as other employable adults receiving such aid, to complete high school, seek additional education, get training, or work. A variety of educational and training alternatives are possible under the program. Participants in JOBS, however, are not expected to leave welfare for work that pays less than their public assistance benefits. As of 1991,

7 percent of the eligible caseload must participate, rising incrementally to twenty percent by 1995. Participants must average twenty hours a week in JOBS-related activities before they can be counted as participating in the program. States must spend at least 55 percent of their JOBS funds on individuals who have been targeted by the legislation as likely to become long-term welfare recipients. These are heads of AFDC families who are (1) parents who are under 24 years old and have not completed high school or who have had little or no work experience from the previous year, (2) parents who have been on public assistance for more than thirty-six of the previous sixty months, or (3) parents whose youngest children are within two years of no longer being eligible for assistance. Two-parent families receiving AFDC must have at least one parent enrolled in the JOBS program or must complete sixteen hours a week of community service work. Enhanced federal funding is available for subsidizing the costs of state JOBS programs if states meet their targets and requirements, but states must first put up the money and only then be reimbursed.

The law's second major provision is for limited extensions of child-care and Medicaid benefits up to one year after a family leaves AFDC for paid employment. The third major component of the 1988 legislation requires that states extend aid up to six months each year to a two-parent family where the principal wage earner is unemployed (AFDC-UP). Finally, the law requires states to establish automatic payroll deductions of child support payments from absent parents of AFDC children and liberalizes the 1984 rule allowing the first $50 each month of such payments to be disregarded in the determination of a family's welfare benefit.[51]

The revisions do offer states distinctive options with which to address welfare dependency, but, given the context, it is entirely possible that these options will be constrained by the symbolic purposes of welfare at the expense of needed benefits and services.

Research Metaphor

The symbolic character of the Family Support Act is revealed in its relationship to social science. The Family Support Act has been touted as an unprecedented example of legislation based on empirical research.[52] All four major components of the legislation, however, have relationships to existing research that are at best weak and are often conflicting; in some cases, real relationships are nonexistent.[53] The Family Support Act's relationship to research parallels that of other policies for which empirical research has largely served as legitimation for halfhearted policy actions rather than as a firm base for informed policy.[54]

The law, for instance, requires states to extend aid for up to six months each year to two-parent families where the principal wage earner is unemployed (AFDC-UP). Before the 1988 legislation passed, twenty-seven states and the District of Columbia provided such aid, and all did so without any limitation on the length of time a family could receive AFDC-UP. This program, originally enacted in 1961 as temporary antirecession legislation, has been repeatedly questioned as to whether it supports or undermines two-parent families.[55] It has often been suggested that extending aid only to single-parent families encourages the breakup of poor families, and that extending aid to two-parent families would alleviate this problem.[56] The evidence, however, is inconclusive on whether this salubrious result is achieved by allowing two-parent families to receive AFDC-UP specifically.[57] Another suggestion is that the UP program actually increases the breakup rate among two-parent families who receive such aid.[58] There are grounds for extending aid to two-parent families, but empirical research that AFDC-UP will protect the two-parent family is not one of them. The UP program is a limited one. State UP programs vary in size from less than 5 percent to about one-quarter of the AFDC basic program population. Moreover, these programs restrict recipients from working more than 100 hours a month. The program therefore discourages work while trying to ensure that only unemployed two-parent families get assistance. By no means does it give aid to all needy two-parent families, and the research available is inconclusive as to its effects on the two-parent family.

Second, much research supports the idea that AFDC families are often reluctant to leave welfare for fear of being unable to replace health insurance and child care.[59] Yet the extension of Medicaid under the Family Support Act to families that leave welfare for work will have at best limited effect. The federal government was already requiring states to extend Medicaid to families leaving welfare for work. The 1988 revisions increase the required time period for the extension of medical benefits from nine to twelve months after a family leaves welfare, but it is a change that affects only the thirty-six states that had not extended Medicaid beyond the federally required time period. This, then, is at best an incremental reform that is unlikely to increase dramatically the willingness of families to leave welfare.

The new child-care provisions, however, constitute a more significant change for many states, including those that already extend child care, because now all families leaving welfare will qualify. Indeed, early reports from states implementing the reforms suggest there is some question as to whether they will be willing and able to provide child care to all families who leave welfare.[60] Most important, for both the extension of Medicaid and child care, no research supports the idea that after one year off welfare poor families will be able to cover these expenses on their own.

Third, the law enhances the ability of states to enforce child support payments for welfare families. This is done primarily through automatic withholding of child support from the absent parent's paycheck for all cases being enforced by a state's child support agency, irrespective of whether the payments are in arrears. Nothing in the legislation, however, speaks to providing services or opportunities, such as education, training, or job placement, for absent parents so they might be better able to offer child support. The admittedly laudable norm of parental responsibility for absent parents is being supported here more than the ability of these parents to fulfill that responsibility. Therefore, it is not surprising that initial research indicates that the child support provisions will marginally reduce the state's welfare burden by shifting a small part of it to a population of largely poor absent parents. In 1986, less than 5 percent of families receiving AFDC in any one month had income from child support, and these payments averaged just over $47.[61] Although routine withholding of child support payments has been found to increase the amount and frequency of such payments by 11-30 percent, automatic withholding has a limited effect on what is supposed to be collected and on what families need in order to leave welfare.[62]

More hope centers on the last component of the 1988 legislation—JOBS. The JOBS program represents the latest instance in the long history of welfare to promote wage work to discourage welfare dependency among the poor. Work requirements have been associated with welfare from its inception in the Western world.[63] JOBS is often associated with newer forms of work requirements stemming from the 1960s, commonly called workfare.[64] Most often, the term workfare has been reserved for the requirement that recipients work for their benefits, usually by accepting some form of public or community work assignment. The JOBS program has been called the "new workfare" in that it does not just mandate participation in work placement programs but also offers opportunities for education, job training, skill development, and job counseling and placement in the private sector, along with other supportive services such as extended child care and health insurance.[65]

Prior to the passage of the Family Support Act, policy discussions emphasized research that highlighted the effectiveness of "new workfare" programs in moving people off welfare.[66] Lawrence Mead stresses that low-cost programs emphasizing work requirements as a general norm are cost-efficient and likely to provide considerable movement from welfare to wage work. Other studies, however, emphasize the modest effects of such programs.[67] A survey of pre-Family Support Act state workfare programs done by the U.S. General Accounting Office suggests that the impact of these programs is greatest for recipients with limited labor market experience and results usually in only marginal increases in labor force participation and earnings.[68] Kathryn Porter reexamined data from studies conducted by the Manpower Demonstration Research Corporation (MDRC), which were very influential during the debates over the Family Support Act, and she found that the workfare programs studied were least effective for those who were most job ready and that low-cost employment services, such as job search programs, had not been very effective in increasing employment or earnings for AFDC recipients with the greatest barriers to employment.[69] Fred Block and John Noakes also reanalyzed MDRC data and found that, once one corrects for welfare benefits received after taking a job, the modest effects of workfare programs have been even smaller than had been reported.[70] Most people were not finding jobs that paid better than welfare and were even less likely to be placed in jobs that would lift them out of poverty.

Similarly, Kathryn Edin and Christopher Jencks found that the increases in employment from programs such as JOBS are hardly a solution to the problems of poor, female-headed families if we take into account the earnings needed to enable these families to get out of poverty.[71] They suggest that, on average, mothers in these families would need jobs that pay two to three times the minimum wage before they could be reasonably expected to leave welfare and cover their own expenses, including child and health care. Edin and Jenck's findings suggest that the research base for the JOBS program was woefully out of touch with the realities of welfare families' attempts to combine wage work and welfare.

Contradictory research findings have also been relied upon to support potentially conflicting dimensions of the JOBS program. The legislation reflects research indicating that simply requiring people to take jobs is the most expeditious way to reduce welfare dependency.[72] Yet the legislation's potentially pathbreaking provisions requiring states to offer educational opportunities to JOBS participants reflects alternative research that indicates that more intensive, long-term educational programs are necessary if we are to move many welfare recipients off the rolls and into positions of self-sufficiency.[73]

Early reports from states on their implementation of the JOBS program underscore this ambivalence, with some states not placing many participants in educational options such as vocational training and postsecondary education and others emphasizing this route. Some states stress the quick placement of participants in wage employment, whereas others look to the long run and offer participants training in skills that the states hope will enable recipients to hold down non-poverty-inuring jobs should they become available.[74]

Symbols at the Expense of Substance

Initial indications from the implementation of the 1988 revisions suggest that some states are concerned about their ability to finance the matching funds required for the JOBS program and related supportive services such as child care. The number of families receiving AFDC increased from 3.9 million in 1989 to 4.6 million in 1991. Expenditures rose from $16 billion to $24 billion in that same period.[75] These figures raise the frightening specter of growing welfare dependency in a stagnant economy. One explanation for the rise is that reforms that were designed to help people leave welfare have "backfired." The reforms, according to this account, have resulted only in making welfare taking more attractive.[76] Policy makers have responded by slashing welfare benefits and tightening eligibility standards.[77] This may be a sign that the changes are valued in some quarters more as politically potent symbolism than as potentially expensive programming. Yet, even if states were to commit fully to the JOBS program, the concern that these revisions sacrifice substantive benefits in the name of symbolic reassurance would still be valid.

The JOBS program's symbolic character is accentuated by the categorical nature of the program. Historically, welfare policy in the United States has resulted in highly fragmented, specialized, and categorical programs for distinctive populations, such as women with children.[78] The JOBS program is consistent with this approach to social policy, and may be a paradigmatic case of this sort of specialism. Specialism in policy—that is, a separate policy to treat a distinctive problem specific to a particular group—implies that the group is different and in need of special treatment.[79] This type of targeting may be necessary in some cases, including female-headed families on welfare, but such categorization also facilitates the symbolism of welfare policy. Welfare becomes more a matter of treating defined problems and meeting imputed needs than of providing people with resources. Poor people receive aid only if they can prove they are poor. Such policies can become self-fulfilling prophecies, with people organizing their lives to qualify for aid rather than using aid to change their lives for the better.[80] And once people can no longer show they fall within the category to be assisted they cannot receive such aid even if they still need it. Welfare becomes a policy dedicated more to treating a conceptualized problem than to helping people cope with their specific circumstances.[81]

In the case of the JOBS program, targeting suggests that it is not so much about improving the long-run self-sufficiency of the poor in general, or even poor families as a specific group, but that JOBS aims mainly at reducing welfare dependency. The JOBS program arises within the highly charged constellation of related concerns about related problems — deterioration of inner-city schools, the rise in births to unmarried teens, growing joblessness, increased drug abuse and crime — all of which are often seen as concentrated among racial minorities and culminating in welfare dependency. By targeting only the AFDC population, the JOBS program addresses these problems strictly in terms of reducing welfare dependency. Such targeting unavoidably means treating only one arguably superficial aspect of a larger problem, without necessarily improving the material conditions of the welfare recipients or of the poor in general. In addition, the program is largely interested in reducing the welfare dependency of a particular subpopulation — women with children. Although male-headed families can participate, they are not the primary focus of the program. All other poor — couples, childless singles, and so on — do not fall within the purview of the program. Despite its symbolism, the program is not about promoting self-sufficiency among the poor generally, but rather about reducing the welfare dependency of a particular group of families.

A separate program for women with children on welfare is all the more logical when the aim is to reduce their welfare dependency without challenging dominant but contradictory notions of work, motherhood, and family.[82] The JOBS program singles out largely female heads of welfare families for specialized treatment, but without being tailored to their particular problems as single mothers who have to shoulder full responsibility for work both at home and on the job. It adopts an androcentric approach that ends up unfairly holding these women with children to the same standards as other families. Single mothers, for instance, might get training and they might even get jobs, but whether they will draw a "family wage" from the labor market in a way that enables them to fulfill their responsibilities at home remains doubtful. This is in no small part because the subtext of the Family Support Act is still tied to dominant notions of work, motherhood, and family. The Family Support Act perpetuates the distinction between nurturing and work in contradictory ways to the disadvantage of women with children. Mothering does not count as work and in most cases will not constitute an exemption from work requirements, and the idea that mothers should be able to earn a wage to support a family is not considered. Participants in such programs will therefore not really be expected to obtain such employment. About two-thirds of all AFDC families are composed of women with children under the age of 6, and many of them will probably remain outside of the purview of the JOBS program, at best affected by it symbolically. Even most program participants will become actors in a symbolic exercise more than beneficiaries of programs that will enable them to work their way out of poverty. Continuing on welfare, working in poverty-wage jobs, and marrying will most often remain their substantive, if limited, options. Holding many of the single women with children who receive welfare to the same standard as wage earners from middle-class and often two-wage-earning families is unrealistic as well as unfair in an economy that tends not to offer family wage jobs for these women.

There are other dangers in singling out welfare recipients as being in need of specialized job services. First, it can contribute to labeling the targeted group as different. This can, in turn, all too easily slide into suggesting that there are characteristics or traits specific to that economic, cultural, or racial group that are the primary reasons for their problems, which can lead to blaming them for their problems and holding them responsible for failing to measure up to standards implicit in welfare policy. This often culminates in specifying the problem to be attacked as one that should be treated by professionals who are trained in counseling such individuals on how to change their behavior. In many ways, this is the narrative implicit in the call of the JOBS program for a separate, distinctive work program for welfare recipients: it is the welfare recipients who need to change, and not the job market.[83]

The JOBS program belies its title. It does not create jobs. It does not assume that job creation is the problem. Instead, it assumes that jobs exist and that the problem is to train and place welfare recipients. In short, we do not need a "jobs program" to create jobs but a "JOBS program" to change the behavior of welfare recipients. Yet the evidence for this view is subject to tremendous debate.[84] A specialized JOBS program for mothers on welfare thus may serve the symbolic purpose of reinforcing the work ethic and the traditional family (i.e., the conventional male breadwinner-family wage system) but do little to enhance the availability of the jobs that women in this program need.

The Family Support Act therefore faces the distinct prospect of becoming another piece of welfare legislation dedicated to sacrificing substantive benefits for symbolic purposes. Grounded in symbolic research tied to contradictory narratives regarding family, work, and individual responsibility, it perpetuates welfare symbolism that reminds us all of the distinction between "good nature," which qualifies for participation in the ordered liberty of society, and "bad nature," which is disorderly and in need of regulation.[85] It does so, however, at the expense of needed resources. The 1988 legislation could seriously limit cash benefits for all poor because it is focused on reinforcing dominant norms. The incentive to keep benefits down is intensified with the attempt to move recipients off welfare. This is especially the case for JOBS participants because they are not required to take jobs with wages lower than their benefits. The emphasis on reducing dependency may also mean that programs that move recipients off welfare will be emphasized even if they do not help families out of poverty. The preoccupation with reinforcing norms may, especially for mother-only families, result in a lack of services for some or services not sufficiently tailored to particular needs for others. The tendency to reduce substantive benefits and intensify the symbolic dimension of welfare is likely to increase in a period of economic decline, job shortages, budget deficits, and swelling welfare rolls.

Conclusion

One of the greatest ironies of the Family Support Act of 1988 is that it is based on hard data and solid research that do not support the legislation in many respects.[86] The research is often silent on key features of the legislation. When it does speak to specific revisions, it often contradicts other parts of the legislation. Other times, concerning work requirements in particular, the research suggests that these changes are not likely to have much effect in providing recipients with the substantive resources they need to escape the poverty that makes them dependent on welfare. The failure of the final legislation to reflect the research lies in part in the compromises endemic to the legislative process, but the tenuous relationship between re-search and policy is also attributable to the fact that the research was used to legitimate preconceived policy approaches. This may be because the sym-bolic dimension of the legislation has been emphasized over the substan-tive reality of what it will take in the way of resource commitments to enable many families to get off welfare and out of poverty. Symbolic research has reinforced symbolic policies.

Historically, welfare as a policy has often been used to serve symbolic purposes at the expense of providing substantive benefits, in good part be-cause a wide variety of groups have sought to address their symbolic con-cerns related to welfare and welfare recipients have remained politically powerless and unable to voice their concerns regarding the provision of sub-stantive benefits. Even liberal groups of professional women have proven at times to be interested more in what welfare symbolizes about women's roles in society than in the provision of benefits that will enable women with children to ensure their families adequate resources. Until women in need of public assistance get to speak for themselves, welfare will in all like-lihood continue to be a realm where symbolic purposes will override the provision of substantive benefits. In the meantime, women on welfare will be increasingly shunted into workfare to the neglect of their child care re-sponsibilities and needed presence in their homes and neighborhoods, while marriage rather than work will remain the primary route off public assistance.

CHAPTER EIGHT

The Feminization of Poverty

From Statistical Artifact to
Established Policy

Substantial proportions of welfare mothers oppose working as maids, and
some say they would decline such work if offered, even though this is often
the only kind of job they can get.
Lawrence M. Mead, *The New Politics of Poverty*

Similarly contradictory is the rhetoric that welfare represents
deplorable "dependence," while women's subordination to husbands
is not registered as unseemly. This contradiction should not be surprising,
for the concept of dependence is an ideological one that reflects
particular modes of production.
Linda Gordon, *Women, the State, and Welfare*

Of course, the welfare system does not deal with women on women's
terms.... Clearly, this system creates a double bind for women raising
children without a male breadwinner.... In effect, it decrees simultaneously
that these women must be and yet cannot be normative mothers.
Nancy Fraser, *Unruly Practices*

A cultural "backlash" against feminism is afoot, with reverberations for
social policy.[1] Electoral politics has provided conservatives with a forum

for suggesting that the problems of increased crime, unemployment, low school performance, family deterioration, and welfare dependency can be blamed on a decadent cultural or "media" elite who support the alleged feminist moves implied in such television sitcoms as *Murphy Brown* and tolerate, if not glorify, the formation of mother-only families. By April 1993, although the Republicans may have lost the election, they seemed to have won the debate in the popular press when the *Atlantic*'s cover story on the deleterious effects of family breakup was headlined "Dan Quayle Was Right."[2]

This propagandizing of the two-parent family no doubt oversells its advantages and discounts its limitations in ways that make it harder to promote social policies that will treat alternative families more equitably. Yet what is most critical for understanding contemporary social policy is not so much how cultural value conflicts help influence social policy. Instead, the growing preoccupation with mother-only families in the current period highlights how social policy itself is a cultural force working to reinforce advantages for the traditional two-parent family over others.[3]

Much has been made in the past of how welfare benefits as material resources are largely available only for one-parent families and therefore are a disincentive to the creation and maintenance of two-parent families.[4] However, this stress on the materiality of welfare overlooks how it operates as a cultural force, reinforcing the two-parent family through the negative symbolic significance attached to welfare taking by female-headed families. Welfare as a cultural formation provides female-headed families benefits but does so under punitive and stigmatizing conditions that reinforce the denigration of female-headed families and help rationalize popular resistance to state efforts on their behalf.

In this chapter, I want to suggest that the statistically documented trend of the "feminization of poverty" can be profitably characterized as an established social policy reflecting the inadequacy of welfare, both as material benefits and as cultural standard. Following a review of the statistical evidence regarding why mother-only families predominate among the officially defined poor, I interrogate contemporary welfare policy so as to highlight how it has been a critical constitutive factor in reproducing poverty in these families. The goal is to promote a destabilization of increasingly insistent and anachronistic distinctions of welfare policy discourse so that we can increase the chances of making public policy in a more democratic way that is more tolerant of the variety of families and the diversity of circumstances.

Women and Welfare Policy in Post-Critical Perspective

The cultural significance of welfare policy is better appreciated when it is seen not as a response to a preexisting problem but instead as something central to the problem's formulation. Political scientists have for some time toyed with inverting the linear, rational problem-policy response paradigm. E. E. Schattschneider long ago noted that "new policies create a new politics." Aaron Wildavsky years later stressed that "policy becomes its own cause" in the sense that, once in place, public policies inevitably are administered in ways that legitimate the need to expand and develop them. Margaret Weir has emphasized how the evolution of policy is contingent upon how previous policies have served to reinforce a prevailing ideational context such that former policies prefigure future policies, sometimes irrespective of the ostensible problems to be attacked. Frances Fox Piven has reminded us that programs create political constituencies at least as much as the other way around.[5] Yet there is a latent literalism in many attempts to invert the positivistic policy paradigm. They underestimate the extent to which policy is partly constitutive of the reality against which it is directed.[6] Policy, therefore, as an ensemble of discursive practices, does not just create its own politics or become its own cause, but it is a critical contributing factor in making up the reality it confronts.[7] Ann Schneider and Helen Ingram have written:

> Social constructions become embedded in policy as messages that are absorbed by citizens and affect their orientations and participation patterns. Policy sends messages about what government is supposed to do, which citizens are deserving (and which not), and what kinds of attitudes and participatory patterns are appropriate in a democratic society. Different target populations, however, receive quite different messages. Policies that have detrimental impacts on ... target populations may not produce citizen participation directed toward policy change because the messages received by these target populations encourage withdrawal or passivity. Other target populations, however, receive messages that encourage them to combat policies detrimental to them through various avenues of political participation.[8]

For the most part, only in this most ironic sense is there something in the right-wing view that welfare causes poverty. The inadequacy of welfare policy for poor women with children is therefore part of a self-fulfilling prophesy that makes it hard for these families to be successful. This paradox consequently reinforces the idea that these families are the cause of their own problems. In its perpetuation of the blind commitment to the two-parent family as a fundamental constitutive element of the market system, welfare policy resists providing assistance to alternative families. These practices are likely to continue the bias in favor of the two-parent family as the route out of poverty and are just as likely to accelerate the trend toward the "femininization of poverty." For Nancy Fraser, this is a discursively constituted reality that is reproduced through public policy:

> Of course, the welfare system does not deal with women on women's terms. On the contrary, it has its own characteristic ways of interpreting women's needs and positioning of women as subjects....
>
> Clearly, this system creates a double bind for women raising children without a male breadwinner. By failing to offer these women day care for their children, job training, a job that pays a "family wage," or some combination of these, it constructs them exclusively as mothers. As a consequence, it interprets their needs as maternal needs and their sphere of activity as that of "the family." Now according to the ideology of separate spheres, this should be an honored social identity. Yet the system does not honor these women. On the contrary, instead of providing them a guaranteed income equivalent to a family wage as a matter of right, it stigmatizes, humiliates, and harasses them. In effect, it decrees simultaneously that these women must be and yet cannot be normative mothers.[9]

The Feminization of Poverty as Established Policy

There is no better evidence that welfare policy is partly constitutive of the problem it addresses than the "feminization of poverty." Although much has been made of the feminization of poverty as a recent and increasing phenomenon, the welfare state has historically been built on gendered distinctions that work to the disadvantage of female-headed families. Single-parent families headed by women have historically had much higher poverty rates than other kinds of families. Closer examination of trend-line data provides a basis for this interpretation. As Table 8.1 indicates, single-parent families headed by women have historically had high poverty rates. Table 8.2 reinforces the idea that the feminization of poverty (i.e., the growing proportion of poor families that are female-headed) is indeed a real and long-standing phenomenon. As the first column in Table 8.2 indicates, the proportion of poor families headed by women has increased from about one-fifth to more than one-half in the past thirty years. During this time, however, compared with other families, female-headed families have consistently had a larger "poverty deficit" (i.e., amount of income needed to be lifted up to the poverty level) (see the second and third columns in the

Table 8.1 Poverty rates for families, 1959–90
(percentage of families below the poverty level)

Year	All families	All Female-headed families	White families	White Female-headed families	Black families	Black Female-headed families	Hispanic families	Hispanic Female-headed families
1990	10.7	33.4	8.1	26.8	29.3	48.1	25.0	48.3
1989	10.3	32.2	7.8	25.4	27.8	46.5	23.4	47.5
1988	10.4	33.4	7.9	26.5	28.2	49.0	23.7	49.1
1987	10.7	34.2	8.1	26.9	29.4	51.1	25.5	52.2
1986	10.9	34.6	8.6	28.2	28.0	50.1	24.7	51.2
1985	11.4	34.0	9.1	27.4	28.7	50.5	25.5	53.1
1984	11.6	34.5	9.1	27.1	30.9	51.7	25.2	53.4
1983	12.3	34.0	9.7	28.3	32.3	53.7	25.9	52.8
1982	12.2	36.3	9.6	27.9	33.0	56.2	27.2	55.4
1981	11.2	34.6	8.8	27.4	30.8	52.9	24.0	53.2
1980	10.3	32.7	8.0	25.7	28.9	49.4	23.2	51.3
1979	9.2	30.4	6.9	22.3	27.8	50.6	20.3	49.2
1978	9.1	31.4	6.9	23.5	27.5	51.0	20.4	53.1
1977	9.3	31.7	7.0	24.0	28.2	52.2	21.4	53.6
1976	9.4	33.0	7.1	25.2	27.9	50.1	23.1	53.1
1975	9.7	32.5	7.7	25.9	27.1	52.2	25.1	53.6
1974	8.8	32.1	6.8	24.8	26.9	52.7	21.2	49.6
1973	8.8	32.2	6.6	24.5	28.1	53.3	19.8	51.4
1972	9.3	32.7	7.1	24.3	29.0	53.5	20.6	–
1971	10.0	33.9	7.9	26.5	28.8	54.3	–	–
1970	10.1	32.5	8.0	25.0	29.5	53.3	–	–
1969	9.7	32.7	7.7	25.7	27.9	54.3	–	–
1968	10.0	32.3	8.0	25.2	29.4	53.3	–	–
1967	11.4	33.3	9.1	25.9	33.9	53.2	–	–
1966	11.8	33.1	9.3	25.7	–	–	–	–
1965	13.9	38.4	11.1	31.0	–	–	–	–
1964	15.0	36.4	12.2	29.0	–	–	–	–
1963	15.9	40.4	12.8	31.4	–	–	–	–
1962	17.2	42.9	13.9	33.9	–	–	–	–
1961	18.1	42.1	14.8	33.5	–	–	–	–
1960	18.1	42.4	14.9	34.0	–	–	–	–
1959	18.5	42.6	15.2	34.8	–	–	–	–

Source: U.S. Bureau of the Census, Poverty in the U.S., Current Population Reports, P-60 series, no. 175 (Washington, D.C.: U.S. Government Printing Office, 1990), Table 4.

table). These data can be read to suggest that women with children have always had a high incidence of poverty, have always been among the poorest of the poor, have probably not benefited from economic growth and related social policies as much as other families, and are perhaps therefore in need of different strategies.[10]

Table 8.2. The feminization of poverty

| Year | Percentage of poor families female-headed | Median income deficit (1990 $s) | | Number of poor female-headed families (thousands) | Number of all other poor families (thousands) |
		Female-headed families	All other families		
1990	53.1	5,661	4,673[a]	3,768	3,330
1989	51.7	5,704	4,663[a]	3,504	3,280
1988	53.0	5,752	4,896[a]	3,642	3,232
1987	52.2	5,669	4,953	3,654	3,351
1986	51.4	5,591	4,846	3,613	3,410
1985	48.1	5,602	4,896	3,474	3,749
1984	48.1	5,470	4,994	3,498	3,779
1983	46.6	5,504	4,986	3,564	4,083
1982	45.7	5,517	5,069	3,434	4,078
1981	47.5	5,307	4,805	3,252	3,599
1980	47.8	5,100	4,741	2,972	3,245
1979	48.4	5,129	4,598	2,645	2,816
1978	50.3	4,973	4,516	2,654	2,626
1977	49.1	4,828	4,565	2,610	2,701
1976	47.9	4,657	4,494	2,543	2,768
1975	44.6	4,981	4,519	2,430	3,020
1974	47.2	5,002	4,539	2,324	2,598
1973	45.4	4,955	4,371	2,193	2,635
1972	42.5	5,047	4,422	2,158	2,917
1971	39.6	5,190	4,319	2,100	3,203
1970	37.1	5,398	4,412	1,952	3,308
1969	36.5	5,217	4,179	1,827	3,181
1968	34.8	5,576	4,335	1,755	3,292
1967	31.3	–	–	1,774	3,893
1966	29.8	–	–	1,721	4,063
1965	28.5	5,600	4,732	1,916	4,805
1964	25.4	–	–	1,822	5,338
1963	26.1	–	–	1,972	5,582
1962	25.2	–	–	2,034	6,043
1961	23.3	–	–	1,954	6,437
1960	23.7	5,961	5,214	1,955	6,288
1959	23.0	–	–	1,916	6,404

[a]Married-couple families.
Source: Data for 1985–90 are from U.S. Bureau of the Census, *Poverty in the U.S.*, Current Population Reports, P-60 series, no. 175. (Washington, D.C.: U.S. Government Printing Office, 1985–90). Data for 1959–84 are from U.S. Bureau of the Census, *Characteristics of the Population below the Poverty Level: 1984*, Current Population Reports, P-60 series, no. 152 (Washington, D.C.: U.S. Government Printing Office, 1984), Table 5, p. 22.

Of particular importance in these data, the last two columns in Table 8.2 point out that the growth in the feminization of poverty is a result of both the increase in poor female-headed families and the decrease in other, especially two-parent, poor families. The former is somewhat overstated because of a Census Bureau undercount until 1983 of teenage mothers who lived at home with their parents.[11] The latter is itself a contradictory phenomenon, caused in part by the increases in out-of-marriage births, divorce, and related trends (e.g., growing sexual permissiveness).[12]

Therefore, the feminization of poverty is actually reflective of a more persistent reality that has in large part become more visible only because of different trends at different times. First, a number of teenage single mothers were poor for years without being counted. Second, during the years of substantial economic growth from the 1960s to the early 1970s, the growth in the proportion of poor families from female-headed households came more from a shrinkage in the number of poor families that were not female-headed than from an increase in the number of poor women with children. Third, from the mid-1970s to the current period, the growth in the proportion of poor families headed by women stems mostly from relatively recent growth in the number of poor single women with children. The number of two-parent poor families, however, also increased in this period, especially from the late 1970s to the mid-1980s (see Figure 8.1). The net result of all these developments has been the feminization of poverty—the growing proportion of the poor made up of single women with children.

John Schwarz and Thomas Volgy, however, add the important point that the much-discussed alleged radical changes in the composition of the poverty population,[13] such as the growing proportion made up of single women with children, are in good part results of the way the poverty level has distorted estimates of the prevalence of poverty over time.[14] Most important for my analysis here, we also find that the poverty population has *not* come to be composed more of nonworking, welfare-dependent, or female-headed families. Instead, only an increasingly irrelevant official poverty measure has led to this conclusion. Therefore, the alleged feminization of poverty is in good part an artifact of the government's poor statistical accounting. Although feminist analysts may be wrong if they stress the newness of the feminization of poverty, it is conservatives who have the most to worry about in these data, for the feminization of poverty is a deep-seated problem embedded in the structure of society and the operations of the welfare state.

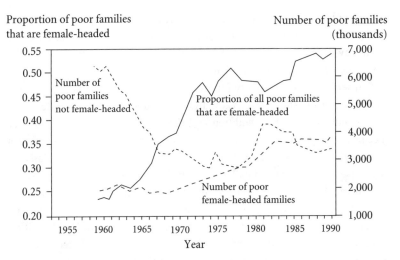

Figure 8.1. The feminization of poverty.

Sources: See Tables 8.1 and 8.2.

The initial growth in the feminization of poverty therefore did not come about because poverty among women was new; it simply became more visible because of declines in poverty for other families. The much-touted feminization of poverty is the product of declines in poor two-parent families and outdated poverty statistics that have allowed poverty among women to become more visible. The feminization of poverty has actually been a persistent problem embedded in the structure of U.S. society, the economy, and public policy.

Materializing Family Structure as Impoverishing

A critical dimension to welfare policy discourse is the presumption that two-parent families have at least the potential for being "self-sufficient" and are therefore "deserving," whereas mother-only families are "dependent" largely for reasons for which they must assume responsibility, and therefore are not deserving of as much support. Invidious distinctions of self-sufficiency/dependency, deserving/undeserving, responsible/promiscuous are deployed in gendered ways. The symbolic significance of welfare lies in its denigration of mother-only families in the name of affirming two-parent families. Welfare policy as a system of symbolic signification serves to reduce the extent to which social institutions, markets, and state policies feel pressure to structure their practices to accommodate mother-only families. The main way it does this is by reinforcing the idea that mother-only families are the cause of their own problems.

Conservatives argue that two-parent families are better than one-parent families for a variety of reasons, including greater ability to provide necessary parental attention to children and the presence of a male role model, specifically for young boys.[15] This argument is particularly a concern for poor minority families, which have distinctively high rates of female-headship, and these themes have in fact been emphasized by moderate and conservative African American politicians, such as Sharon Pratt Kelly, the former mayor of Washington, D.C., and Douglas Wilder, former governor of Virginia.[16] Others have suggested that it will be extremely difficult to build political coalitions with the white working class unless there is a shared commitment to valuing the two-parent family.[17] Yet the growth of female-headed families among whites has also been a cause for concern in recent years.[18]

The growth of poor female-headed families among both whites and blacks is indeed a troubling development in certain respects, most significantly in that it poses increased risks for children regarding such matters as schooling completed, earnings potential, out-of-wedlock childbearing, and future welfare dependency.[19] There is evidence that children in two-parent families are much less likely to be poor, and that the growth in female-headed families is strongly associated with sharp increases in child poverty, especially among minorities.[20] Yet the genesis and implications of the growth of female-headed families are more complicated than universal condemnations suggest.

Divorce often reduces the number of poor two-parent families while increasing the number of poor mother-only families. Even the issues of births outside marriage and especially unmarried teen births are more complicated than two-parent family advocates imply. Although close to 30 percent of children are now born outside marriage and more than 65 percent of black children are born to mothers who are serving as single parents,[21] the supposed epidemic of unmarried and teen births is largely a statistical artifact of declining fertility rates, especially for married women.[22] Whereas expected lifetime births for unmarried women has risen slightly over the past thirty years, the expected lifetime births for married women has decreased markedly, so that the proportion of births occurring outside of marriage has risen sharply, especially for black women. It is important to note that the apparent sharp increase for black women is in no small part a result of the fact that the lifetime birthrate for married women declined from 3.49 to .87 between 1960 and 1987. The teen birthrate actually declined for the period 1960–86, from 40 to 21 per 100 white women and from 80 to 51 per 100 black women. The percentage of lifetime births occurring in the teen years remained basically static for white women over this period, going from 11.3 to 12.1, while rising only slightly for black women, from 17.6 to 22.9. Thus, increases in the proportion of children born out of wedlock or the proportion of women living with children and without husbands are in part explained by declines in fertility among married women. Therefore, even if single parenthood is assumed to be bad or at least problematic for children, it needs to be stressed that although an increasing percentage of children are so situated, the rate at which women are having children outside marriage and especially in their teen years, when this is apt to be the most troublesome, is not skyrocketing. Instead, the statistical reality is quite different. Static and declining rates for births outside marriage combined with steeply decreasing birthrates for married, non-teenage women throughout most of the 1980s made for sharp increases in the *percentages* of children born to single mothers.[23] Adolph Reed Jr. puts it well:

> As for out-of-wedlock birth, insofar as it is not a subset either of the female-headed household concern or the teenage childbearing concern, it is simply nobody's business. "Teen pregnancy," though is a more complicated issue, largely because of its power as a condensation symbol. It is the big trump in the underclass pundits arsenal of pathologies.... the actual object of public and policy concern — and record-keeping — is not teenage pregnancy but teenage childbearing. The rhetorical focus on pregnancy both conveniently sidesteps the significance of restrictions on access to abortion for increases in adolescent fertility and trades on adult anxieties about youthful promiscuity to foment a tone of often hysterical urgency.[24]

There is, however, evidence that births to unmarried women increased in the years 1985–90, especially among African Americans (see Figure 8.2).[25] There is also evidence that as the fertility rates for teenagers continue to fall, the rates for births outside marriage for teens have risen; from 1955 to 1988, they rose slightly for blacks (from 77.6 to 98.3 per thousand) and dramatically for whites (from 6 to 24.8 per thousand).[26] Arlene Geronimus has emphasized how this trend, especially for poor, young African Americans, is not as irrational as many critics would have it.[27] First, it is important to recognize that this trend takes place in a society that discourages sex education, birth control, and abortion (especially among the poor, by

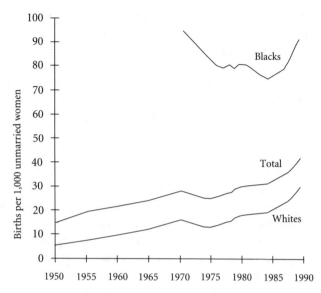

Figure 8.2. Births to unmarried women, 1950–89.

Source: Reprinted from Philip K. Robins and Paul Fronstin, "Welfare Benefits and Family-Size Decisions of Never-Married Women," discussion paper no. 1022-93, Institute for Research on Poverty, Madison, Wis., 1993. Data are from U.S. Bureau of the Census, *Statistical Abstract of the United States* (Washington, D.C.: U.S. Government Printing Office, 1992).

limiting medical assistance for this procedure) and simultaneously resists investing in poor communities so that the formation of female-headed families would not be either so likely or so often resulting in increased welfare taking. Geronimus's most striking point, however, is that the longer a poor young woman waits to have a child, the more she risks ill health and infertility and the less likely her mother is to be alive to help her rear her children. Kristin Luker reinforces this perspective when she says, relying on the 1988 National Survey of Family Growth, that "a little over 70 percent of the pregnancies to teens were reported as unplanned; the teenagers described the bulk of these pregnancies as wanted, just arriving sooner than they had planned."[28] Mike Males takes this a step further, noting that approximately 70 percent of teen pregnancies are caused by men over 20 years of age and that two-thirds of teen mothers and pregnant teens had been raped or sexually abused, nearly always by parents or other guardians or relatives.[29] These figures point toward the conclusion that births outside marriage are about more than teenage irresponsibility; they are related to larger questions of the deterioration of the quality of life for poor communities.

Therefore, although the recent rise in births to poor unmarried women and especially teenagers is undoubtedly an issue of critical concern for society, the growth in this phenomenon has often been exaggerated, and when not exaggerated it has been placed within an all-too-convenient and insufficiently challenged perspective that this trend signals an increase in irrational and irresponsible behavior. Instead, we need to specify the cultural, political, and economic changes taking place in postindustrial America that are making for the growth in births outside marriage. Poor teenage girls may be choosing to have children outside marriage with greater frequency than in the recent past, but this may be a small part of the teen pregnancy problem and itself may be more a sign of growing hopelessness and lack of access to needed services, including abortion, than anything else. Therefore, there is good reason to suggest that this trend is more a symptom than a cause of growing poverty and desperation.

Focusing on teen pregnancy outside marriage is an easy, if contestable, target. Highlighting teen pregnancy overlooks the evidence that even if teens delay having children outside marriage these same individuals would like to have babies a few years later, especially if their economic circumstances remain the same.[30] In and of itself, ending teen pregnancy would probably do very little to reduce poverty or welfare taking. Yet shortsightedness is only one feature of family policy discourse in these trying times. Even accepting that the increased percentage of children born outside marriage to young, poor women is a bad thing, showing a correlation between family structure and poverty is not the same as proving causation.[31] According to some analysts, family structure may not be critical in producing poverty, especially for minority families.[32] Instead, it may be that female-headed families are now, because of changing mores, a consequence of how people respond to poverty that already confronts them.[33] In the face of difficult economic circumstances and declining access to adequate public assistance, it may now be more convenient for two-parent families not to form or to dissolve.

In fact, according to a 1993 Census Bureau report on data concerning the past decade, "poor two-parent families were about twice as likely as non-poor two-parent families to be discontinued within two years."[34] Poor female-headed minority families are often the product of a "reshuffling of poverty" from already poor two-parent families not forming or splitting up.[35] There is reason to think that the causal arrows between family breakup and poverty run both ways, and emphasizing how family structure causes poverty backgrounds the critical reality that poverty does much to erode family ties. The Census Bureau report cited above concludes that poverty is at least as much a factor in the dissolution of two-parent families as the reverse. The report also notes that the effects of poverty on family breakup vary by race and ethnicity. For example, the study found that 12 percent of poor white two-parent families had dissolved within two years, but only 7 percent of white families above the poverty line had broken up. Among black two-parent families, 21 percent of those who were poor broke up within two years, compared with only 11 percent of those who were not in poverty. Among Hispanic families, the dissolution rates were about the same for poor and nonpoor households: 11 percent and 9 percent, respectively. Those in many new poor one-parent families had already been poor as members of two-parent families before breakup occurred: 26 percent of the white families and 39 percent of the black families without fathers were poor before the fathers left.[36] These figures should remind us that class and race differences are more important than family structure in determining poverty.[37] Therefore, it should not be too surprising to find that poverty for black children in two-parent families is almost as pervasive a reality as it is for their counterparts in female-headed families.[38]

The feminization of poverty occurs not because two-parent families are better or will always prove a more effective institutional structure for escaping poverty. The trend to single-parent families is the product of a confluence of factors, some negative and others positive, and some quite complicated, including the trend toward leaving abusive marital relationships and the increase in pregnancies outside of marriage.[39] The problem is the reverse of what pro-family values advocates wish to suggest: it is as often the case that poverty creates female-headed families than that female-headed families create poverty. A number of recent studies have documented that teen pregnancy and out-of-wedlock childbearing are most common among children who have been raised in low-income, less educated, more mobile families.[40] Poverty often leads, among young males as well as females, to a lack of information about birth control, a lack of understanding about skills in parenting, and a general sense of hopelessness that might make having a child attractive even to an unmarried teenager. Young poor males who father children may be reluctant to form two-parent families because of the lack of economic opportunities available for them.[41] Yet, as long as the prevailing discourse helps re-create the idea that family structure causes poverty, rather than the other way around, many people will continue to accept the invidious notion that single-parent families are the cause of their own poverty.[42]

Welfare Policy Re-creates Its Own Reality

Existing social policies are implicated in this problem. They have helped construct female-headed, single-parent families as the marginal "other" and set them up for inferior benefits and punitive therapeutic practices.[43] From this perspective, it is a mistake to see the growth in female-headed families as an autonomous "pathology" generated independent of policy and social institutions. Instead, it is more important to address how welfare policy is a critical constitutive factor reproducing the female-headed family as a stigmatized and disadvantaged social formation.[44]

Linda Gordon emphasizes that public assistance is founded on a "family wage" system based on the assumption that families have two parents and the male is the breadwinner.[45] Diana Pearce argues that even the public assistance program that primarily serves women with children — Aid to Families with Dependent Children — continues to be organized along the lines of the "male pauper model," which assumes that welfare benefits should be low enough so they do not discourage family heads from taking even the lowest-paying jobs as a means of supporting a family.[46] Under these circumstances, two-parent families are more likely to benefit from such varying phenomena as economic growth and jobs programs, which tend to be designed with the two-parent family in mind. Although neither males nor females are likely to do well in a labor market that increasingly consists of low-wage jobs, women with children will lag behind as they struggle to make do with policies and programs not designed to accommodate their particular needs and circumstances as single mothers.[47]

Policies geared toward women with children tend to offer inferior benefits or are lacking in commitment to the services and strategies, such as child care and pay equity, women need in order to become self-sufficient.[48] In particular, a major reason for the increased poverty of women with children is that AFDC has been less effective than programs such as social security and unemployment compensation in lifting families out of poverty.[49] The debased value of public assistance programs focused on poor women with children is a major factor in explaining the sharp increases in their poverty rate in recent years. The average cash benefit in constant dollars received from all public assistance programs over the 1973–87 period declined dramatically. Also, benefits to female-headed families have flagged relative to those going to other families: female-headed households went in real terms from a mean cash transfer (in 1987 $s) of approximately $7,000 in 1973 to $4,400 in 1987, or a 37 percent decline, compared with a corresponding drop from approximately $8,000 to $6,000, or a 25 percent decline, for male-headed families.[50]

These trends exacerbate a historic divide. Programs focused on poor women with children have historically been inadequate to lift their recipients out of poverty. Danziger and Stern have examined the rate at which families and the elderly are lifted over the official poverty line by cash assistance. They have found that whereas the elderly's rate is quite high, because of social security, female-headed families have a very low rate, with no more than 10 percent escaping poverty today through government transfers.[51] This discrepancy is almost entirely the result of the extent to which welfare programs focused on these families continue to offer benefits well below the poverty level for most families.[52]

Whether it was because public assistance was tied to the "family wage" system that promoted women's dependence on a male breadwinner or because it was tied to a market logic that sought to ensure that benefits were below the lowest wages, women on welfare have been denied adequate benefits under invasive treatment.[53] There is a need to highlight how welfare policies designed to be consonant with the low-wage labor market work together to promote more poverty. During a time of decreased welfare benefits, deterioration of job opportunities for the relatively unskilled, and increases in the numbers of female-headed families, the growth of female-headed families in poverty is symptomatic of the cultural biases embedded in social policy. Social policy operates to disadvantage women with children, materially as well as symbolically. Reinforcing their inferior status, social policy logically provides them inferior benefits.[54]

Welfare Policy as a Culture in Denial

The foregoing analysis is not meant to suggest that change will flow easily once welfare politics comes to be a cultural politics centered on what welfare signifies about families. Given its active involvement in promoting two-parent families, the welfare state has vested interests in perpetuating its own cultural construction.[55] Therefore, welfare policy discourse continues to construct poverty as a problem of family structure and seeks to find its solution in the two-parent family. In fact, discursive moves on behalf of the two-parent family wage system intensify especially as that ideal becomes harder to sustain. Insisting that family breakdown is a cause rather than a symptom of growing poverty allows social policy to continue to legitimate itself in spite of the failure of social policy to address the collapse of the family wage system. To be sure, blaming female-headed families for growing poverty provides a convenient and culturally ascendant way to deflect attention from the deleterious effects of the changing economy on the poorer segments of society.[56] The scapegoating of family structure for problems embedded in the sexist, racist, and economic exclusionary practices of the "contemporary postindustrial society of economic decline" propels popular resistance to public assistance and aggressively silences attempts to articulate a family policy that could ensure that all families have the resources to avoid poverty. Moving from a "culture of poverty" argument, which blames the poor for their problems, policy discourse has hit upon a "culture of single motherhood" to promote a punitive approach to poor women with children that obviates the need to address the dwindling economic opportunities associated with the current economic transition.[57]

Social policy then becomes ever more easily and explicitly dedicated to supporting only the two-parent family, blaming one-parent families for their problems, punishing women with children who fail to marry, refusing to address problems of sexism, exploitation, and abuse within the two-parent family, and so on. Overall, public assistance becomes less readily available, more temporary, more contingent on moral and social regulation, more premised on state surveillance of sexual, medical, social, and parental practices, and more attached to work requirements that move recipients from welfare to work irrespective of the lack of improvement in their economic condition. Even the outright abolition of welfare now gains ascendancy in policy circles, and some states pass legislation promising to do just that.[58]

Many of these changes overlook that family structure is in all likelihood far less significant in determining the economic well-being of family members than it is often made out to be. Most important, there is a tendency to emphasize the deleterious effects of family breakup while neglecting the fact that poverty itself is a major factor undermining the two-parent family among the poor. Also lost is the possibility that improved schooling, enhanced employment prospects, less sexism and racism in both areas, improved sex education, and a generally more hopeful horizon for poor children, especially from minority communities, would go a long way toward minimizing the significance of family structure and reducing the welfare burden on the state. Relatively stable marriages would likely increase among disadvantaged populations and alternative families that did form would be less likely to pose high welfare costs. Yet, in the current period, the incentive grows to blame symptoms, such as changing family patterns, rather than address the cultural biases that social policies actively reinforce.[59]

Conclusion

The feminization of poverty is an important phenomenon in need of increased attention; however, it is not new and its growing visibility is an artifact of bad statistics. The feminization of poverty is a manifestation of how welfare policy has historically served to create its own reality—stigmatizing female-headed families in order to reinforce two-parent families. The inadequacy of welfare policy for poor women with children is part of a self-fulfilling prophesy that makes it hard for these families to be successful and, consequently, reinforces the idea that these families are the cause of their own problems.

Women heading these families do not have access to other programs, often for no other reason than that their spouses chose to leave them rather than died, became disabled, or ended up out of work. Reflecting the biases of the broader society, the welfare state is not structured to provide such women with "family insurance" or "divorce insurance" policies that could correspond to programs that protect families when the primary wage earner dies, becomes disabled, or becomes unemployed. Cultural biases persist in perpetuating a welfare state that will insure families against some hazards but not others.

In spite of, and actually because of, rising numbers of single-parent families, society continues to resist the idea that women need to be protected from the risks of bearing and raising children on their own. Alternative arguments stress holding women responsible, getting "deadbeat dads" to pay child support, or some combination of both.[60] Yet, why is it that the risk of bearing and raising children on one's own is still considered largely a private responsibility, when coping with losing a job, becoming disabled, or losing a wage-earning spouse through death is accepted as a state that makes one deserving of support by government-sanctioned and funded "insurance" programs? Gender biases persist in relegation of women's risks to the private realm and prevent us from seriously confronting the need to guarantee all families minimally adequate resources after private sources of support, such as alimony and child support, have been tapped. Instead, poor women with children who do not qualify for the more generous types of assistance must confront the harsh reality of an underfunded and punitive welfare system. They are seen as "dependent" welfare recipients, whereas others can claim the name of "beneficiaries" or "insurees." Until we recognize that these women are just as deserving on average as recipients of the benefits from other programs, the biases of the existing welfare state and its failure to provide women either equality of treatment or special protection are likely to endure.[61]

In particular, we need to recognize that these allegedly dependent women are often actually establishing their independence by taking welfare. Many instances of the formation of female-headed families are the result of women coping with difficult social and economic circumstances. This is especially the case for women who are leaving abusive familial or work relationships.[62] By taking public assistance, these women with children are asserting their right to provide for their families in some minimally adequate way under desperate economic circumstances and independent of physical and emotional danger.[63] Until we are prepared to help change those circumstances, we might as well be prepared to expect that these families will continue to receive inadequate assistance even as they continue to form, either out of ignorance and hopelessness, especially among teenagers, or out of resilience and defiance, especially among women escaping abusive and impoverishing relationships.

More important, we need to overcome the resistance to supporting mother-only families that is grounded in the prevailing cultural anxiety about women acting in autonomous fashion. Even attempts to shift from welfare to "assured child support" or "children allowances" will not address this issue, for they tie assistance to the needs of children rather than legitimate and support women in the important work they do as mothers and nurturers in the realm of reproduction. Until reproduction is valued not only as much as production but in fact as another form of productive work, supporting women with children will continue to be at risk of inadequate funding and invasive bureaucratic practices. Nor will it be sufficient simply to "insure" women from risk of divorce or the absence of a husband, for such policies will serve to emphasize mother-only families as a problem rather than support mothering as worthwhile work in its own right. As unpopular as the idea currently is, guaranteeing families a minimally adequate income would avoid these problems. Until we are ready to commit to women with children and value women's reproductive work as integral to the well-being of society, these families will not receive support in any way commensurate with that received by the retired, disabled, and unemployed. In other words, until women's attempts at independence are valued as much as anyone else's, the feminization of poverty will remain established policy.

CHAPTER NINE

Waltzing with the Rapper: Industrial Welfare Policy Meets Postindustrial Poverty

Karl Marx in his early writings confessed his need to find a class whose aspirations would establish universal values, a class with "radical chains." He found that class in the proletariat, the liberation of which was supposed to end the domination of man by man. The underclass plays a similar role for Civic Liberalism, but in reverse fashion, a villain rather than hero. It is a class whose values are so inimical to America's potential universal culture that its negation, and transformation, will allow those universal values to flower.

Mickey Kaus, *The End of Equality*

As obstacles to its efficacy multiply, the state increasingly sustains collective identity through theatrical displays of punishment and revenge against those elements that threaten to signify its inefficacy.... The welfare class thus becomes a permanent demonstration project in the theatricality of power.

William E. Connolly, *Identity\Difference*

It is a symptom of society's reluctance to accept the reality that underlies all kinds of labor in late capitalist society: the national economy simply no longer requires the vast army of labor that seeks wages and salaries.

Stanley Aronowitz, *The Politics of Identity*

U.S. Senator Daniel Patrick Moynihan from New York has written, "Just as unemployment was the defining issue of industrialism, dependency is becoming the defining issue of postindustrial society."[1] His response is "postindustrial social policy," which concentrates on reducing welfare dependency by getting recipients to take what work the changing economy will provide. For Moynihan, postindustrial social policy is so critical to refashioning the welfare state in the 1990s that in early 1993 he threatened to hold the Clinton Administration's health care proposal hostage to welfare reform.[2] But what Moynihan takes as given is a discourse of denial in need contestation.[3]

The postindustrial age is an age of denial, and welfare policy discourse bears the marks of postindustrialism in denial. What is being called "postindustrial social policy" signifies that denial, as do "the feminization of poverty," "the underclass," and so many other terms of art that circulate in social policy circles today. The special significance of "postindustrial social policy" is that it represents a paradigmatic case of how postindustrial welfare discourse denies the extent to which postindustrial economic change is in good part responsible for growing welfare dependency.[4]

"Postindustrial social policy" is a self-legitimating performative that rationalizes itself just by saying so, even in the face of countervailing evidence.[5] Its self-legitimating performance authorizes anachronistic industrial and even preindustrial biases about who is poor and why to masquerade as innovative policy developed for a brave new world order. Postindustrial poverty meets industrial welfare policy and the state is waltzing with the rapper. Postindustrial social policy ends up blaming the poor for their own problems, so that its inability to respond to an increasingly deterritorialized global political economy will not be called into question.[6] As the twentieth century rushes to a close, we can see that this adherence to anachronistic discourse is not a disability limited to policy makers in the Reagan years. Instead, the attempt to insist on an industrial discourse for deciding how people will be valued in a postindustrial era had its boldest statement in the Clinton administration's desire to "end welfare as we know it," until Republicans made welfare disenfranchisement the centerpiece of their 1994 "Contract with America."[7]

Postindustrial Social Policy

The denial implicit in the phrase *postindustrial social policy* is foreshadowed by the term *postindustrial,* from which it is derived. Postindustrialism can at times sound like the culture of a future age of convenience and leisure.[8]

Yet postindustrialism means more than, for instance, a growing reliance on high technology. It also involves the decline of manufacturing, the rise of service industries, increased use of temporary employment, and the stagnation of wages for American workers in an increasingly competitive global economy.[9] Although postindustrial growth has meant more economic opportunities for the technologically proficient, including "symbolic analysts" and others associated with new information technologies, it has meant declining opportunities for others.[10] Postindustrialism has intensified economic inequality.[11] Postindustrialism has meant working more, getting by on less, or both, for many Americans. Declining wage rates for the average worker tell a good part of the story. "Had the average wage continued to grow after 1973 at the rate it did from 1947 to 1973, toilers in 1992 would be earning almost $19 an hour instead of $10.56 — a difference of more than $17,000 for full-time workers."[12] John Schwarz and Thomas Volgy estimate that there are 30 million working poor, and that there are 7 million poor working full-time, year-round.[13] Laurence Lynn Jr. has emphasized how the past decade has seen an exacerbation of this problem:

> As the economy restructures itself, relative demand rises for those with higher order skills — and there is net job creation — but falls precipitately for the relatively unskilled.... The effect of race is striking. Full-time employment rates for young black men with some college education have deteriorated from 48 percent in 1967 to 37 percent in 1989. Nonemployment rates among young black high school dropouts have risen from 10 percent in 1967 to over 35 percent in 1989....
>
> Thus, it is increasingly difficult for low-income families, whether headed by a couple or by a woman, to earn their way out of poverty in the legitimate economy.[14]

"Postindustrialism" is itself a cultural artifact, a discursive practice in service of attempts to make sense of the political, economic, social, and cultural changes of the contemporary period. Operating as its own self-legitimating rationalization, "postindustrialism" is often used in policy discourse to rationalize the dislocations of the emerging economy as part of a brave new world of technological convenience.[15] "Postindustrialism" promotes remaking the political economy so that this new world will be accepted even if it can deliver its benefits only to a selected population at the expense of others. "Postindustrialism" engenders a symbolic politics about legitimating changes that are presented as necessary for realizing that new order. The North America Free Trade Agreement (NAFTA) is an exemplary case. NAFTA's importance lies primarily in its symbolic value in rationalizing dominant versions of postindustrial change as inevitable.[16] Its symbolic significance in legitimating disinvestment from domestic manufacturing outweighs the material consequences in the number of jobs that will be affected by the agreement. "Postindustrial social policy" operates like "postindustrialism," and recent welfare reforms are the poverty-related analogues of NAFTA.

The symbolic character of postindustrialism raises questions about whether the economy can grow to create decent-paying jobs for all who need them. Postindustrialism challenges us to rethink the "work dogma" and to begin to imagine the necessity of calling forth a "postwork" society in which people's ability to achieve a minimally adequate standard of living need not and should not be tied to employment as much as it was in the past.[17] Finding alternative ways to redistribute the increasing productivity of a postindustrial economy becomes the agenda for a more enlightened postindustrial social policy.[18] Shortening the workday, raising wages, creating environmentally and socially productive public employment, and replacing welfare with a guaranteed income that ensures all families minimally adequate basic resources start to make more sense given the realities of postindustrialism. Given the growing chasm between the increasing productivity of the postindustrial economy and its decreasing potential to create jobs with decent wages, these ideas begin to take on the form of the agenda for the coming "postindustrial welfare state."

Yet what is currently being called "postindustrial social policy" is something that fails to account for many of the consequences of postindustrialism. In fact, postindustrial social policy amounts to an attempt to rationalize systematically the emerging economic system's inability to generate adequate economic opportunities for all who need them. Moynihan's call for a postindustrial social policy assumes that it is reasonable that reducing welfare dependency by promoting work requirements ought to replace eliminating poverty as a central concern of the state. "Postindustrial welfare policy" represents a convenient device for overlooking the ongoing erosion in adequate-paying jobs in the increasingly bifurcated, dual labor market of the emerging "postindustrial economy of limited choice."[19] A welfare policy that focuses on alleged "underclass" behaviors deflects attention from the growing underlying poverty that gives rise to them in the first place.[20] Postindustrial welfare policy's refusal to address these issues leads it to reinforce the work ethic in ways that are neglectful of the conditions confronting people living in poverty today. It is denial masquerading as public policy and justifying the "end of welfare" as the basis of a new "Contract with America."

The End of Welfare

At present, there are many signs that welfare is ending not in ways that create opportunities for a saner social policy but in ways that suggest that poor people must fend for themselves more intensely than they have had to in years. While Clinton and the Republican Congress contemplate the end of welfare, states are ending welfare on their own by slashing benefits, tightening regulations, and introducing punitive behavioral requirements.[21]

It is a time of ferment regarding the alleged curse of "welfare dependency." In the push to institute work requirements for welfare recipients through what was to become the Family Support Act of 1988, Ronald Reagan, as president, said of welfare in 1987: "It is time to reform this outdated social dinosaur and finally break the poverty trap."[22] Five years after the passage of the Family Support Act's Job Opportunities and Basic Skills (JOBS) program, Bill Clinton began his tenure as president proposing to "end welfare as we know it." President Clinton has proposed a two-year time-limit for receiving welfare after completion of a training program. Republicans go further, calling for the denial of aid to young single mothers, prohibitions on additional assistance for children born to mothers on welfare, refusal to provide benefits to legal immigrants, a crackdown on illegal immigrants, and the wholesale conversion of welfare entitlements into discretionary block grants that states can dole out largely as they see fit.[23] "Welfare dependency" has therefore become the major object of political concern in social policy circles.

Is, then, the current period the beginning of the end of welfare? Public assistance benefits, especially the main cash-benefit program for nonaged poor families with children — Aid to Families with Dependent Children — have been declining for almost two decades. Inflationary pressures followed by the onset of a deindustrializing economy with stagnant wages and slower job growth in the 1970s helped initiate the decline in benefits. In addition, since then, raising welfare benefits has once again become the political bête noir it was before the years of liberalization in the late 1960s and early 1970s. Increased talk in the states about "welfare magnets" has led relatively high benefit states to let their benefits decline faster than other states.[24] Also since 1972, the intergovernmental system of financing welfare has made it costly for states to raise benefits because they will lose approximately $.30 in food stamps for every $1.00 increase in public assistance benefits.[25] The current era of fiscal retrenchment is then likely only to exacerbate the already well-entrenched political, governmental, and fiscal pressures operating on all states to forgo raising public assistance benefits. The changes in 1991 were particularly dramatic:

> 2.9 million needy children and their caretakers — more than one third of the entire Aid to Families with Dependent Children (AFDC) caseload — were plunged deeper into poverty by drastic cuts in AFDC benefit levels in seven states and the District of Columbia during 1991. Their total income loss over the course of a year will be well over 400 million dollars. Additional children suffered losses as 5 states eliminated certain benefits given to families with special needs.

> Another 5.2 million needy children and their caretakers — over three-fifths of the national caseload — saw some of their meager income eaten up by inflation as 33 states held 1991 AFDC benefits at levels set in 1990 or earlier.

> Fewer than half a million children and their caretakers — less than 6% of the caseload — saw any increase in AFDC benefits in 1991. Those increases were often no more than or less than the 5.4% increase in the cost of living over the course of the previous year.

> These cuts followed a 15 year period during which the numbers of children and others in poverty grew, AFDC benefit levels and total AFDC expenditures fell, and the number of poor children served by AFDC declined.

> The numbers served began growing in 1989, and have now [in 1991] surpassed the previous high [growing 21 percent in the last year]. Expenditures per recipient in real dollars have continued to shrink.[26]

AFDC benefits levels are set by the states, which share the cost of funding them with the federal government according to a reimbursement formula; the federal government covers from 50 to 83 percent of the costs, depending on the state's average personal income. State benefits also vary widely. In 1993, the highest monthly benefits for a family of three were $924 in Alaska, $693 in Hawaii, and $633 in California. The lowest benefits were $185 in Tennessee, $184 in Texas, and $120 in Mississippi. The average state benefit was $391. In no state did AFDC benefits, even when combined with food stamps, bring a family's income up to the government's official poverty line.[27]

All states in fact have let AFDC benefits decline from highs in the early 1970s to levels undercutting the real value of benefits at the outset of the 1960s (see Table 9.1). Updating those figures, we find that the median state monthly AFDC benefit for a family of four fell 42 percent in real dollars from 1970 to 1990. Even if food stamps are counted as part of the welfare benefits package, in recent years in the average state they are worth not much more than cash public assistance was alone in 1960 (see Table 9.2). The cash value of food stamps and AFDC combined, however, declined 27 percent

Table 9.1. State monthly AFDC Benefits for a four-person family with
no other income by benefit levels in 1960 (in 1989 $s)

| Year | States by Benefit Level in 1960[a] | | | All states |
	Low	Medium	High	
1960	362.75	611.59	821.69	603.23
1964	377.69	600.08	773.71	587.71
1968	411.77	679.41	821.83	641.43
1970	399.62	715.15	804.63	643.17
1975	383.74	660.84	730.73	594.61
1980	335.79	563.04	640.73	515.78
1985	308.44	481.11	553.27	449.77
1989	298.19	472.06	513.35	429.63
N	16	16	17	49
Percentage change				
1960–89	−17.80	−22.81	−37.53	−28.78
1975–89	−22.29	−28.57	−29.75	−27.75

Note: The numbers in the table are averages for each group of states. Alaska and Hawaii are not included because 1960 data for them are not available. District of Columbia is included.
[a]States are divided into thirds according to their AFDC benefit levels in 1960.
Sources: Data for 1960, 1964, and 1968 are from U.S. House of Representatives, Committee on Ways and Means, Background Material and Data on Programs with the Jurisdiction of the Committee on Ways and Means (Washington, D.C.: U.S. Government Printing Office, 1969), Table 17, p. 576. Data for 1969–81 are from Richard Kasten and James Todd, Transfer Recipients and the Poor during the 1970s (Durham, N.C.: Duke University Press, 1983). Data for 1982–83 are from the U.S. Department of Health and Human Services publication Quarterly Public Assistance Statistics, April–June 1982, Table 25; April–June 1983, Table 24. Data for 1984–89 are from unpublished material supplied by the U.S. Department of Health and Human Services.

from 1972 to 1990. Even adding Medicaid benefits to food stamps and AFDC results in no net gain in benefits from 1969 to 1989 for the average state.[28] Adding housing allowances would make a significant increase in benefits, but less than one-third of all poor tenants in the United States receive some form of government housing subsidy, and only about one-fifth of AFDC families receive such aid.[29] For much of the 1980s, states allowed the real value of benefits to decline simply by not raising benefits to keep up with the rising cost of living. Now in the 1990s, however, states increasingly are taking the extra step of actually reducing the nominal value of benefits.

In addition to reductions in benefits, the work requirements of the JOBS program continue to be phased in for welfare recipients (see the discussion of JOBS in chapter 7). Beyond reducing benefits and work requirements, there is a "new paternalism" afoot that has states moving to increase regula-

Table 9.2.   State monthly AFDC-food stamp benefits for a four-person family
with no other income by benefit levels in 1960 (in 1989 $s)

Year	States by Benefit Level in 1960[a]			All states
	Low	Medium	High	
1960	362.75	611.59	821.69	603.23
1964	377.69	600.08	773.71	587.71
1968	588.96	776.31	876.00	749.79
1970	582.77	803.66	866.27	753.25
1975	615.58	809.55	858.47	763.18
1980	762.25	707.86	762.25	674.79
1985	523.78	644.64	695.15	622.70
1989	511.73	633.44	662.35	603.73
N	16	16	17	49
Percentage change				
1960–89	41.07	0.04	−19.39	0.00
1975–89	−16.87	−22.91	−22.85	−20.89

Note: The numbers in the table are averages for each group of states. Alaska and Hawaii are
not included because 1960 data for them are not available. District of Columbia is included.
[a]States are divided into thirds according to their AFDC benefit levels in 1960.
Sources: Data for AFDC benefits are the same as those for Table 9.1. Food stamp data for
1969–86 are from unpublished material supplied by the U.S. Department of Agriculture.
Food stamp data for 1987–89 are from U.S. House of Representatives, Committee on Ways
and Means, *Background Material and Data on Programs with the Jurisdiction of the
Committee on Ways and Means: "The Green Book"* (Washington, D.C.: U.S. Government
Printing Office, 1990), Table 9, p. 1275.

tion of recipients' behavior, all in attempts to reduce the welfare population.[30]
The preoccupation with welfare dependency has also encouraged states to
seek federal waivers in mushrooming numbers for rules changes regarding
the provision of public assistance so that they can tighten the restrictions
for receiving assistance.[31] Penalties for lack of school attendance, and for
having children while on public assistance, are matched in some states
with rewards for getting married and accepting Norplant contraceptive
implants and requirements that teen mothers live at home with their parents.[32] Lower benefits for recipients who have arrived recently from out of
state and even now the idea of a two-year time limit for the receipt of welfare have been approved as experiments under the waiver process. Additional efforts outside the public assistance system designed to promote
further reductions in "welfare dependency" have come to include expedited
approaches for collecting child support from absent parents and even attempts to reduce the availability of divorce. The new paternalism suggests
that even the work requirements of the Family Support Act of 1988 have

proven, at least to enough policy makers in some states, to be insufficiently coercive.[33]

Although benefit reductions, eligibility restrictions, welfare-to-work programs, and other schemes proliferate, these efforts often lack evidence that they will significantly trim the welfare rolls.[34] More important even less research looks to evaluate the impacts of such measures on welfare recipients' well-being. The new paternalism is about reducing the number of people receiving assistance, irrespective of whether they leave the rolls under improved circumstances. As such, it is an attempt to reduce the visibility of the poverty problem and to deny responsibility for having to address it. Therefore, it is unlikely that many studies will be done that focus on the effects on recipient well-being.

The Brave New World of Welfare Policy

Appearances can be deceiving. The draconian budget compromise of 1990 between Congress and the Bush administration ironically included several improvements in social supports for the "working" poor, including health and infant care tax credits and promised increases in the availability of Head Start and various nutrition assistance programs, including the WIC (Women, Infants and Children) program.[35] After more than ten years of cutting back on social programs and tightening conditions regarding the receipt of public assistance, these particular changes conceivably represented the beginnings of a salubrious shift from punishing welfare taking to rewarding work.

"Making work pay" through added tax benefits has been the coming strategy for about a decade. Its most ambitious idea is an employer mandate to guarantee health insurance to all employees. Less dramatic is the idea of tax credits for low-wage workers. Increases in tax credits in 1975, 1986, 1989, 1990, and 1992 have improved the ability of poor families with wage earners to get needed health insurance, infant care, and child care. These were superseded by the 1993 changes in the earned income tax credit (EITC) for "working" poor families, who by 1995 can receive up to $2,040 if they earn less than $23,760 and have one child and up to $3,033 if they earn less than $26,000 and have more than one child.[36] These tax credits represent maximum annual increases over 1993 levels of approximately $700 for families with one child and $1,500 for families with more than one child. As dramatic as these changes are, they will still leave in poverty most poor families relying on a minimum-wage job even with full-time employment.[37]

New Liberal Strategies Are Old Conservative Ones

The prospects for a distinctively different approach to welfare reform dim once we see how liberals have become wedded to the conservative agenda of reducing "welfare dependency" at the expense of other considerations. "Making work pay" is designed to reduce "welfare dependency" by making work more attractive than welfare. Rewarding work is therefore a relative phenomenon, and in a "postindustrial economy of limited choice" it necessarily involves punishing welfare taking.

Beginning in the early 1980s, liberals became more willing to participate in the conservative agenda to devalue public assistance.[38] Liberal complicity came relatively easily, given liberals' long-standing ambivlance about welfare. David Ellwood accurately notes that no one really likes welfare: conservatives think it creates dependency, liberals think its benefits are inadequate, and the poor find it oppressive. But liberals in particular have had a very ambivalent attitude about welfare.[39] Theda Skocpol has argued that programs for the poor make for poor programs.[40] From this perspective continuing to hope for low-cost welfare solutions to the persistent problems of poverty is no solution at all. Proponents of a more universalistic social welfare state would replace welfare with policies on which all families could rely. Poor people would then be getting a hand up, not a handout. The universal availability of decent schools, adequate child care, affordable health insurance, and meaningful job training, coupled with a concerted effort to develop non-poverty-wage jobs, would go a long way to creating that sustained foundation. Rather than wasting time waging war on welfare, the state would be building a better alternative. Yet, while talk about a universalistic social welfare state continues, the current system of public assistance has eroded. In fact, the emphasis on universalistic programs can contribute to the neglect and even delegitimation of welfare programs for the poor. Even liberals have become uncomfortable with welfare and have talked in ways that may not be very helpful in protecting public assistance from further cutbacks.[41]

Such a policy strategy plays into the hands of conservatives, who are busy trying to prop up the old market ideology: public assistance should be limited and temporary because whatever work is available is the best cure for poverty.[42] In spite of the fact that most unemployment continues to be structural and not frictional,[43] this belief in the power of the "free market" continues to feed the all-too-convenient attitude that the state must tighten welfare eligibility and cut benefits so as to promote a willingness to work. Whereas some analysts persist in arguing that there are ample jobs available,[44] many others point out that the numbers of adequate-paying jobs that could serve as the source for escaping poverty have rapidly diminished during the current period of economic transformation and declining global competitiveness.[45] The net result is that the ongoing denigration of the concept of welfare and a corresponding decline in public assistance benefits are likely to continue as long as both liberals and conservatives agree on concentrating on reducing welfare dependency to the neglect of addressing poverty. In the long run, the continual denigration of the poor and welfare taking serves only to undercut the case for public assistance; in the short run, it leads to the scratching out of marginal or even questionable improvements in services at the expense of increasingly coercive regulation of welfare recipients.[46]

Clinton and the Neoliberal Welfare Imaginary

Clinton's welfare reforms have followed the path of the new paternalism, with its lineage in Reaganism and state attempts to discipline the poor. Clinton is allegedly a "New Democrat." New Democrats embrace a "neoliberalism" that says that there is much to learn from conservatives, especially about being fiscally responsible and using social policy to reinforce traditional institutions like work and family. Nancy Fraser has pointed out that the "neoliberal political imaginary" shares much in common with the "neoconservative political imaginary" of Reagan-Bush, especially over what can be called the "political imaginary of social welfare."[47]

Regarding welfare, Fraser sees very little difference between the neoconservative political imaginary of Reagan-Bush and the neoliberal political imaginary of Clinton.[48] Although Clinton wants to subsidize work, especially through changes in the tax code by way of expanding the EITC, the neoliberal political imaginary he reflects is only slightly more committed than conservatives to the idea that the government has an obligation to ensure a "social wage" that makes a nonpoverty existence affordable. Clinton is, however, more committed than conservatives to ensuring that some basic needs are considered so important that they must be treated as guaranteed public goods and their provision should not be left to the vagaries and inequities of the market. Clinton's preoccupation with "ending" welfare dependency while not talking about social security or people's dependence on other major social policies suggests that he is just as committed as conservatives to maintaining the bifurcated character of the contemporary U.S. welfare state.[49] Clinton's agenda shares with the conservative agenda the "independence versus dependence" distinction, which asserts that receiving welfare is dependency whereas relying on social insurance is not. His agenda also shares the conservatives' assumption that we must move beyond guaranteeing rights to "entitlements" to enforcing the alleged "obligations" that go with entitlements.[50] Finally, Clinton's version of "mutual responsibility" remains vague, and although it might portend a greater sense of the community's obligation to ensure all people the "capacity" to participate in mainstream institutions and enjoy the fruits of society, it may also imply that individuals must exhibit "competence" in order to qualify as functioning members of society. Under the former, social policy will be more committed to removing barriers that exclude poor persons from participation in the broader society. Under the latter, social policy will be more committed to enforcing standards that regulate people's behavior.

Clinton's Industrial Welfare Policy and Postindustrial Poverty

The welfare philosophy of the Clinton administration is based on certain explicit assumptions and leads to some very specific program initiatives. The principles are untenable in today's postindustrial economy, and the program initiatives will therefore do little more than "recycle" the poverty and "redistribute" the burden that currently exists without significantly increasing the "well-being" of the families affected by such changes.

The first principle of the Clinton administration's welfare philosophy is "making work pay."[51] As postindustrialism continues to remake the job structure of the United States, it becomes harder and harder to sustain the idea that the economy has a non-poverty-wage job for everyone who needs one. Whether people are prepared to accept it or not, postindustrialism more and more means that many people, workers included, must derive part of their standard of living from government support. Whether it is untaxed fringe benefits, tax deductions, earned income tax credits, social security, disability compensation, unemployment insurance, or even public assistance, the "citizen's wage" as a component of people's total income has become an enduring and growing feature of economics in a postindustrial economy.[52] Even if jobs are to be obtained, for the poor these are jobs that increasingly must be subsidized with supplemental wages, tax credits, or the extension of public assistance benefits if they are to serve as a likely means of subsistence for persons currently receiving public assistance. Job supplementation in these forms costs money, and the Clinton proposals in the face of the administration's attempts to reduce the federal deficit suggest that efforts to make more jobs worth taking will in all likelihood fall seriously short.[53]

The second major principle of the Clinton administration's welfare philosophy is that the government is obligated to help welfare recipients be able to take what work is available. The New Democrats emphasize work training and placement, whereas liberals are more prone to emphasize education. Their differences come to a head on the second major Clinton campaign promise, to put a two-year time limit on the receipt of welfare.[54] A draconian version of this policy is being implemented in Wisconsin under a federal waiver for a two-county experiment that assumes that after two years an employable recipient should have had enough time to find employment. A more tolerant version is being implemented as a seven-county experiment in Minnesota; this version requires that after two years recipients must accept placement in a program designed to lead eventually, at some unspecified time in the future, to work through education, training, or placement.[55] In either case, government assistance is designed to treat behavioral deficiencies or at least inadequacies in the recipient population. It is not designed to restructure existing labor markets so that more better-paying jobs start to appear in the bottom of the segmented postindustrial economy. Clinton did push for a job-creating economic stimulus package, but when it failed he allowed himself to be prodded into proposing reforms to push welfare recipients into a workforce that has very few prospects for them. A serious program that would create jobs for all who need them would not only cost far more than the deficit-conscious Clinton administration is prepared to pay, it would probably attract onto the welfare rolls many additional poor people currently not receiving assistance, simply because the jobs crisis extends well beyond the public assistance population.[56]

The third principle of the Clinton welfare philosophy is increasing parental responsibility. This starts with addressing the problem of teen pregnancy by denying unmarried teen mothers public assistance unless they stay at home with their parents.[57] Another feature is the denial of aid for any additional children born to a mother on public assistance. The more tolerant version of this principle involves getting noncustodial fathers more involved in assuming responsibility for ensuring the well-being of their children. Parents need not be married, but they must accept the responsibility for their children. This principle takes the programmatic form of expanding efforts to establish paternity, mandating universal routine withholding of child support from the paychecks of working noncustodial parents, instituting some sort of percentage-of-income method of establishing child support obligations, achieving a 100 percent ratio of child support payments to obligations, supplementing poor noncustodial parent payments, and providing increased job training and placement opportunities for poor fathers.[58] Again, the goal is laudable; fathers should accept an appropriate share of parental responsibility irrespective of whether they live with their children or not. But most poor fathers lack the means of livelihood to fulfill that responsibility. Insisting on it without effectively creating the conditions for them to meet their obligations will only "redistribute" the poverty of female-headed families to include these noncustodial parents without appreciably changing the circumstances of either. Given the Clinton administration's acceptance of the deficit as a real obstacle to government initiatives, we again face the prospect of welfare reforms that institute requirements without establishing corresponding programmatic efforts, such as calling for automatic withholding of child support without finding some way to increase the incomes of those whose earnings are being withheld.[59]

Full funding of even the most liberal approaches is problematic. First, this focus on the welfare population overlooks the pervasiveness of the structural dislocation taking place. Therefore, well-funded education and training programs that lead to real jobs will end up either attracting many people onto public assistance so that they can qualify for such opportunities or creating demand for such programs to be extended beyond the welfare population, at unavoidably greater expense than the Clinton administration has estimated. Second, such programs focus largely on reducing the welfare population. They reinforce the notion that people who have to rely on welfare are somehow different and deficient.[60]

The postindustrial denial involved in the Clinton program becomes explicit with the provision to help finance the job training of welfare recipients by denying assistance to immigrants. It is true that immigrants absorb a growing proportion of public assistance, especially in the Supplemental Security Income program for low-income elderly and disabled; the number of immigrants receiving SSI increased from 127,900 in December 1982 to 601,430 in December 1992, or from 3.3 to 10.9 percent of recipients. Yet immigrants remain a small proportion of the total public assistance population. Exploiting xenophobia while projecting the growing sense that the state cannot be effective in the face of increasingly global forces, the Clinton administration hopes to cut off aid to immigrants even though they are less likely to take public assistance than are citizens. Even though "there is no evidence that access to federal programs acts as a magnet to foreigners or that further restrictions would discourage illegal immigrants," the symbolism of denying aid to immigrants is potent in an era where industrial social policy is inadequate to confront postindustrial poverty. The Clinton program has been surpassed, however, by the Republicans' "Contract with America" and its proposed Personal Responsibility Act. This act would demonize welfare recipients as deviant others by denying aid not only to illegal and legal immigrants but also to young single mothers, while disenfranchising the poor in general by converting welfare entitlements into block grants that states can largely dole out as they see fit, and not necessarily to all who qualify.[61]

The industrial welfare philosophy of the Clinton administration is no match for the postindustrial poverty it ostensibly addresses. Strauss meets L.L. Cool J — the result is the policy equivalent of waltzing with the rapper. Whether New Democrat or social democrat, it does not matter — Bill Clinton is committed to a philosophy that is blind to the character of postindustrial poverty in a postwork society.[62] Whether investing in people or enforcing behavioral standards, the near-term future of welfare policy is one that refuses to address the structural sources of welfare dependency and growing likelihood that the changing postindustrial economy will continue to fracture with decreasing wages and job opportunities for low-skilled workers. Instead, Clinton's approach continues to locate the problems of nonwork in individual welfare recipients and poor people more generally. The problem is attitude more than economics. This "politics of attitude" perpetuates a "welfare political imaginary" that easily slips into rationalizing the growing inability of work to ensure independence and self-sufficiency by blaming it on lack of motivation and a culture of resistance and resignation among the poor. The politics of attitude suggests that if people would simply work they could escape poverty, but the reality is that millions of people already working full-time, year-round, are still poor.[63] The politics of attitude becomes the handmaiden of a new ethic of labor discipline that forces workers into low-wage jobs and continued poverty so as to allow corporations to win profits in the emerging postindustrial global economy.[64]

Reencoding Otherness in Contemporary Welfare Policy

Even the Clinton administration's promise to end welfare as we have known it reencodes the welfare recipient as the deficient "other" failing to conform to ascendant notions of the self-sufficient self, but this time in a postindustrial context.[65] The old canard that the poor are different when it comes to work and family becomes a bad joke in the context of deindustrialization, the evaporation of decent-paying low-skill work, and the decline of wages. Welfare dependency comes to be seen as a cop-out when in fact it is often nothing more than an inadequate last resort for those who cannot find the means of even basic survival in a deindustrializing economy and a fissuring society.[66]

As the gap between those who have and those who do not widens, it becomes harder for the privileged, including those in policy-making roles, to envision just what it would take to enable those dependent on welfare to rely on other means for their well-being.[67] The stress on rewarding paid labor may create further divisions between families who have jobs and those that do not.[68] These divisions are likely to persist when public policy that rewards paid labor makes only marginal changes to address the fact that work itself is less able in the postindustrial present of today than it was in the industrial past of twenty years ago to ensure independence and self-sufficiency. Public policies that insist that work and welfare distinguish the independent and the dependent only help re-create the ugly reality of a poverty based on neglect and indifference. Such neglect conveniently reinforces the old theme of the "worthy" versus the "unworthy" poor in a way that further discourages extension of aid to families whose heads do not have paid jobs, in particular mothers with children. In turn, this invidious distinction reinforces a bifurcated welfare state that divides along gender, race, and class lines, with women and minorities often being relegated to programs with inferior benefits.[69]

Welfare Policy as Symbolism in Denial

What is being called "postindustrial social policy" is a case of how welfare policy discourse is a self-legitimating interpretive structure that denies its own inadequacies and exculpates its own participation in the problems it ostensibly is designed to address. It helps remake the alleged pregiven reality it is supposed to address in ways that rationalize injustices to the people who are expected to conform to ascendant notions of a self-sufficient self. Postindustrial social policy reinforces the age-old social construction of poverty as individual deviance while de-emphasizing the extent to which postindustrial economic transition is involved in the manufacturing of much of the poverty prevalent today. In the process, postindustrial social policy becomes a mask for an anachronistic industrial welfare policy discourse that fails to account for the emerging postindustrial poverty. It helps rationalize neglect of all those who find themselves increasingly passed over in the transition to the brave new world of a global postindustrial political economy. Persistent reliance on the anachronistic discursive practices of industrial welfare policy discourse ensures a policy that emphasizes that industrialized versions of traditional ideas about work, family, and individual responsibility will be nothing more than cruel vices within which marginalized populations must squeeze their postindustrial circumstances before they can hope for any assistance from the state. Postindustrial welfare discourse, with its references to "welfare dependency," and even "the homeless" and "the hungry," represents a displacement that distracts attention from the persistence and even intensification of poverty as the main problem of the postindustrial era.

Ending welfare will not end postindustrial poverty. From one presidential administration to the next, the inefficacy of the state in the face of global postindustrialism is rationalized by theatrical displays of power directed at regulating the poor and stigmatizing them as responsible for their own failure to survive in the face of an inadequate welfare state. William Connolly underscores the symbolic character of contemporary postindustrial social policy when he writes:

> As obstacles to its efficacy multiply, the state increasingly sustains collective identity through theatrical displays of punishment and revenge against those elements that threaten to signify its inefficacy. It launches dramatized crusades against the internal other (low-level criminals, drug users, disloyalists, racial minorities, and the underclass), the external other (foreign enemies and terrorists), and the interior other (those whose strains of abnormality, subversion, and perversity that may reside within anyone)....
>
> To the degree that this heterogeneous constellation of misfits and outcasts is fashioned into an object of political disposability — that is, into a welfare class — the theatricality of state power is magnified and its inefficacy remains deniable....
>
> The welfare class thus becomes a permanent demonstration project in the theatricality of power. It becomes a dispensable subject of political representation and an indispensable object of political disposability.[70]

Neither can the persistence of postindustrial poverty be wished away by what can be called a "politics of attitude." Conservatives (e.g., Lawrence Mead) and liberals (e.g., William Julius Wilson) alike have helped amplify the age-old idea that if the poor had a better attitude there would far less poverty, as if being chipper can increase employment, raise productivity, and lift the standard of living. The Clinton effort remains within the politics of attitude, hoping against hope that people will lift themselves out of poverty or at least into better-paying jobs without restructuring job creation practices in the postindustrial economy of temporary and low-wage work. Subsidizing work through the earned income tax credit has merit, and attention should be paid to any effects the Clinton changes in the EITC have. But the therapeutic and regulatory impulses in Clinton's neoliberal welfare imaginary mean that welfare policy is likely to change little, if at all, while Republican proposals try to intensify the regulative role of welfare to a nearly unprecedented degree.

Nothing short of an interrogation of the animating categories of contemporary welfare policy discourse will suffice. It is time to examine seriously work and family as assumptions. They are cultural norms that are integral for the functioning of the political economy and increasingly undermined by it. As postindustrial society makes them harder to realize for everyone at all times, postindustrial welfare policy is animated to insist on them so as to help sustain the existing social, political, and economic arrangements. The emergence of the idea of a postindustrial welfare policy reflects the growing preoccupation with reinforcing both the two-parent family and the work ethic in the face of the postindustrial economic deterioration that threatens them.

Alternatives begin to emerge once postindustrial social policy is seen as the fraudulent self-legitimating performance that it is. The inability of the state to ensure full employment at adequate levels of remuneration in the face of a deterritorialized global political economy becomes increasingly visible in spite of the theatrics of state power that stigmatize the welfare class. The idea of planning for a "postwork" society begins to receive attention under these circumstances.[71] There is growing recognition that work no longer can signify the exhaustive source of self-sufficiency that it never was but once could claim to be. Political resistance to this new logic is likely to be substantial until the deleterious consequences of deindustrialization spread far enough into the middle class, and might mean tying income support to uses that are more consistent with middle-class concerns about enforcing "delayed gratification." Reform then might mean tying income support to uses that not only meet a family's immediate needs but also are "investments in a future of self-sufficiency."[72] At the same time, in an age of fiscal austerity, it might mean promoting programs aimed specifically at the poor.[73] It might mean recognizing the need to create many more subsidized jobs. It might mean reducing the workweek without lowering wages. It might mean finally accepting the necessity of a guaranteed income in a productive economy that does not need anywhere near the workforce of its predecessor. It might mean reinvesting in communities rather than focusing on changing behavior. It might mean leaving welfare alone and restoring funding for schools in poor neighborhoods, improving job training, increasing the standard deduction and exemptions for dependents in the income tax and extending them to all families—in other words, recognizing that welfare has been reduced to serving symbolic purposes of behavioral regulation and that the solutions to poverty lie elsewhere. It might mean doing many things that currently are not given much discussion. In any case, in the "mean" time, eliminating benefits for single males, punishing single women with children, and reducing benefits to all other families will not help us get to that more hopeful future. Relying on anachronistic industrial welfare policy discourse to decide which individuals, workers, and families will be valued and in what ways is simply not helpful. In fact, it hurts.

Notes

Foreword

1. See especially David T. Ellwood and Mary Joe Baine, "The Impact of AFDC on Family Structure and Living Arrangements," *Research in Labor Economics* 7 (1986): 137–207. For a discussion, see William Julius Wilson and Kathryn M. Neckerman, "Poverty and Family Structure: The Widening Gap between Evidence and Public Policy Issues," in *Fighting Poverty: What Works and What Doesn't,* ed. Sheldon H. Danziger and Daniel H. Weinberg (Cambridge: Harvard University Press, 1986). See also Frances Fox Piven and Richard A. Cloward, "The Contemporary Relief Debate," in *The Mean Season: The Attack on the Welfare State,* ed. Fred Block, Richard A. Cloward, Barbara Ehrenreich, and Frances Fox Piven (New York: Pantheon, 1987).

2. See especially Murray Edelman, *Symbolic Uses of Politics* (Chicago: University of Illinois Press, 1964).

3. Karl Polanyi, *The Great Transformation: The Political and Enconomic Origins of Our Time* (Boston: Beacon, 1957), 102.

Introduction

1. For an analysis that begins to point in this direction, see Nancy Fraser and Linda Gordon, "A Genealogy of *Dependency*: Tracing a Keyword of the U.S. Welfare State," *Signs* 19 (Winter 1994): 328. See also Nancy Fraser, "Women, Welfare, and the Politics of Need Interpretation," in *Unruly Practices: Power, Discourse, and Gender in Contemporary Social Theory* (Minneapolis: University of Minnesota Press, 1989), 144–60.

2. On the myth of autonomy for science in general, see Helen E. Longino, *Science as Social Knowledge: Values and Objectivity in Scientific Inquiry* (Princeton, N.J.: Princeton University Press, 1990).

3. For a defense of the position that textual analysis even in the form of a "cultural studies" that construes texts broadly is necessarily not political intervention and should concern itself with analyzing texts strictly for their literary possibilities, see Stanley Fish, "Why Literary Criticism Is Like Virtue," *London Review of Books,* June 10, 1993, 11–15.

4. Michael J. Shapiro, *Reading "Adam Smith": Desire, History and Value* (London: Sage, 1993), 48–49.

5. Evelyn Z. Brodkin, "The Making of an Enemy: How Welfare Policies Construct the Poor," *Law and Social Inquiry* 18 (Fall 1993): 647–70; Joel F. Handler and Yeheskel Hasenfeld, *The Moral Construction of Poverty: Welfare Reform in America* (Newbury Park, Calif.: Sage, 1991).

6. Some people consider the material value of benefits to be inadequate, in that public assistance leaves recipients in poverty; others view the material value of benefits as overly generous, such that public assistance undermines commitments to work and family and generates "welfare dependency." For the former position, see David T. Ellwood, *Poor Support: Poverty in the American Family* (New York: Basic Books, 1988); for the latter position, see Charles Murray, *Losing Ground: American Social Policy 1950–1980* (New York: Basic Books, 1984).

7. William E. Connolly, *Identity\Difference: Democratic Negotiations of Political Paradox* (Ithaca, N.Y.: Cornell University Press, 1991), 206–8.

8. Charles E. Lindblom, *Inquiry and Change: The Troubled Attempt to Understand and Shape Society* (New Haven, Conn.: Yale University Press, 1990), 189. Leslie Dunbar, in *The Common Interest: How Social Welfare Policies Don't Work and What We Can Do about Them* (New York: Pantheon, 1988), 18, notes that "social science ... treats the poor like a foreign nation or fashions them into objects unlike us, against a discipline that speaks mainly for the approval of other social scientists and of legislators, and seldom consults the poor themselves."

9. Michael B. Katz, *The Undeserving Poor: From the War on Poverty to the War on Welfare* (New York: Pantheon, 1989), 122.

10. For a survey of the development of poverty research as an applied social science, see Robert H. Haveman, *Poverty Policy and Poverty Research: The Great Society and the Social Sciences* (Madison: University of Wisconsin Press, 1987). For an overview of the network of institutes and think tanks and their growing role in public policy making, see David Ricci, *The Transformation of American Politics: The Rise of Washington Think-Tanks* (New Haven, Conn.: Yale University Press, 1993).

11. For a critique of the emphasis on behavior to the exclusion of the political-economic and institutional context, see Michael B. Katz, "The Urban 'Underclass' as a Metaphor for Social Transformation," in *The "Underclass" Debate: Views from History,* ed. Michael B. Katz (Princeton, N.J.: Princeton University Press, 1993), 3–23.

12. For a look at the discursive practices of economists, with some attention to their policy implications, see Donald N. McCloskey, *The Rhetoric of Economics* (Madison: University of Wisconsin Press, 1985); Donald N. McCloskey, *If You're So Smart: The Narrative of Economic Expertise* (Chicago: University of Chicago Press, 1990). For a wider-ranging look at the discursive practices of contemporary social sciences, see John S. Nelson et al., eds., *The Rhetoric of the Human Sciences: Language and Argument in Scholarship and Public Affairs* (Madison: University of Wisconsin Press, 1987).

13. For a critique of how poverty research discourse has helped construct and legitimate the idea of the "underclass" in ways consonant with popular prejudices, see Adolph Reed Jr., "The Underclass as Myth and Symbol: The Poverty of Discourse about Poverty," *Radical America* (January 1992): 21–38.

14. Robert Moffitt, "An Economic Model of Welfare Stigma," *American Economic Review* 73 (December 1983): 1023–35.

15. For a review of the literature on welfare that evaluates it in terms of incentive effects, see Robert Moffitt, "Incentive Effects of the U.S. Welfare System: a Review," *Journal of Economic Literature* 30 (March 1992): 1–61. In reviewing research on the effects of welfare on family formation (which he concludes are probably at least as significant as the effects on work effort), Moffitt writes in an economistic vein: "The more important evidence should come from econometric analyses that are based upon rigorous economic models that control for other determinants of female headship. The underlying theoretical model most commonly used to analyze headship is based loosely on the [Gary] Becker model of marriage. In that model marital unions form when there are utility gains to both parties doing so and dissolve when utility gains disappear" (p. 29). For a critique of this sort of reasoning applied to family life, see Alan Wolfe, *Whose Keeper? Social Science and Moral Obligation* (Berkeley: University of California Press, 1989), 51–77.

16. See Haveman, *Poverty Policy and Poverty Research,* 32–34.

17. See David T. Ellwood, *Targeting the Would-Be Long Term Recipient: Who Should Be Served?* report to the U.S. Department of Health and Human Services (Princeton, N.J.: Mathematica Policy Research, 1986); Mary Jo Bane and David T. Ellwood, *The Dynamics of Dependence: The Routes to Self-Sufficiency,* report to the U.S. Department of Health and Human

Services (Cambridge, Mass.: Urban Systems Research & Engineering, 1983); David T. Ellwood and Mary Jo Bane, "The Impact of AFDC on Family Structure and Living Arrangements," *Research in Labor Economics* 7 (1986): 137–39.

18. For the suggestion that economic modeling particularly relying on notions of cost-benefit ratios began to become dominant in the 1960s as the basis for evaluating the desirability of public policies, see Peter W. House and Roger D. Shull, *The Practice of Policy Analysis: Forty Years of Art and Technology* (Washington, D.C.: Compass, 1991), 15–21.

19. Ellwood, *Poor Support.*

20. On the growing role of econometric modeling in the development of social policy, see Constance F. Citro and Eric A. Hanushek, "Microsimulation Models for Social Welfare Programs: An Evaluation," *Focus* 15 (Winter 1993–94): 13–21.

21. See Haveman, *Poverty Policy and Poverty Research,* 236; Katz, *The Undeserving Poor,* 117–23.

22. Philip K. Robins and Paul Fronstin, "Welfare Benefits and Family-Size Decisions of Never-Married Women," discussion paper no. 1022-93, Institute for Research on Poverty, Madison, Wis., September 1993.

23. Murray, *Losing Ground,* 156–77.

24. Haveman makes this quite clear in *Poverty Policy and Poverty Research,* 236. See also Katz, *The Undeserving Poor,* 121.

25. See Longino, *Science as Social Knowledge,* 4–7.

26. The dynamic relationship between material macrostructure and symbolic microdiscourse parallels the relationship between structure and agency emphasized by Anthony Giddens in *The Constitution of Society* (Cambridge: Harvard University Press, 1984) and others, such as Alex Callinicos, *Making History: Agency, Structure and Change in Social Theory* (Ithaca, N.Y.: Cornell University Press, 1988), 9–10. In my reading, however, macrostructures are stabilized discourses that get institutionalized to the extent that they are reproduced in the daily practices of people's lived experiences. The relationship of macrodiscursive structures to microdiscursive structures better parallels the relationship of exterior to interior found in John Fiske, *Power Plays Power Works* (London: Verso, 1993), 11–14, although for Fiske, power, practice, and discourse are more important than structure, ideology, and consciousness for understanding how power blocs get to dominate in a postconsensual society. The issue for Fiske is more how the powerful get to deploy cultural interpretations to their advantage rather than how hegemonic structures constrain people to think in ways advantageous for the powerful.

27. Walter Truett Anderson, *Reality Isn't What It Used to Be* (San Francisco: Harper, 1990).

28. It is entirely appropriate to suggest that postmodernism as an emerging sensibility can be characterized as emphasizing some concerns over others. The essays that follow, in fact, seek to do just that and to offer an example of what a postmodern policy analysis looks like. I, however, want to resist the idea that we should try to define the essence of what postmodernism, or for that matter anything else, is. In fact, if one were to try to specify the core, essence, or critical focus of postmodernism, one would probably have to adopt the ironic position that postmodernism is at its essence about how there are no essences. Jacques Derrida and Michel Foucault both resist the idea that there is one uniformly agreed-upon form of postmodernism that in particular can be dismissed for the same reasons. See Jacques Derrida, "But Beyond ... (Open Letter to Anne McClintock and Rob Nixon)," *Critical Inquiry* 13 (1986): 162–78; Michel Foucault, "Critical Theory/Intellectual History," in *Michel Foucault: Politics, Philosophy, Culture: Interviews and Other Writings 1977–1984,* ed. Lawrence D. Kritzman, trans. Alan Sheridan et al. (New York: Routledge, 1989), 33–54.

29. See Murray Edelman, *Constructing the Political Spectacle* (Chicago: University of Chicago Press, 1988), 115–19.

30. See Shapiro, *Reading "Adam Smith"*, 45–48; Michel Pecheux, "Discourse: Event or Structure," in *Marxism and the Interpretation of Culture*, ed. Cary Nelson and Lawrence Grossberg (Urbana: University of Illinois Press, 1988), 638.

31. See Michel Foucault, "Questions of Method," in *The Foucault Effect: Studies in Governmentality*, ed. Graham Burchell, Colin Gordon, and Peter Miller (Chicago: University of Chicago Press, 1991), 76–78.

32. This phrase is perhaps most visibly associated with Jacques Derrida's work on deconstruction as the textual practice of amplifying how all text, narrative, discourse, and even what he calls Western logocentrism are contradictory structures whose logical order is always premised on assumed givens that cannot be accounted for by those structures themselves. See Jacques Derrida, *Of Grammatology*, trans. Gayatri Chakravorty Spivak (Baltimore: Johns Hopkins University Press, 1974), 141–64. Derrida has been accused of not only resisting politics and political theorizing but making politics itself impossible. I do not find such conclusions necessary; instead, I want to suggest that interrogating discursive structures is an important critical element in contesting entrenched power. For a thoughtful reconsideration of how deconstruction can be connected to institutional revision, see Dominick LaCapra, *Soundings in Critical Theory* (Ithaca, N.Y.: Cornell University Press, 1989), 17–23.

33. The pervasiveness of textuality is discussed in LaCapra, *Soundings in Critical Theory*, 19–20.

34. M. E. Hawkesworth, *Theoretical Issues in Policy Analysis* (Albany: State University of New York Press, 1988), 186–88. See also Deborah A. Stone, *Policy Paradox and Political Reason* (Boston: HarperCollins, 1988).

35. See Edelman, *Constructing the Political Spectacle*, 12–36. On the role of state-sanctioned narrative in helping reinforce cultural formations, see LaCapra, *Soundings in Critical Theory*, 133–81. On the role of contemporary welfare policy in reinforcing invidious distinctions between the "deserving" and the "unworthy," see Connolly, *Identity\Difference*, 208.

36. In discussing the causes of homelessness for what he calls the "visible homeless" of people on the streets and in shelters, Christopher Jencks suggests that although structural causes are important, we must still recognize that the "visible homeless" have also made choices for which they must accept responsibility. Although Jencks is at some level correct, he fails to interrogate how prevailing discursive practices operate within the matrix of institutionalized society to marginalize such people such that the choices they get to make are highly constrained ones, often on the order of choosing different ways to be poor. See Christopher Jencks, *The Homeless* (Cambridge: Harvard University Press, 1994), 117–18.

37. The idea of hybrids that are based on recognizing the artificialness of such distinctions as politics and science comes from Bruno Latour, *We Have Never Been Modern*, trans. Catherine Porter (Cambridge: Harvard University Press, 1994), 1–12.

38. A good initial consideration of these issues in general terms is found in Pierre Bourdieu and Loic J. D. Wacquant, *An Invitation to Reflexive Sociology* (Chicago: University of Chicago Press, 1992).

39. For a call for a new science that is neither pseudo nor innocent, see Donna J. Haraway, *Simians, Cyborgs, and Women: The Reinvention of Nature* (New York: Routledge, 1991), 175.

1. Suffer in Silence: The Subtext of Social Policy Research

1. For an incisive analysis of how social science has participated in the welfare reform movement, see Michael B. Katz, *The Undeserving Poor: From the War on Poverty to the War on Welfare* (New York: Pantheon, 1989), 185–235.

2. See Adolph Reed Jr., "The Underclass as Myth and Symbol: The Poverty of Discourse about Poverty," *Radical America* (January 1992): 21–40.

3. Laurence E. Lynn Jr., "Ending Welfare Reform as We Know It," *The American Prospect* 15 (Fall 1993): 90.

4. For a thorough overview, see Robert H. Haveman, *Poverty Policy and Poverty Research: The Great Society and the Social Sciences* (Madison: University of Wisconsin Press, 1987). In his epilogue, Haveman notes that he expects the next generation of social research on poverty to be "less narrow and measurement-oriented" and less dominated by economics and the estimation of formal causal models.

5. For an initial examination of how the prevailing "juridical-administrative-therapeutic state apparatus" (JAT) is a discourse that imputes identity and interest to poor women, see Nancy Fraser, "Women, Welfare, and the Politics of Need Interpretation," in *Unruly Practices: Power, Discourse, and Gender in Contemporary Social Theory* (Minneapolis: University of Minnesota Press, 1989), 144–60. An overly neat formula suggests that the relationship of JAT to ETM is one of a prevailing macrodiscourse to a disciplinary microdiscourse; however, the interplay between the two is probably more complicated than that.

6. For a thoughtful internal critique of the embedded biases of welfare policy research, see Robert H. Haveman, "The Nature, Causes, and Cures of Poverty: Accomplishments of Three Decades of Poverty Research and Policy," in *Confronting Poverty: Prescriptions for Change*, ed. Sheldon H. Danziger, Gary D. Sandefur, and Daniel H. Weinberg (Cambridge: Harvard University Press, 1994), ch. 16. Haveman and Sawhill confine their analysis largely to emphasizing how a field like welfare policy research, which is dominated by economists' interest in marginal analysis, logically focuses on the effects of incremental changes.

7. See Helen E. Longino, *Science as Social Knowledge: Values and Objectivity in Scientific Inquiry* (Princeton, N.J.: Princeton University Press, 1990), 4–7. Longino underscores how both the contextual values of the broader society and the constitutive values implicit in a discipline's theories and methods work in combination to make ostensibly neutral and objective science profoundly biased and anything but autonomous.

8. See Fred Dallmayr, *G. W. F. Hegel: Modernity and Politics* (London: Sage, 1993).

9. See William E. Connolly, *Political Theory and Modernity* (Oxford: Basil Blackwell, 1988); William E. Connolly, *Identity\Difference: Democratic Negotiations of Political Paradox* (Ithaca, N.Y.: Cornell University Press, 1991), 16–35.

10. See Connolly, *Identity\Difference*, 198–222.

11. Michael J. Shapiro, *Reading "Adam Smith": Desire, History and Value* (London: Sage, 1993), 59–83.

12. See Andrew J. Polsky, *The Rise of the Therapeutic State* (Princeton, N.J.: Princeton University Press, 1991), for an analysis of the historical, cultural, political, and economic roots in the United States of state intervention that stressed therapeutic treatment as the primary way to get persons in poverty to respond to economic incentives. Polsky argues that therapeutic discourse has been supplanted by economistic discourse as economists have replaced social workers as the dominant group of welfare policy analysts (pp. 186–87). Nancy Fraser and Linda Gordon, in "A Genealogy of *Dependency*: Tracing a Keyword of the U.S. Welfare State," *Signs* 19 (Winter 1994): 328–29, suggest that both therapeutic and economistic orientations are dominant today in promoting a behavioral orientation to examining policy. See also Murray Edelman, *Political Language: Words That Succeed and Policies That Fail* (New York: Academic Press, 1977); Frances Fox Piven and Richard A. Cloward, *Regulating the Poor: The Functions of Public Welfare*, updated ed. (New York: Vintage, 1993). For more global theorizing on the therapeutic impulse in modernity, see Jacques Donzelot, *The Policing of Families* (New York: Pantheon, 1979); Michel Foucault, *Discipline and Punish: The Birth of the Prison*, trans. Alan Sheridan (New York: Vintage, 1979).

13. For examples, see Haveman, *Poverty Policy and Poverty Research*. For a critique, see Charles E. Lindblom, *Inquiry and Change: The Troubled Attempt to Understand and Shape Society* (New Haven, Conn.: Yale University Press, 1990), 257–83.

14. See Fraser and Gordon, "A Genealogy of *Dependency*," 328–29. Fraser and Gordon see two streams of contemporary thought dominating discourse on "welfare dependency": personal pathology and rational man. Inducing behavioral change is the logical response in both cases, with therapeutic treatment for the former and a revised economic incentive structure in welfare programs for the latter. Fraser and Gordon stress how both liberals and conservatives fail to interrogate their shared commitment to the discursive practices that reflect these views. "Certainly, there are real and significant differences [between liberals and conservatives on the issue of welfare dependency], but there are also important similarities. Liberals and conservatives of both schools rarely situate the notion of dependency in its historical or economic context; nor do they interrogate its presuppositions. Neither group questions the assumption that independence is an unmitigated good nor its identification with wage labor. Many poverty and welfare analysts equivocate between an official position that dependency is a value-neutral term for receipt of (or need for) welfare and a usage that makes it a synonym for *pauperism*."

15. For an excellent sampler of the sophistication of such work even as it strives to be relevant to public policy making, see Sheldon H. Danziger, Gary D. Sandefur, and Daniel H. Weinberg, eds. *Confronting Poverty: Prescriptions for Change* (Cambridge: Harvard University Press, 1994). For a thorough review, see Robert Moffitt, "Incentive Effects of the U.S. Welfare System: A Review," *Journal of Economic Literature* 30 (March 1992): 1–61.

16. On the role of outside researchers in checking ideology in public policy making, see David Ricci, *The Transformation of American Politics: The Rise of Washington Think-Tanks* (New Haven, Conn.: Yale University Press, 1993). On the same for welfare policy research, see Haveman, *Poverty Policy and Poverty Research*, 236. A strong case for welfare policy research's potential to influence public policy is found in Richard P. Nathan, *Social Science and Government: Uses and Misuses* (New York: Basic Books, 1988), 97–121. See also Erica B. Baum, "When the Witch Doctors Agree: The Family Support Act and Social Science Research," *Journal of Policy Analysis and Management* 10 (Fall 1991): 603–15. For a discussion of how the poverty research community has since the 1960s come to comprise a variety of experts not all tied to elite interests and who therefore can challenge apologetics on behalf of attempts to subordinate the poor, see Frances Fox Piven and Richard A. Cloward, "The Contemporary Relief Debate," in *The Mean Season: The Attack on the Welfare State*, ed. Fred Block, Richard A. Cloward, Barbara Ehrenreich, and Frances Fox Piven (New York: Pantheon, 1987), 45–52.

17. See Center on Social Welfare Policy and Law, *The Rush to Reform* (Washington, D.C.: Center on Social Welfare Policy and Law, November 7, 1993). For a survey of state waivers to institute many of these changes, see Center on Social Welfare Policy and Law, *Recent Developments in the Use of HHS Waiver Authority* (Washington, D.C.: Center on Social Welfare Policy and Law, November 8, 1993); Michael Wiseman, "Welfare Reform in the States: The Bush Legacy," *Focus* 15 (Spring 1993): 18–36. Wiseman does emphasize that waivers must include their own experimental research evaluation components, but this does not mean that the changes being proposed are based on credible research.

18. Although much research has indicated that the wide variety of reforms instituted by the states in recent years, such as penalizing parents on public assistance for the low school attendance of their children (Wisconsin's "learnfare") or penalizing mothers who have additional children while receiving welfare (New Jersey's "family cap"), are having little or no effect, state policy makers have often been unmoved even after evaluations have shown the need to rethink these proposals. See Center on Social Welfare Policy and Law, *The Rush to Reform*, 2–3.

19. See Lynn, "Ending Welfare Reform," 90; Haveman and Sawhill, "The Nature, Causes, and Cures of Poverty."

20. See Reed, "The Underclass as Myth and Symbol"; Fraser and Gordon, "A Genealogy of *Dependency*," 328–29; and Piven and Cloward, "The Contemporary Relief Debate."

21. For an insufficiently critical commentary on the dominance of welfare policy discourse by experts, especially concerning services for women as mothers, see Theda Skocpol, *Protecting Soldiers and Mothers: The Political Origins of Social Policy in the United States* (Cambridge: Harvard University Press, Belknap Press, 1992), 537. Skocpol writes: "But to whom, and for whom, are today's advocates of maternalist ideals American social policy speaking? Like most members of what Hugh Heclo calls 'issue networks' in U.S. politics today, these fine people are professionals working for various public agencies, foundations, universities, and public-interest lobbying associations. Most of them work in Washington, DC, New York City, or major university centers across the country. Using a specialized discourse, they talk mostly to one another—and to the staffs of legislative committees charged with overseeing very specific public programs that they want to defend, expand, or incrementally improve to better help children, mothers, and families."

22. A good initial foray into this issue is found in Katz, *The Undeserving Poor*, 79–235.

23. On the lack of studies tying welfare taking to attempts to escape abusive relationships and the need for new scholarship, see Linda Gordon, "The New Feminist Scholarship on the Welfare State," in *Women, the State, and Welfare*, ed. Linda Gordon (Madison: University of Wisconsin Press, 1990), 26–30. For a discussion of the limited work done on the high percentage of teen mothers (60–70 percent) estimated to have suffered physical abuse by parents as well as rape by adult family members, see Mike Males, "In Defense of Teenaged Mothers," *The Progressive*, August 1994, 22–23.

24. Bruno Latour, *The Pasteurization of France, Followed by Irreductions: A Politico-Scientific Essay* (Cambridge: Harvard University Press, 1988), as cited in Donna J. Haraway, *Simians, Cyborgs, and Women: The Reinvention of Nature* (New York: Routledge, 1991), 248.

25. Patricia Ticineto Clough, *The End(s) of Ethnography: From Realism to Social Criticism* (Newbury Park, Calif.: Sage, 1992), 179; Stanley Aronowitz, *The Politics of Identity: Class, Culture, Social Movements* (New York: Routledge, 1992), 125–74; Stanley Aronowitz, *Science as Power: Discourse and Ideology in Modern Society* (Minneapolis: University of Minnesota Press, 1988).

26. Reed, "The Underclass as Myth and Symbol," 32.

27. For a critique of how welfare policy research fails to provide alternative points of view for the policy making process, see Peter Marris, "How Social Science Could Inform Debate over Urban Problems," *Chronicle of Higher Education*, May 20, 1992, A40.

28. Haveman, *Poverty Policy and Poverty Research*, 33.

29. Katz, *The Undeserving Poor*, 117–18.

30. Haveman, *Poverty Policy and Poverty Research*, 51–52.

31. Katz, *The Undeserving Poor*, 120.

32. Ibid., 121–22. Welfare policy research's innovativeness has arguably been in service of not just perennial issues regarding welfare dependency, but particularly conservative ones. Albert O. Hirschman, in *The Rhetoric of Reaction: Perversity, Futility, Jeopardy* (Cambridge: Harvard University Press, Belknap Press, 1991), 40–42, suggests that conservative rhetoric historically has sought to discourage government intervention on the grounds that it is most often likely to produce unanticipated consequences that have perverse effects. The preoccupation of welfare policy researchers with incentives and disincentives in public assistance reflects this classic conservative concern. An alternative perspective would be one that minimizes the importance of welfare's behavioral effects and instead emphasizes meeting people's basic needs as the overriding consideration of how to design social policy.

33. See Frank Levy, "The Labor Supply of Female Heads, or AFDC Work Incentives Don't Work Too Well," *Journal of Human Resources* 14 (Winter 1979): 76–97; Robert Moffitt, "Work Incentives in Transfer Programs (Revisited): A Study of the AFDC Program," in *Research in Labor Economics*, vol. 8, ed. Ronald G. Ehrenberg (Greenwich, Conn.: Jai, 1986), 389–439.

34. The 1981 change in the earnings disregard was subsequently amended several times, but it still has not returned to the open-ended benefit that it was before the Reagan reforms. See George E. Peterson, "Federalism and the States: An Experiment in Decentralization," in *The Reagan Record: An Assessment of America's Changing Priorities*, ed. John L. Palmer and Isabel V. Sawhill (Cambridge, Mass.: Ballinger, 1984), 219–20; Sanford F. Schram "The New Federalism and Social Welfare: AFDC in the Midwest," in *The Midwest Response to the New Federalism*, ed. Peter K. Eisinger and William Gormley (Madison: University of Wisconsin Press, 1988), 264–67.

35. Lawrence M. Mead, *The New Politics of Poverty: The Nonworking Poor in America* (New York: Basic Books, 1992), 160–61; Janet D. Griffith and Charles L. Usher, "A Quasi-Experimental Assessment of the National Impact of the 1981 Omnibus Budget Reconciliation Act (OBRA) on the Aid to Families with Dependent Children (AFDC) Program," *Evaluation Review* 10 (June 1986): 313–33; Janet D. Griffith and Charles L. Usher, "Measuring the Effects of the Reagan Welfare Changes on the Work Effort and Well-Being of Single Parents," *Focus* 8 (Spring 1985): 1–6.

36. David T. Ellwood and Mary Jo Bane, *The Impact of AFDC on Family Structure and Living Arrangements*, report prepared for the U.S. Department of Health and Human Services under grant no. 92A-82 (Cambridge: Harvard University, March 1984), 1–6.

37. For the argument that Ellwood and Bane's research was used by the media to suggest that welfare does not lead to illegitamacy, see Charles Murray, "Does Welfare Bring More Babies?" *Public Interest* 115 (Spring 1994): 17–30.

38. Ellwood and Bane, *The Impact of AFDC*, 7.

39. Along with Bruce Reed, deputy assistant to the president for domestic policy, Ellwood and Bane served as chairs of the Clinton administration's Working Group on Welfare Reform, Family Support and Independence. A full list of the group's members is found in Center on Social Welfare Policy and Law, *Status of Administration's Welfare Reform Proposal*, (New York: Center on Social Welfare Policy and Law, October 28, 1993), 6.

40. See David T. Ellwood, *Targeting the Would-Be Long Term Recipient: Who Should Be Served?* report to the U.S. Department of Health and Human Services (Princeton, N.J.: Mathematica Policy Research, 1986); Mary Jo Bane and David T. Ellwood, *The Dynamics of Dependence: The Routes to Self-Sufficiency*, report to the U.S. Department of Health and Human Services (Cambridge, Mass.: Urban Systems Research & Engineering, 1983).

41. Greg J. Duncan, *Years of Poverty, Years of Plenty* (Ann Arbor: University of Michigan, Institute of Social Research, 1984); June O'Neill, Douglas A. Wolf, Laurie J. Bassi, and Michael T. Hannan, *An Analysis of Time on Welfare*, final report to the U.S. Department of Health and Human Services (Washington, D.C.: Urban Institute, 1984).

42. Relying on Ellwood and Bane, Mickey Kaus notes that the average length of stay on welfare for those receiving assistance at any one point in time is 11.6 years. Those who stay on welfare for more than eight years constitute 65 percent of those receiving assistance at any one point in time and 30 percent of all those who ever use the program. The average stay of those going on welfare for the first time is 6.6 years. Only about 30 percent of all those who have received welfare do so for less than two years. For overheated rhetoric accusing those who disagree with him of lying, see Mickey Kaus, *The End of Equality* (New York: Basic Books, 1992), 118.

43. Mead, *The New Politics of Poverty*, 197.

44. Kaus, *The End of Equality*, 246.

45. Ellwood, *Targeting the Would-Be Long Term Recipient*, 5, Table I.1.

46. U.S. House of Representatives, Committee on Ways and Means, *Background Material and Data on Programs within the Jurisdiction of the Committee on Ways and Means* (Washington, D.C.: U.S. Government Printing Office, 1987), Table 30.

47. Piven and Cloward, "The Contemporary Relief Debate," 63.

48. Kaus, *The End of Equality*, 246.

49. Mark Greenberg, *The Devil Is in the Details: Key Questions in the Effort to "End Welfare as We Know It"* (Washington, D.C.: Center for Law and Social Policy, 1993), 6.

50. LaDonna A. Pavetti, *The Dynamics of Welfare and Work: Exploring the Process by Which Young Women Work Their Way Off Welfare*, (Cambridge: Harvard University, John F. Kennedy School of Government, 1993), ch. 2, p. 18, as cited in U.S. House of Representatives, Committee on Ways and Means, *The Green Book* (Washington, D.C.: U.S. Government Printing Office, 1993). Also see John Fitzgerald, "Welfare Durations and the Marriage Market: Evidence from the Survey of Income and Program Participation," *Journal of Human Resources* 26 (Summer 1993): 545–61.

51. Rebecca Blank and Patricia Ruggles, "When Do Women Use AFDC and Food Stamps? The Dynamics of Eligibility vs. Participation," paper presented at the Summer Workshop on Problems of Low Income Populations, Institute for Research on Poverty, Madison, Wis., June 1993, 27, 37–38.

52. Pavetti, *The Dynamics of Welfare and Work*, 18.

53. For critical commentary on the new paternalism, see Mimi Abramovitz, "The New Paternalism," *The Nation*, October 5, 1992, 368–71; Sanford F. Schram, "Finding New Ways to Blame the Poor," *Minneapolis Star Tribune*, March 14, 1994. A12.

54. Mead, *The New Politics of Poverty*, 197–98; Kaus, *The End of Equality*, 118–20.

55. Mead, *The New Politics of Poverty*, 197; Kaus, *The End of Equality*, 116–20. Blank and Ruggles suggest that about 35 percent of spells of eligibility and about 16 percent of all spells of participation in AFDC at any one point in time involve heads of households who are working. "When Do Women Use AFDC and Food Stamps?" 16.

56. Piven and Cloward, *Regulating the Poor*, 373–81; Timothy J. Casey and Mary R. Mannix, *Quality Control in Public Assistance: Victimizing the Poor through One-Sided Accountability* (New York: Center on Social Welfare Policy and Law, October 1988).

57. Haveman, *Poverty Policy and Poverty Research*, 192.

58. On guaranteed income experiments, see Philip K. Robins et al., *A Guaranteed Income: Evidence from a Social Experiment* (New York: Academic Press, 1980). For a survey of major findings on workfare experiments, see Judith M. Gueron and Edward S. Pauly, *From Welfare to Work* (New York: Russell Sage Foundation, 1991).

59. Wiseman, "Welfare Reform in the States."

60. See the Center on Social Welfare Policy and Law's publications, *The Rush to Reform* and *Recent Developments in the Use of HHS Waiver Authority*. The more liberal experiments emphasize rewarding work through allowing recipients to keep benefits and receive child care when employed. New York State's Child Assistance Program (CAP) and the Minnesota Family Investment Plan are the two most supportive experiments. See Jean Hopfensperger, "State Begins Experiment Aimed at Helping Parents Work Free of Welfare," *Minneapolis Star Tribune*, March 29, 1994, 1A, 14A.

61. On the case for experimentation, see Peter Passell, "Like a New Drug, Social Programs Are Put to the Test," *New York Times*, March 9, 1993, C1. See also Nathan, *Social Science and Government*, 97–121; Richard P. Nathan, *Turning Promises into Performance: The Management Challenge of Implementing Workfare* (New York: Columbia University Press, 1993), 108–9; Baum, "When the Witch Doctors Agree." For assessment of the utility of experimentation, see James J. Heckman, "Randomization and Social Policy Evaluation," in *Evaluating Welfare and Training Programs*, ed. Charles F. Manski and Irwin Garfinkel (Cambridge: Har-

vard University Press, 1992); James J. Heckman and Joseph V. Hotz, "Choosing among Alternative Nonexperimental Methods for Estimating the Impact of Social Programs: The Case of Manpower Training," *Journal of the American Statistical Association* 84 (December 1989): 862–74. Moffitt, in "Incentive Effects," emphasizes that experimentation overlooks that "nationwide implementation of a pure workfare program would certainly change the types of women applying for AFDC—those who expect to get little from the program may no longer apply, for example. This would, in turn, make the estimates of earnings effects obtained from a randomized experiment on the existing caseload of questionable relevance" (p. 49).

62. The federal government evaluates waiver applications according to criteria that include whether there is adequate provision for assessment of impact through rigorous evaluation. The Bush administration made random assignment the norm for conducting such evaluations, which meant that recipients could be placed in "treatment" or "control" groups without their consent. See Wiseman, "Welfare Reform in the States," 18. The issue of whether informed consent is required when recipients are at risk of harm was raised but not disposed of in *Beno* v. *Shalala* 30 f.3d 1057 (9th Cir. 1994).

63. On efforts by welfare rights groups to end forced sterilization of welfare recipients in the 1970s, see Linda Gordon, *Woman's Body, Woman's Right: Birth Control in America* (New York: Penguin, 1990), 431–36. The long history of experimentation on disadvantaged groups in the United States has had many questionable moments, including the Tuskegee Syphilis Experiment, in which African American males suffering from syphilis were periodically examined without being treated, for purposes of studying the disease. See James H. Jones, *Bad Blood: The Tuskegee Syphilis Experiment* (New York: Free Press, 1981).

64. See Sheryl Stolberg, "An Experiment in Medical Ethics," *Minneapolis Star Tribune,* January 18, 1994, 4A.

65. Recent state initiatives to get welfare recipients to use Norplant are covered in Martha F. Davis, *The New Eugenics: A Legal and Policy Analysis of State Proposals to Control Poor Women's Reproduction through Norplant* (New York: NOW Legal Defense and Education Fund, April 1993).

66. William J. Wilson, *The Truly Disadvantaged: The Inner City, the Underclass, and Public Policy* (Chicago: University of Chicago Press, 1987), 6–7; Isabel V. Sawhill, "The Underclass: An Overview," *Public Interest* (Summer 1989): 3–11; Erol R. Ricketts and Isabel V. Sawhill, "Defining and Measuring the Underclass," *Journal of Policy Analysis and Management* 7 (Winter 1988): 316–18; Ronald B. Mincy, Isabel V. Sawhill, and Douglas A. Wolf, "The Underclass: Definition and Measurement," *Science* 248 (April 1990): 450–53.

67. Reed, "The Underclass as Myth and Symbol," 24.

68. For an examination of the term that concludes that, on balance, it is useful, see Robert Kuttner, "Notes from Underground: Clashing Theories about the 'Underclass,'" *Dissent* (Spring 1991): 212–17.

69. See Douglas S. Massey and Nancy A. Denton, *American Apartheid: Segregation and the Making of the Underclass* (Cambridge: Harvard University Press, 1993), 148–85.

70. Reed, "The Underclass as Myth and Symbol"; Michael B. Katz, "Reframing the 'Underclass' Debate," in *The "Underclass" Debate: Views from History,* ed. Michael B. Katz (Princeton, N.J.: Princeton University Press, 1993), 440–78; Herbert J. Gans, "The Dangers of the Underclass: Its Harmfulness as a Planning Concept," in *People, Plans, and Policies: Essays on Poverty, Racism, and Other National Urban Problems* (New York: Columbia University Press, 1991), 328–44.

71. Lou Turner, "American Apartheid," *Labor News and Notes,* July 1993, 1, 8.

72. The danger of disembodied information about persons living in poverty has been pointed out by John E. Schwarz and Thomas J. Volgy, *The Forgotten Americans: Thirty Million Working Poor in the Land of Opportunity* (New York: W. W. Norton, 1992), 16; see also Mark Robert Rank, *Living on the Edge: The Realities of Welfare in America* (New York: Columbia University Press, 1994), 7–11.

73. In Alan Wolfe, *The Seamy Side of Democracy: Repression in America*, 2d ed. (New York: Longman, 1978), 209.

74. For an analysis of how a perspective grounded in the biases of the work ethic tends to emphasize the independence of individuals and to focus on individual behavior, whereas a care ethic recognizes the interconnectedness of individuals and focuses on community and institutional development, see Joan Tronto, *Moral Boundaries: A Political Argument for an Ethic of Care* (New York: Routledge, 1993), 165–66.

75. Wilson, *The Truly Disadvantaged*, 144.

76. Many of these studies were commissioned by the federal government and discussed the issue in terms of "the underclass." For a survey, see William R. Prosser, "The Underclass: Assessing What We Have Learned," *Focus* 13 (Summer 1991): 1–18. In particular, see Ricketts and Sawhill, "Defining and Measuring the Underclass," 316–25; Ronald B. Mincy, *Underclass Variations by Race and Place: Have Large Cities Darkened Our Picture of the Underclass?* (Washington, D.C.: Urban Institute, February 1991); Paul Jargowsky and Mary Jo Bane, *Neighborhood Poverty: Basic Questions* (Cambridge: Harvard University, John F. Kennedy School of Government, Center for Health and Human Resources Policy, March 1990); M. Anne Hill and June O'Neill, *Underclass Behaviors in the United States: Measurement and Analysis of Determinants* (New York: City University of New York, March 1990); Douglas A. Wolf, Rebecca Clark, and Vicki Freedman, *Modeling the Growth of the Underclass: Neighborhood Effects and Neighborhood Dynamics* (Washington, D.C.: Urban Institute, May 1990). For a study that puts neighborhood effects in the broader context of metropolitan racial segregation but still focuses on isolating individual behavior, see Douglas S. Massey, Andrew B. Gross, and Mitchell L. Eggers, "Segregation, the Concentration of Poverty, and the Life Chances of Individuals," *Social Science Research* 20 (1991): 397–420.

77. See Henry J. Aaron, *Politics and the Professors: The Great Society in Perspective* (Washington, D.C.: Brookings Institution, 1978), 26–27.

78. See Haveman, *Poverty Policy and Poverty Research*, 236. Haveman hopes for a welfare policy research that can check the role of ideology in setting social policy.

79. Charles Murray, *Losing Ground: American Social Policy 1950–1980* (New York: Basic Books, 1984), 154–66.

80. See Sheldon Danziger and Peter Gottschalk, "Social Programs—A Partial Solution to, but Not a Cause of Poverty: An Alternative to Charles Murray's View," in *Losing Ground: A Critique*, Special Report Series, no. 38, ed. Sara McLanahan et al. (Madison. Wis.: Institute for Research on Poverty, August 1985), 73–91.

2. Discourses of Dependency: The Politics of Euphemisms

1. See Russell Jacoby, *Dogmatic Wisdom: How the Culture Wars Divert Education and Distract America* (Garden City, N.Y.: Doubleday, 1994), 60–91.

2. See Murray Edelman, *Political Language: Words That Succeed and Policies That Fail* (New York: Academic Press, 1978); Nancy Fraser, *Unruly Practices: Power, Discourse, and Gender in Social Theory* (Minneapolis: University of Minnesota Press, 1989), 144–60.

3. See Michael J. Shapiro, *Reading "Adam Smith": Desire, History and Value* (London: Sage, 1993), 45–48.

4. On structure and discourse, see John Fiske, *Power Plays Power Works* (London: Verso, 1993), 3–33, 251–57. Fiske asserts that the power of aligned groupings, rather than the structural insistences of institutionalized ideological formations, makes the use of existentially lived categories of race, class, gender, and other distinctions oppressive for marginalized groups. For an analysis of how a structural account of welfare politics incorporates considerations of discourse, see France Fox Piven and Richard A. Cloward, *Regulating the Poor: The Functions of Public Welfare*, updated ed. (New York: Vintage, 1993), 344–99.

5. See Shapiro, *Reading "Adam Smith,"* 30–41.

6. For an examination of the political uses of the keyword *dependency* that resists insisting on one right term to characterize welfare use, see Nancy Fraser and Linda Gordon, "A Genealogy of *Dependency:* Tracing a Keyword of the U.S. Welfare State," *Signs* 19 (Winter 1994): 309–36.

7. Jacoby, in *Dogmatic Wisdom,* 64–68, notes that critics as diverse H. L. Mencken and George Orwell saw euphemistics as a profoundly American practice tied to denying difference in a society that aspires to equality. For a similar commentary, see Robert Hughes, *Culture of Complaint: The Fraying of America* (New York: Oxford University Press, 1993), 18–37. Hughes includes *family values* in the grab bag of right-wing euphemisms.

8. See Kathleen T. Bartlett, "Surplus Visibility," in *Beyond PC: Toward a Politics of Understanding,* ed. Patricia Aufderheide (St. Paul, Minn.: Greywolf, 1992), 124.

9. See Mike Budd, Robert M. Entman, and Clay Steinman, "The Affirmative Character of U.S. Cultural Studies," *Critical Studies in Mass Communication* 7 (Winter 1990): 169–84.

10. Stanley Aronowitz, *The Politics of Identity: Class, Culture, Social Movements* (New York: Routledge, 1993), 225–52; Herbert J. Gans, "Scholars' Role in Planning a 'Post-Work' Society," *Chronicle of Higher Education,* June 9, 1993, B3.

11. On space as an alternative metaphor to either structure or discourse for characterizing the processes of inclusion and exclusion, see Michel Foucault, "Of Other Spaces," *Diacritics* 16 (Fall 1986): 22–27; Edward Soja, "History: Geography: Modernity," in *The Cultural Studies Reader,* ed. Simon During (New York: Routledge, 1993), 136.

12. For a consideration of texts broadly construed as the discursively constituted institutionalized context from which people impart meaning to their exchanges in organized daily life, see Dominick LaCapra, *Soundings in Critical Theory* (Ithaca, N.Y.: Cornell University Press, 1989), 18–29.

13. Relatedly, there is good reason to suggest that the new politics of multiculturalism will flounder if it is not tied to the older politics of class action. Efforts at achieving "recognition" will be most effective when connected to movements dedicated to producing "redistribution." See Nancy Fraser, "Redistribution or Recognition: Political Dilemmas for a Post-Socialist Age," paper presented at Macalester College, March 3, 1994.

14. See William E. Connolly, *Identity\Difference: Democratic Negotiations of Political Paradox* (Ithaca, N.Y.: Cornell University Press, 1991), 158–222; Lawrence Grossberg, "It's a Sin: Politics, Post-Modernity and the Popular," in *It's a Sin: Essays on Postmodernism, Politics, and Culture,* ed. Lawrence Grossberg, et al. (Sydney: Power, 1988), 6–71; Budd, Entman, and Steinman, "The Affirmative Character," 174–75.

15. See Shapiro, *Reading "Adam Smith,"* 30–41.

16. See Fiske, *Power Plays Power Works,* 251–53.

17. The argument in this chapter should not be confused with one that suggests that autonomous consciousness in the form of conceptualization overrides discursive practices in setting the terms of debate and political exchange. For this argument, which otherwise makes several sound points, see Steven Pinker, "Let Concepts, Not Words, Rule," *Minneapolis Star Tribune,* April 15, 1994, 21A.

18. See Michael Sherraden, *Assets and the Poor: A New American Welfare Policy* (Armonk, N.Y.: M. E. Sharpe, 1991); Don Fraser, "How Children Fared in Clinton's Message," *Minneapolis Star Tribune,* January 30, 1994, 19A.; William J. Wilson, *The Truly Disadvantaged: The Inner City, the Underclass, and Public Policy* (Chicago: University of Chicago Press, 1987), 164; Jonathan Kozol, *Rachel and Her Children: Homeless Families in America* (New York: Crown, 1988), 191–93. For a discussion of how even in a political economy organized as "market socialism," the level of investment in the next generation that is optimal for achieving a productive society may be below what is socially optimal according to noneconomic standards,

see John E. Roemer, *A Future for Socialism* (Cambridge: Harvard University Press, 1994), 109–16.

19. In a more structural idiom, the problem for Andre Gorz is avoiding status quo-reinforcing "reformist-reform" while pursuing transformative "nonreformist reform." See Andre Gorz, *A Strategy for Labor: A Radical Proposal* (Boston: Beacon, 1964), 6–8.

20. Walter Truett Anderson, *Reality Isn't What It Used to Be* (San Francisco: Harper, 1990), 49.

21. Jeffrey Goldfarb, *The Cynical Society: The Culture of Politics and the Politics of Culture in American Life* (Chicago: University of Chicago Press, 1991).

22. See Jacques Derrida, *Of Grammatology*, trans. by Gayatri Chakravorty Spivak (Baltimore: Johns Hopkins University Press, 1974), 6–26.

23. See Jacoby, *Dogmatic Wisdom*, 64–68.

24. Ibid., 71–72.

25. See Hughes, *Culture of Complaint*, 12–14. For an extended discussion of the issue of balancing sameness and difference, especially for women pursuing both equal rights and special protections, see Bonnie Honig, *Political Theory and the Displacement of Politics* (Ithaca, N.Y.: Cornell University Press, 1993), 206–11; Martha Minow, *Making All the Difference: Inclusion, Exclusion, and American Law* (Ithaca, N.Y.: Cornell University Press, 1990), 373–90; Martha Albertson Fineman, *The Illusion of Equality: The Rhetoric and Reality of Divorce Reform* (Chicago: University of Chicago Press, 1991), 189–90.

26. See Susan Moller Okin, *Justice, Gender, and the Family* (New York: Basic Books, 1989), 180–86.

27. See Hughes, *Culture of Complaint*, 15.

28. See Adolph Reed Jr., "The Underclass as Myth and Symbol: The Poverty of Discourse about Poverty," *Radical America* (January 1992): 37–38. The critique of emphasizing culture is an important part of Reed's disagreement with William Julius Wilson. For Wilson's position, see William Julius Wilson, "Cycles of Deprivation and the Underclass Debate," *Social Service Review* 59 (December 1985): 541–59.

29. See Reed, "The Underclass as Myth and Symbol," 38–39. Brett Williams, in a critique of Christopher Jenck's *Rethinking Social Policy: Race, Poverty, and the Underclass* (Cambridge: Harvard University Press, 1992), notes that "Jencks both reifies and denigrates culture, evoking it to make sense of his facts and placing it at the heart of his arguments, while understanding it through introspection and guesswork.... All quantitative researchers spin qualitative stories to interpret their facts, but some check the ethnographic evidence to test the personal, political vision that shapes those tales. "Us and Them," *The Nation*, October 5, 1992, 371–72.

30. Derrick Bell supplies a nuanced discussion of the unavoidable necessity in a white-dominated society for African Americans to forgo at times criticizing other African Americans or to resist discussing such topics as male violence against women in the African American community so as to not provide ammunition to the enemy. *Faces at the Bottom of the Well: The Permanence of Racism* (New York: Basic Books, 1992), 47–64. On the Anita Hill-Clarence Thomas hearings, John Fiske has written: "Two Blacks fighting in front of a white audience is a recurrent event in US history, and one whose only beneficiary is white power." *Power Plays Power Works*, 263.

31. See Cornel West, "Nihilism in Black America: A Danger That Corrodes from Within," *Dissent* (Spring 1991): 221–26, for the argument that "culture is quite as structural as the economy or politics" and that poor inner-city African American youths lack the cultural armor to defend themselves from the temptations of the broader consumeristic society.

32. See Rose Brewer, "Black Women in Poverty: Some Comments on Female-Headed Families," *Signs* 13 (Winter 1988): 31–39; Carole B. Stack, *All Our Kin: Strategies for Survival in a Black Community* (New York: Harper & Row, 1974).

33. For the latest installments in the "culture of poverty" genre, see Lawrence M. Mead, *The New Politics of Poverty: The Nonworking Poor in America* (New York: Basic Books, 1992); Mickey Kaus, *The End of Equality* (New York: Basic Books, 1992).

34. Henry Louis Gates, "Writing, Race and the Difference It Makes," *Critical Inquiry* 12 (Autumn 1985): 1–20.

35. See Henry Louis Gates Jr., "What's in a Name: Some Meanings of Blackness," *Dissent* (Fall 1989): 487–95.

36. Herbert Gans has highlighted how racially coded terms such as *underclass* allow for racist distinctions without using racial categories. See Herbert J. Gans, "Deconstructing the Underclass: The Term's Dangers as a Planning Concept," *Journal of the American Planning Association* 56 (Summer 1990): 271–77.

37. Gates, "What's in a Name," 494. See also Houston A. Baker Jr., "Caliban's Triple Play," *Critical Inquiry* 13 (Autumn 1986): 182–98.

38. The double bind of pariah versus parvenu is from Arendt's characterization of the dilemma facing Jews on the question of assimilation into gentile culture. See Hannah Arendt, *The Origins of Totalitarianism* (New York: Harcourt, Brace & World, 1966), 56.

39. See Christopher Jencks, "The Homeless," *New York Review of Books*, April 21, 1994, 20–27, for the suggestion that homeless advocates Robert Hayes and Mitch Snyder had by 1981 given people living on the streets the then-new name of "the homeless." For a criticism of this rhetorical move by these activists on the grounds that it displaced attention from the growing need for affordable housing by a much broader population of persons living in poverty, see Theresa Funiciello, "Give Them Shelters," *The Nation*, April 2, 1988, 469. Funiciello writes: "In fact, the label 'homeless family' was in many ways more destructive than helpful in the long run. As it came into fashion, it redefined a population largely to suit the advocacy imperative of the social-welfare professionals. This distorted any accurate picture of the real problem: poverty (coupled with the meanest welfare system New York City has seen in at least half a century)." For a discussion on the political implications of how the "homeless" get constructed, see Fiske, *Power Plays Power Works*, 27–33. See also Peter Marcuse, "Neutralizing Homelessness," *Socialist Review* 18 (1988): 69–96; Peter Marin, "Helping and Hating the Homeless," *Harper's*, January 1987, 39–69.

40. The literature on the homeless is extensive. Recent works include Martha R. Burt, *Over the Edge: The Growth of Homelessness in the 1980s* (New York: Russell Sage Foundation, 1993); Peter H. Rossi, *Down and Out in America: The Origins of Homelessness* (Chicago: University of Chicago Press, 1989); David Wagner, *Checkerboard Square: Culture and Resistance in a Homeless Community* (Boulder, Colo.: Westview, 1993).

41. Michael B. Katz, *The Undeserving Poor: From the War on Poverty to the War on Welfare* (New York: Pantheon, 1989), 194; Mark Stern, "The Emergence of the Homeless as a Public Problem," *Social Service Review* 58 (June 1984): 291–301.

42. For an attempt to justify the narrow focus on the "visible homeless," see Christopher Jencks, *The Homeless* (Cambridge: Harvard University Press, 1994), 3–7.

43. See Joel Blau, *The Visible Poor: Homelessness in the United States* (New York: Oxford University Press, 1992), 15–30; Rossi, *Down and Out in America*, 45–81. Estimates of the number of homeless in the United States range from 250,000–350,000 to 3–4 million, according to Theresa Funiciello, *The Tyranny of Kindness: Dismantling the Welfare System to End Poverty in America* (New York: Atlantic Monthly Press, 1993), 163. For the lower estimates, see U.S. Department of Housing and Urban Development (HUD), *A Report to the Secretary on the Homeless and Emergency Shelters* (Washington, D.C.: Office of Policy Development and Research, 1984). For an estimate that is approximately double that of HUD, see Martha R. Burt and Barbara E. Cohen, *Feeding the Homeless: Does the Prepared Meals Provision Help?* vols. 1–2 (Washington, D.C.: Urban Institute, 1987); Burt, *Over the Edge*. Funiciello's

higher estimates stem from her decision to add to the homeless on the street and in the shelters those who are "temporarily" housed in welfare hotels or who are "doubled up" — living
with friends or relatives. For an analysis of the causes of homelessness using both types of estimates, see Marjorie Honig and Randall K. Filer, "Causes of Intercity Variation in Homelessness," *American Economic Review* 83 (March 1993): 248–55. For an analysis that embraces
both the high and low estimates while limiting the definition of the homeless to people on
the streets and in shelters, see Jencks, *The Homeless,* 8–20. Jencks, as the quintessential bare-
foot empiricist who positions himself as one who unabashedly and meticulously scrutinizes
all data irrespective of how they are framed, accepts the whole range of estimates on the
grounds that the low ones (i.e., 200,000–600,000) reflect those who are currently homeless at
any one point in time and the high estimates (i.e., 6–7 million) reflect how many people suffered a bout of homelessness at any time over an extended period. Jencks, however, frames
his own analysis strictly in terms of what he calls the "visible homeless" on the streets and in
the shelters, thereby allowing the focus to shift away from the argument that the bulk of the
homeless are people whose primary problem is lack of affordable housing. *The Homeless,*
3–7. See also Jencks, "The Homeless," 20–27.

44. This is the population that conservatives emphasize. See Alice S. Baum and Donald
W. Burnes, *A Nation in Denial: The Truth about Homelessness* (Boulder, Colo.: Westview,
1993); Richard W. White Jr., *Rude Awakenings: What the Homeless Crisis Tells Us* (Washington, D.C.: Institute for Contemporary Studies, 1993); William Tucker, "Where Do the Homeless Come From?" *National Review* 25 (September 1987): 32–43. Baum and Burnes admit
that the homeless population increased in the 1980s; White doubts that it did.

45. Blau, *The Visible Poor,* 29–30; Irving Piliavin, Michael Sosin, and Herb Westerfeldt,
"Conditions Contributing to Long-Term Homelessness: An Exploratory Study," discussion
paper no. 853-87, Institute for Research on Poverty, Madison, Wis., 1987.

46. Honig and Filer, "Causes of Intercity Variation," 248–55.

47. Although much of the literature has suggested that the homeless population is largely
male if families that are doubled and tripled up in residential housing are not included, a
growing proportion of this limited population is made up of individual women, women with
children, women with men, and women with men and children. See Stephanie Golden, *The
Women Outside: Meanings and Myths of Homelessness* (Berkeley: University of California Press,
1992), ix–x.

48. See HUD, *A Report to the Secretary.*

49. See Marin, "Helping and Hating the Homeless," 39–41; Randy Diamond, "Homeless
Face a Cold Shoulder across US," *Christian Science Monitor,* December 10, 1990, 9; Isabel
Wilkerson, "Shift in Feelings on the Homeless: Empathy Turns into Frustration," *New York
Times,* September 2, 1991, 10; Rick Bragg, "Homeless Seeing Less Apathy, More Anger," *New
York Times,* February 25, 1994, 1.

50. Funiciello, *The Tyranny of Kindness,* 162–211.

51. See Katz, *The Undeserving Poor,* 194; Dennis P. Culhane, "Poorhouse Revisited," *New
York Times,* November 18, 1991, A15.

52. See Tucker, "Where Do the Homeless Come From?" 32–43; Thomas Main, "What
We Know about the Homeless," *Commentary* 85 (May 1988): 27–31.

53. See Celia W. Dugger, "Families Seek Out Shelters as Route to Better Homes," *New
York Times,* September 4, 1991, A1.

54. See Joan Minieri, "Traumatic Experience" (letter to the editor), *New York Times,*
September 23, 1991, A14. After the fact, other studies providing an alternative point of
view surfaced. See Maria Newman, "Homeless Found to Go Slowly to Shelters," *New York
Times,* December 23, 1991, B3. Newman reports on a study by Anna Lou Dehavenon that
found that "more than three-quarters of those asking for emergency assistance said they

had been 'doubling up' with friends or relatives and that they left chiefly because of over-crowding."

55. Dugger, "Families Seek Out Shelters"; "A Hotel Is Not a Home," *New York Times,* September 1, 1991, E10; Celia W. Dugger, "Housing Setbacks Temper a Mayor's Hopes," *New York Times,* July 5, 1993, B12. By the end of 1992 the waiting list for Housing Authority apartments in New York City had reached its highest level ever at 240,000, nearly equaling "the total number of units in all of the city's public housing projects and subsidized apart-ments." Shawn G. Kennedy, "Applications to Public Housing in New York City Reach Record High," *New York Times,* December 27, 1992, A14.

56. Thomas Morgan, "Dinkins's Chief Homeless Policy Adviser Resigns," *New York Times,* September 4, 1991, B21; Dugger, "Housing Setbacks," B12.

57. See Funiciello, *The Tyranny of Kindness,* 162-211, for an indictment of Cuomo on grounds that he tried to push the definition of the homeless to accord with the type of hous-ing and services that his nonprofit agency, Housing Enterprise for the Less Privileged (HELP), provided.

58. See Blau, *The Visible Poor,* 15-16; Funiciello, *The Tyranny of Kindness,* 205-11.

59. On the tendency of television reporters to report only on the "well" homeless, see Walter Goodman, "The TV Journalists' Urge to Prettify the News," *New York Times,* Febru-ary 2, 1992, C20.

60. Celia W. Dugger, "Gambling on Honesty on the Homeless," *New York Times,* Febru-ary 17, 1992, B1. Dugger quotes Cuomo as saying that he was hopeful that the public would be galvanized to action by the findings in the report. Yet, given the findings in the report, the action seemed to be directed toward a therapeutic approach rather than the provision of housing. See New York City Commission on the Homeless, *The Way Home: A New Direction in Social Policy* (New York: New York City Commission on the Homeless, 1992).

61. With the ascension of Rudolph Guiliani to the office of mayor of New York City, the Cuomo Commission's emphasis on the homeless as a population in need of treatment more than permanent housing has been ratified, and acceptance of required services and training placement has come to be used as a condition for admission to shelters, even for families with children. See Celia W. Dugger, "Plan Ties Shelter for the Homeless to Social Services," *New York Times,* May 7, 1994, A1.

62. Blau, *The Visible Poor,* 15-30; Fiske, *Power Plays Power Works,* 28-29.

63. Honig and Filer, "Causes of Intercity Variation," 249.

64. Funiciello, *The Tyranny of Kindness,* 210-11; Blau, *The Visible Poor,* 15-30.

65. Cuomo, now assistant secretary for community planning and development at the U.S. Department of Housing and Urban Development, has changed his tack. He has drafted a plan, outlined in a report titled "Priority: Home! The Federal Plan to End Homelessness," that recognizes there are two pools of homeless — the smaller and more visible group of men-tally ill and drug addicts and the larger group of individuals and families who cannot afford housing. According to the report, an estimated 7 million people were homeless in the United States at some point between 1985 and 1990. This estimate is based on Bruce Link et al., "Re-considering the Debate about the Size of the Homeless Population," paper presented at the annual meeting of the American Public Health Association, October 1993. See Jencks, "The Homeless," 21; Jason DeParle, "Report to Clinton Sees Vast Extent of Homelessness," *New York Times,* February 17, 1994, A1, A10.

66. Sam Roberts, "Dinkins to Study Homeless Proposals," *New York Times,* February 22, 1992, 27.

67. For an ethnography reporting shockingly ignorant opinions among the British press, politicians, and community leaders, including the clergy, indicting the homeless as beggars

and suggesting that most, if not all, beggars are actually well-off, see Andrew O' Hagan, "On Begging," *London Review of Books* 15 (Summer 1993): 9–12.

68. Fiske, *Power Plays Power Works,* 20–33. Fiske writes, "When homelessness is semiotically deviant but economically structural, the social conflict between the privileged (the 'normal') and the homeless (the 'deviant') becomes explicit" (p. 29).

69. Katz, *The Undeserving Poor,* 194.

70. See Fraser and Gordon, "A Genealogy of *Dependency.*" For a discussion of how the meaning of *welfare* was transformed from well-being to ill-being, see Linda Gordon, *Pitied but Not Entitled: Single Mothers and the History of Welfare* (New York: Free Press, 1994), 1–13.

71. Wilson, "Cycles of Deprivation" and *The Truly Disadvantaged,* 20–21.

72. See Nicholas Lemann, *The Promised Land: The Great Black Migration and How It Changed America* (New York: Knopf, 1991), 176–77.

73. Reed, "The Underclass as Myth and Symbol," 25–26. A tabulation of articles on topics related to the Moynihan Report (e.g., female-headed families, teen pregnancy, unmarried mothers) and listed in the *Social Sciences Index* from 1960 to 1990 indicates that rather than scholarship being silenced on the issue it continued along at a rather low rate, just as it had before the Moynihan Report appeared (e.g., 10 articles in 1966), only to peak at much higher levels in the mid-1970s (20 articles in 1974), and then again in the last half of the 1980s (37 articles in 1988 and 55 articles in 1990). If there is any trend, it has been upward, and was increasingly so by the 1980s.

74. Reed, "The Underclass as Myth and Symbol."

75. Wilson, *The Truly Disadvantaged,* 163–64; Theda Skocpol and William Julius Wilson, "Welfare as We Need It," *New York Times,* February 9, 1994, A15.

76. Thomas Byrne Edsall with Mary D. Edsall, *Chain Reaction: The Impact of Race, Rights, and Taxes on American Politics* (New York: W. W. Norton, 1991).

77. See Will Marshall and Martin Schram, eds., *Mandate for Change* (New York: Berkeley, 1993).

78. Fraser and Gordon, "A Genealogy of *Dependency,*" 323–31.

79. See, for instance, Frances Fox Piven and Richard A. Cloward, "The Contemporary Relief Debate," in *The Mean Season: The Attack on the Welfare State,* ed. Fred Block, Richard A. Cloward, Barbara Ehrenreich, and Frances Fox Piven (New York: Pantheon, 1987), 45–108.

80. Reed, "The Underclass as Myth and Symbol," 21–40.

81. Ibid.

82. John E. Schwarz and Thomas J. Volgy, *The Forgotten Americans: Thirty Million Working Poor in the Land of Opportunity* (New York: W. W. Norton, 1992), 3–15.

83. Fraser and Gordon, "A Genealogy of *Dependency,*" 325–28.

84. For an analysis of how the Planned Parenthood profamily discourse has come to be challenged and even supplanted by feminists emphasizing reproductive freedom, see Linda Gordon, *Woman's Body, Woman's Right: Birth Control in America* (New York: Penguin, 1990), 337–474. For an analysis of how attempts to tie the provision of mothers' pensions to the familial discourse that embraced a "family wage" led only to the reinforcement of dominant patriarchal assumptions about the family and low and uneven benefits for single mothers with children, see Gordon, *Pitied but Not Entitled,* 53–64.

85. See Martha F. Davis, *The New Eugenics: A Legal and Policy Analysis of State Proposals to Control Poor Women's Reproduction through Norplant* (New York: NOW Legal Defense and Education Fund, April 1993).

86. Gordon, *Woman's Body, Woman's Right,* 400–416, 475–88. Gordon also notes that feminist advocates for reproductive freedom have erred in the past in emphasizing reproduc-

tive freedom in overly individualistic terms, when it would be better to stress how it is a so-cial good central to achieving a more just and equal society that is better equipped to care for children.

87. John Fiske asserts that it is power rather than ideology that best explains how domi-nance is perpetuated in a postconsensual society: "Social categories such as race, age, gender and class still matter, but they matter because they work as guiding principles in the forma-tion of alliances and the promotion of interests, not because they determine the structure of experience.... But if race, gender and other social relations no longer function within solely ideological structures, their field of operation is far from structureless. They operate always within a field of power, and their particularities typically take the form of hegemonic strug-gles. *Power Plays Power Works*, 251–52.

88. Linda Gordon shows how although welfare reformers in the early twentieth century won the linguistic battle to tie "mothers' pensions" to the honorific "Civil War pensions," they lost the material battle to have those mothers' pensions to be of much economic value. See Gordon, *Pitied but Not Entitled*, 333 n. 113.

89. Invoking the material/culture dichotomy also means an obligation to show how ma-terial and culture are interrelated, especially in the way culture creates material value and how materialized (i.e., institutionalized) structures constrain cultural practice. On the mate-rial/culture of the late-capitalist United States, see Fiske, *Power Plays Power Works*, 35–56.

90. Connolly, *Identity\Difference*, 206–8.

91. Ibid.

92. See Mike Davis, *City of Quartz: Excavating the Future in Los Angeles* (London: Verso, 1990).

93. Fraser and Gordon note that a "genealogy cannot tell us how to respond politically to today's discourse about welfare dependency. It does suggest, however, the limits of any re-sponse that presupposes rather than challenges the definition of the problem that is implicit in that expression." "A Genealogy of *Dependency*," 331.

94. Emphasizing the inability of dominant structures to prohibit alternative readings of social relationships, Fiske writes: "Language is multiaccentual. That is, it always has the po-tential to be spoken with different accents that inflect its meanings towards the interests of different social formations. The imperializing use of language represses this multiaccentual potential and attempts to establish the singular accent of the power-bloc as the only, the nat-ural, the correct one. The language of imperializing power is uniaccentual. Localizing power, on the other hand, exploits the multiaccentuality." *Power Plays Power Works*, 31–32.

95. See Sara M. Evans, "The Politics of Public Relations," in *Beyond PC: Toward a Politics of Understanding*, ed. Patricia Aufderheide (St. Paul, Minn.: Greywolf, 1992), 180–81. On change, Andrew Ross has noted: "The linear model of advance and retreat (there is nowhere else to go) is an ... inadequate way of representing the life of civil rights movements, which diversify their 'gains' almost immediately, each step forward being a step sideways (what Vik-tor Shklovsky called 'knight's move') into an alternate world where new and often unfore-seen relations of power come into play, and where what had been seen as 'advances' at the previous stage now take on a different and less straightforward appearance." "Chicago Gang-ster Theory of Life," *Social Text* 35 (Summer 1993): 110.

96. John Fiske, *Understanding Popular Culture* (Winchester, Mass.: Unwin Hyman, 1989), 168. For an analysis of how the struggle of meaning can be politically efficacious only to the extent that it is grounded in ongoing social movements, see Budd, Entman, and Steinman, "The Affirmative Character"; Mike Budd and Clay Steinman, "Television, Cultural Studies, and the 'Blind Spot' Debate in Critical Communications Research," in *Television Studies: Tex-tual Analysis*, ed. Gary Burns and Robert J. Thompson (New York: Praeger, 1989), 9–20. For a response that recognizes the importance of prevailing political economic structures but

stresses the relative autonomy of culture as a site for popular resistance, see John Fiske, "Popular Television and Commercial Culture: Beyond Political Economy," also in *Television Studies*, 21–38. For an overly deterministic structural account, see Aijaz Ahmad, *In Theory: Classes, Nations, Literatures* (London: Verso, 1992).

3. Inverting Political Economy: Perspective, Position, and Discourse in the Analysis of Welfare

1. For example, see Robert H. Haveman, *Poverty Policy and Poverty Research: The Great Society and the Social Sciences* (Madison: University of Wisconsin Press, 1987). A notable counterexample is Frances Fox Piven and Richard A. Cloward, *Regulating the Poor: The Functions of Public Welfare*, updated ed. (New York: Vintage, 1993). A recent analysis of how welfare policy frames concerns in ways that are tied to a particular state-centered, managerial PPD, see Nancy Fraser, "Clintonism, Welfare, and the Antisocial Wage: The Emergence of a Neoliberal Political Imaginary," *Rethinking Marxism* 6 (Spring 1993): 9–23 A good example of statistical work on welfare policy written from an explicit point of view that is attentive to the consequences policy has for recipients, see Fred Block and John Noakes, "The Politics of the New-Style Workfare," *Socialist Review* 18 (July–September 1988): 31–60.

2. See Michael J. Shapiro, *Reading the Postmodern Polity: Political Theory as Textual Practice* (Minneapolis: University of Minnesota Press, 1992), 37–53; Jonathan Diskin and Blair Sandler, "Essentialism and the Economy in the Post-Marxist Imaginary: Reopening the Sutures," *Rethinking Marxism* 6 (Fall 1993): 28–48.

3. For a survey of such research, see Haveman, *Poverty Policy and Poverty Research*.

4. See Patti Lather, *Getting Smart: Feminist Research and Pedagogy with/in the Postmodern* (New York: Routledge, 1991).

5. See Joan Scott, "The Evidence of Experience," *Critical Inquiry* 17 (Summer 1991): 773–97; Shulamit Reinharz, *Feminist Methods in Social Research* (New York: Oxford University Press, 1992).

6. See Aaron Wildavsky, *Speaking Truth to Power: The Art and Craft of Policy Analysis* (Boston: Little, Brown, 1979), 401–6.

7. Charles E. Lindblom, *Inquiry and Change: The Troubled Attempt to Understand and Shape Society* (New Haven, Conn.: Yale University Press, 1990), 189. For a characterization of how welfare policy research tends to be done by men for men in power, to the neglect of the perspective of women on welfare, see Mimi Abramovitz and Frances Fox Piven, "Scapegoating Women on Welfare," *New York Times*, September 2, 1993, op-ed, where they state: "Johnnie Tillmon, leader of the National Welfare Rights Organization in the 1960s, used to call the welfare system 'The Man' because, she said, it ruled women's lives. The term still fits. Men are the welfare 'experts,' and the system they have designed is increasingly abusive of poor women struggling to raise children."

8. The issues addressed in the following discussion are rehearsed in Reinharz, *Feminist Methods in Social Research*, 46–75, 126–44; Patti Lather, "Feminist Perspectives on Empowering Research Methodologies," *Women's Studies International Forum* 11 (1988): 569–81.

9. See James Clifford and George E. Marcus, eds., *Writing Culture: The Poetics and Politics of Ethnography* (Berkeley: University of California Press, 1986); Patricia Ticineto Clough, *The End(s) of Ethnography: From Realism to Social Criticism* (Newbury Park, Calif.: Sage, 1992).

10. For one of the best examinations of the narrative character of social statistics, see Joseph Gusfield, *The Culture of Public Problems: Drinking-Driving and the Symbolic Order* (Chicago: University of Chicago Press, 1984).

11. For an analysis of how African American counterhistories narrate a bottom-up analysis of white racism and its devastating effects for African Americans today in a way that does

not need to meet top-down objectivist criteria of empirical truth in order to be persuasive, see John Fiske, *Power Plays Power Works* (London: Verso, 1993), 238–48, 284–89.

12. Alison Mitchell, "An Agency Head's Odyssey through the Welfare Maze," *New York Times,* February 5, 1993, B16.

13. See Murray Edelman, *Political Language: Words That Succeed and Policies That Fail* (New York: Academic Press, 1978).

14. This is what happens when increases in public assistance benefits undertaken to placate landlords who want to charge higher rents in turn produce reductions in the amount of food stamps recipients can receive. See chapter 5.

15. The phrase is from Nancy Fraser, "The Struggle over Needs: Outline of a Socialist-Feminist Critical Theory of Late Capitalist Political Culture," in *Unruly Practices: Power, Discourse, and Gender in Contemporary Social Theory* (Minneapolis: University of Minnesota Press, 1989), 161–90. See also Edelman, *Political Language.*

16. Fraser, "The Struggle over Needs," 166–75.

17. Ibid., 174–75.

18. Two examples from the realm of welfare include Carol Stack, *All Our Kin: Strategies for Survival in a Black Community* (New York: Harper & Row, 1974); Prudence Mors Rains, *Becoming an Unwed Mother: A Sociological Account* (Chicago: University of Chicago Press, 1971). Both detail the efforts of recipients themselves to resist bureaucratic practices that read them as deficient and to offer alternative categories that provide the basis for practices that would be more geared to meeting their understandings of what they need.

19. See Mark Rank, *Living on the Edge: The Realities of Welfare in America* (New York: Columbia University Press, 1994).

20. Nathan Glazer, "Poverty and Poverty Research, Then and Now," *Focus* 9 (Summer 1986): 16–17.

21. Ibid., 16.

22. Ibid., 17.

23. See Thomas Sowell, *Ethnic America: A History* (New York: Basic Books, 1981).

24. Glazer, "Poverty and Poverty Research," 17.

25. Mark Seltzer, "Statistical Persons," *Diacritics* 17 (Fall 1987): 82–98. Also see Henry Louis Gates, "Statistical Stigmata," in *Deconstruction and the Possibility of Justice,* ed. Drucilla Cornell, Michel Rosenfeld, and David Gray Carlson (New York: Routledge, 1992), 330–45.

26. For extensive bibliographies concerning statistical work just on the issue of teenage pregnancy and families composed of women with children, see Chong-Bum An, Robert Haveman, and Barbara Wolfe, "Reducing Teen Out-of-Wedlock Births: The Role of Parental Education and Family Stability," discussion paper no. 944–91, Institute for Research on Poverty, Madison, Wis., 1991; David J. Eggebeen and Daniel T. Lichter, "Race, Family Structure, and Changing Poverty among American Children," *American Sociological Review* 56 (December 1991): 801–17; Sara S. McLanahan, Irwin Garfinkel, and Dorothy Watson, "Family Structure, Poverty, and the Underclass," in *Urban Change and Poverty,* ed. M. G. H. McGreary and L. E. Lynn Jr. (Washington, D.C.: National Academy Press, 1988), 102–47.

27. See Michel Foucault, "Governmentality," in *The Foucault Effect: Studies in Governmentality,* ed. Graham Burchell, Colin Gordon, and Peter Miller (Chicago: University of Chicago Press, 1991), 99; Ian Hacking, "Biopower and the Avalanche of Printed Numbers," *Humanities in Society* 5, nos. 3–4 (1982): 279–95; Mary Poovey, "Figures of Arithmetic, Figures of Speech: The Discourse of Statistics in the 1830s," *Critical Inquiry* 19 (Winter 1993): 256–76.

28. For the most recent insistence that the poor are trapped in a "culture of poverty," which includes inadequate attitudes and practices that perpetuate their poverty, see Lawrence M. Mead, *The New Politics of Poverty: The Nonworking Poor in America* (New York: Basic Books, 1992).

29. For an excellent discussion of the prevailing biases in professional white ethnography of poor black culture, see Mitchell Duneier, *Slim's Table: Race, Respectability, and Masculinity* (Chicago: University of Chicago Press, 1992), 137–55.

30. Clough, *The End(s) of Ethnography.*

31. Ibid., 26–27.

32. See Joan Scott, "The Evidence of Experience," 776–77, where she quotes Michel de Certeau on historical discourse as that which "gives its credibility in the name of the reality which it is supposed to represent, but this authorized appearance of the 'real' serves precisely to camouflage the practice which in fact determines it. Representation thus disguises the praxis that organizes it." See Michel de Certeau, "History: Science and Fiction," in *Heterologies: Discourse on the Other,* trans. Brian Massumi (Minneapolis: University of Minnesota Press, 1986), 203.

33. Leslie Dunbar, *The Common Interest: How Social Welfare Policies Don't Work and What We Can Do about Them* (New York: Pantheon, 1988); Susan Sheehan, *Life for Me Ain't Been No Crystal Stair* (New York: Pantheon, 1993); John E. Schwarz and Thomas J. Volgy, *The Forgotten Americans: Thirty Million Working Poor in the Land of Opportunity* (New York: W. W. Norton, 1992); Rank, *Living on the Edge*; Duneier, *Slim's Table: Race, Respectability, and Masculinity*; Nicholas Lemann, *The Promised Land: The Great Black Migration and How It Changed America* (New York: Knopf, 1991); Alex Kotlowitz, *There Are No Children Here: The Story of Two Boys Growing Up in the Other America* (Garden City, N.Y.: Doubleday, 1991). See the discussion of the Urban Poverty and Family Life Study in William Julius Wilson, "The Truly Disadvantaged," *Political Science Quarterly* 106 (Winter 1991–92): 639–56.

34. The earlier articles include Nicholas Lemann, "The Origins of the Underclass," *Atlantic,* June 1986, 31–55; July 1986, 54–68.

35. Lemann, *The Promised Land,* 281–91.

36. Much of this criticism is anticipated by Duneier, who emphasizes how Lemann misleadingly focuses on sharecroppers to represent the whole of black migration from the South to the North after World War II. See *Slim's Table,* 150–55.

37. Kotlowitz, *There Are No Children Here,* xi.

38. On the issue of allegedly neutral documentary work that denies the whiteness of its appropriation of black experience to the neglect of how such appropriations will be read by white audiences, see bell hooks, *Black Looks: Race and Representation* (Boston: South End, 1992), 145–56.

39. Ibid., 177.

40. William J. Wilson, *The Truly Disadvantaged: The Inner City, the Underclass, and Public Policy* (Chicago: University of Chicago Press, 1987).

41. Wilson, "The Truly Disadvantaged," 639–56.

42. Duneier finds Wilson's thesis about middle-class role models to be lacking evidence, and he asserts that it seriously shortchanges the role models remaining in poor neighborhoods. See *Slim's Table,* 121–29.

43. See Stack, *All Our Kin*; Rank, *Living on the Edge,* 172–73. See also Andrew Billingsley, *Black Families in White America* (Englewood Cliffs, N.J.: Prentice Hall, 1968).

44. Duneier poses the issue in terms of reversing the common equation of Jews studying blacks to contemplate what ethnographies would look like if the almost never even imagined occurred — blacks studying Jews. See *Slim's Table,* 137. This issue is pursued in the context of Hollywood cinema in Michael Rogin, "Blackface, White Noise: The Jewish Jazz Singer Finds His Voice," *Critical Inquiry* 18 (Spring 1992): 417–53.

45. Donna J. Haraway, *Simians, Cyborgs, and Women: The Reinvention of Nature* (New York: Routledge, 1991), 191.

46. See Michel Foucault, *The History of Sexuality,* vol. 1, *An Introduction* (New York: Vintage, 1980), 58–67.

47. The phrase "civilization of productivity" is from William E. Connolly, "Civic Disaffection and the Democratic Party," *Democracy* 2 (July 1982): 18–27.

48. See Antonio Gramsci, *Selections from the Prison Notebooks of Antonio Gramsci,* ed. and trans. Q. Hoare and G. Nowell Smith (New York: International, 1971), 419.

49. This argument is perhaps most forcefully and explicitly stated for the United States in Frances Fox Piven and Richard A. Cloward, *The New Class War: Reagan's Attack on the Welfare State and Its Consequences* (New York: Pantheon, 1982). See also Kenneth Dolbeare, *Democracy at Risk: The Politics of Economic Renewal* (Chatham, N.J.: Chatham House, 1986).

50. See Frances Fox Piven and Richard A. Cloward, "The American Road to Democratic Socialism," *Democracy* 3 (Summer 1983): 58–69.

51. See James Scott, *Domination and the Arts of Resistance: Hidden Transcripts* (New Haven, Conn.: Yale University Press, 1990), 1–16.

52. This term is a play on Nancy Fraser's "actually existing democracies," which itself plays off "actually existing socialist systems" and other phrases used to distinguish regimes in power from the theories and ideologies they claim to represent. See Nancy Fraser, "Rethinking the Public Sphere: A Contribution to the Critique of Actually Existing Democracy," *Social Text* 25/26 (1990): 56–80.

53. See Nancy Fraser, "Sex, Lies and the Public Sphere: Some Reflections on the Confirmation of Clarence Thomas," *Critical Inquiry* 18 (Spring 1992): 595–612; Toni Morrison, ed. *Race-ing Justice, En-gendering Power: Essays on Anita Hill, Clarence Thomas, and the Construction of Social Reality* (New York: Pantheon, 1992).

54. For an analysis that situates an ethnographic examination of domestics within the political economy of contemporary U.S. capitalism, see Mary Romero, *Maid in the USA* (New York: Routledge, 1991).

55. Fraser, "Sex, Lies and the Public Sphere," 595–612.

56. See Romero, *Maid in the USA,* 47–49.

57. See Christopher Jencks and Kathryn Edin, "The Real Welfare Problem," *The American Prospect* 1, no. 1 (1990): 31–50.

58. See Michel Foucault, "The Dangerous Individual," and "Social Security," in *Michel Foucault: Politics, Philosophy, Culture: Interviews and Other Writings 1977–1984,* ed. Lawrence D. Kritzman, trans. Alan Sheridan et al. (New York: Routledge, 1989), 125–51, 159–77.

59. Haraway, *Simians, Cyborgs, and Women,* 192.

4. Bottom-Up Discourse: Narrating the Privatization of Public Assistance

1. See John Fiske, *Power Plays Power Works* (London: Verso, 1993), 35–53, for an analysis of how top-down discourses tend to be monocultural, univocal, homogenizing, and individuating consensual discourses of coercive power and regimentation, whereas bottom-up discourses tend to be multicultural, multiaccentual, diversifying, and individualizing nonconsensual discourses of empowerment and liberation. My use of *bottom-up discourse* differs in that I use the term to suggest a strategic attempt not so much to give voice from below as to narrate the consequences of structured practices in terms of the effects for those on the bottom or margin.

2. See Daniel P. Moynihan, "Toward a Postindustrial Social Policy," *Public Interest* 96 (Summer 1989): 16–27.

3. See Theresa Funiciello and Sanford F. Schram, "Post-mortem on the Deterioration of the Welfare Grant," in *The Reconstruction of Family Policy,* ed. Elaine A. Anderson and Richard C. Hula (Westport, Conn.: Greenwood, 1991), 149–64. AFDC grants declined in real value even more precipitously from highs in the 1970s to the current period, falling from

1970 to 1991 "42 per cent in the typical state, after adjusting for inflation" according to Nancy Folbre, "Beltway Bandits Bash the Poor," *Voice Literary Supplement,* November 1992, 31–33. From 1975 to 1992, the drop in the real value in the average state was 34 percent according to Center on Social Welfare Policy and Law, *Living at the Bottom: An Analysis of AFDC Benefit Levels,* publication no. 210 (New York: Center on Social Welfare Policy and Law, 1993), 25. See also chapter 9.

4. Joel Blau, *The Visible Poor: Homelessness in the United States* (New York: Oxford University Press, 1992), 57.

5. Ibid.

6. Michael B. Katz, *The Undeserving Poor: From the War on Poverty to the War on Welfare* (New York: Pantheon, 1989), 236–39.

7. Interview with Roberta Ericson, Salvation Army of Minneapolis, Minnesota, June 21, 1990.

8. See Jeffrey R. Henig, "Privatization in the United States: Theory and Practice," *Political Science Quarterly* 104 (Winter 1989–90): 649–70.

9. For discussion of the theoretical issues involved in the privatization of public assistance, see Evelyn Brodkin, "Making Sense of Privatization: What Can We Learn from Political and Economic Analysis?" in *Privatization and the Welfare State,* ed. Sheila B. Kamerman and Alfred J. Kahn (Princeton, N.J.: Princeton University Press, 1989).

10. See Robert Kuttner, "False Profit: The Perils of Privatization," *New Republic,* February 2, 1989, 21–23.

11. The term is from Ivan Illich, *Shadow Work* (Boston: Marion Boyars, 1981), who uses it to characterize all those nonpaid activities that are tied to the market in that they help make paid activities in the market possible. This sort of work could include all the many responsibilities associated with child rearing, housework, community volunteerism, and the like. See also Marjorie L. DeVault, *Feeding the Family: The Social Organization of Caring as Gendered Work* (Chicago: University of Chicago Press, 1991), 237–41, for an analysis of what happens when we define work as including some activities but not others. The parallel for the privatization of public assistance is what happens when some practices that are critical for meeting the needs of families, such as the provision of food assistance, are privatized in ways that submerge them from public view, thereby diminishing public understanding of people's needs.

12. The research for this section was done in collaboration with Dorothy Dodge during a period stretching from the summer of 1990 to the fall of 1992. In-person interviews were conducted with more than fifty Twin Cities food shelf staff members, advocates for the hungry, and food shelf users. Additional telephone interviews were conducted with directors of food banks around the country in a variety of locations, including California, Texas, Pennsylvania, and Massachusetts.

13. Our own attempts to secure food for others with very young children at various food shelves resulted in our either being asked to have the person in need make an appointment or being allowed to make an appointment for the person in question and then being given baby food or nothing at all. Not all shelves followed this procedure; in some cases, some would give a small amount of food for purposes of assisting until an appointment could be made.

14. Michael Lipsky, *Street Level Bureaucracy: Dilemmas of the Individual in Public Services* (New York: Russell Sage Foundation, 1980); Jon Elster, *Local Justice: How Institutions Allocate Scarce Goods and Necessary Burdens* (New York: Russell Sage Foundation, 1992).

15. See Michel Foucault, *Discipline and Punish: The Birth of the Prison,* trans. Alan Sheridan (New York: Vintage, 1979); Hubert L. Dreyfus and Paul Rabinow, *Michel Foucault: Beyond Structuralism and Hermeneutics* (Chicago: University of Chicago Press, 1982), ch. 7.

16. See Foucault, *Discipline and Punish*; Andrew J. Polsky, *The Rise of the Therapeutic State* (Princeton, N.J.: Princeton University Press, 1991), 42–61; Nancy Fraser, "Women, Welfare and the Politics of Need Interpretation," and "Struggle over Needs: Outline of a Social-ist-Feminist Critical Theory of Late Capitalist Political Culture," in *Unruly Practices: Power, Discourse, and Gender in Contemporary Social Theory* (Minneapolis: University of Minnesota Press, 1989), 144–87.

17. For an analysis of how ironically the push for privatization has led to a growing re-liance on nonprofit agencies that become sites for the extension of government and corpo-rate regulation of private charitable efforts, see Michael Lipsky and Stephen Rathgeb Smith, "Nonprofit Organizations, Government, and the Welfare State," *Political Science Quarterly* 104 (Winter 1989–90): 625–49.

18. On the prevailing discourse of dependency, see Nancy Fraser and Linda Gordon, "A Genealogy of *Dependency*: Tracing a Keyword of the U.S. Welfare State," *Signs* 19 (Winter 1994): 309–36.

19. On the political advantages of stressing food and hunger in the discussion of welfare and poverty, see Nick Kotz, *Let Them Eat Promises: The Politics of Hunger in America* (Engle-wood Cliffs, N.J.: Prentice Hall, 1969), 1–19, 147–62.

20. For two accounts that premise children's access to food on grounds of social justice but point to how others feel the need to rationalize such access in terms of ensuring the pro-ductivity of students, see ibid., 57–60; J. Larry Brown and H. F. Pizer, *Living Hungry in Amer-ica* (New York: Macmillan, 1987), 28–34.

21. See Marcel Maus, *The Gift: Forms and Functions of Exchange in Archaic Societies*, trans. Ian Cunnison (London: Coehn & West, 1954).

22. See Michael J. Shapiro, *Reading "Adam Smith": Desire, History and Value* (London: Sage, 1993), 59–69.

23. Lipsky and Smith, "Nonprofit Organizations," 625–49.

24. See ibid.

25. See Anne Hamre and Peter Rode, *Hunger Hurts: How Government and the Economy Are Failing Minnesota Families* (Minneapolis: Urban Coalition and the Minnesota Food Bank Network, February 1991).

26. See Hennepin Couty Office of Planning and Development, *Description and Evalua-tion of the Emergency Food Distribution System in Hennepin County* (Minneapolis: Hennepin County Office of Planning and Development, March 1994), ii-11, for an estimate that "food shelf usage has increased at a rate of seven percent per year over the past five years. Emergency needs have become more chronic, and the food distribution system addresses a need that is unlikely to be filled by other organizations" (p. ii).

27. Interview with Tammy McKenna, Dorothy Day Center, St. Paul, Minnesota, March 1, 1993.

28. Interview with Noelle Fallin, executive director, Emergency Food Shelf Network, Min-neapolis, Minnesota, June 5, 1990.

29. "Food Banks Established as Part of Help Network," *Northern Virginia Sun*, Decem-ber 27, 1990.

30. Second Harvest, *Second Harvest Annual Report: 1990* (Chicago: Second Harvest, 1990).

31. *Second Harvest Update: New & Issues*, Summer 1992, 7.

32. Solicitation letter from Second Harvest dated March 1, 1993.

33. See Theresa Funiciello, *The Tyranny of Kindness: Dismantling the Welfare System to End Poverty in America* (New York: Atlantic Monthly Press, 1993), 136–39, for evidence of dumping by Atlanta and New York City food banks. Funiciello emphasizes that dumping be-comes all the more plausible for food banks because much of the "product" received is what normally would be considered waste. Kroger Foods, for instance, implemented a company-

wide policy concerning surplus product for its stores under the banner "Donate, Don't Dump." In fact, Second Harvest officials, along with others in the emerging system of privatized food assistance, were concerned that they might be liable for passing on unhealthy food and successfully lobbied state legislatures and Congress to pass "Good Samaritan" laws that provide "immunity from both criminal and civil liability to a donor of food when that food inadvertently, or even negligently, harms the recipient of the food" (p. 158).

34. Interview with Noelle Fallin, executive director, Emergency Food Shelf Network, Minneapolis, Minnesota, June 5, 1990.

35. Hennepin County Office of Planning and Development, *Description and Evaluation*, 18.

36. Ibid.

37. Ibid., 26.

38. Hamre and Rode, *Hunger Hurts*, ii–iii.

39. Dennis P. Culhane, "Poorhouse Revisited," *New York Times*, November 18, 1991, A15.

5. Home Economists as the Real Economists

1. For an initial analysis of how the economistic biases of government statistics help construct "the poor" and reinforce their marginal status, see Frances Fox Piven and Richard A. Cloward, *Regulating the Poor: The Functions of Public Welfare*, updated ed. (New York: Vintage, 1993), 448–49.

2. "Economics," as the Greek *oikonomikos*, was classically management of the "home," only to be transformed with modernity to be concerned with resource production and consumption in the society writ large. Therefore, "home" economists were the unquestioned "real" economists at one point in time. On the transformation of economics as part of the emergence of "governmentality" and the assignment of economic coordination to the state, see Michel Foucault, "Governmentality," in *The Foucault Effect: Studies in Governmentality*, ed. Graham Burchell, Colin Gordon, and Peter Miller (Chicago: University of Chicago Press, 1991), 92–104.

3. See Mollie Orshansky, "Children of the Poor," *Social Security Bulletin* 26 (July 1963): 2–21; Deborah A. Stone, "Making the Poor Count," *The American Prospect* 17 (Spring 1994): 84–88.

4. See John E. Schwarz and Thomas J. Volgy, *The Forgotten Americans: Thirty Million Working Poor in the Land of Opportunity* (New York: W. W. Norton, 1992), 32–65.

5. Mollie Orshansky, comment made at a roundtable, "30th Anniversary of Mollie Orshansky's Poverty Line," held at the annual meeting of the American Political Science Association, September 2–5, 1993. For an analysis of how, in the years leading up to the New Deal, academic male economists pushing a "social insurance" approach to welfare reform marginalized the concerns of female social workers expressing a "social work" orientation about the poverty of single mothers, see Linda Gordon, *Pitied But Not Entitled: Single Mothers and the History of Welfare* (New York: Free Press, 1994), 145–81.

6. This quote is attributed to Eugene Smolensky. See Gordon M. Fisher, "The Development of the Orshansky Poverty Thresholds and Their Subsequent History as the Official U.S. Poverty Measure," unpublished paper, May 1992, 22.

7. Orshansky was not professionally trained as a home economist; her bachelor's degree from Hunter College is in math and statistics. She did work in the Bureau of Human Nutrition and Home Economics in the U.S. Department of Agriculture before joining the staff of the Social Security Administration. She also regularly attended professional meetings for home economists. More important, it is her orientation as a policy analyst who invoked the perspective of the families who had to live on the budgets she estimated that makes her a real home economist in the sense that I am using that term. Orshansky herself once stated, "If I write about the poor, I don't need a good imagination—I have a good memory." Quoted in ibid.

8. See Deborah Stone, *Policy Paradox and Political Reason* (New York: HarperCollins, 1988), and Stone's comments at a roundtable, "30th Anniversary of Mollie Orshansky's Poverty Line," held at the annual meeting of the American Political Science Association, September 2–5, 1993. Orshansky's stories therefore parallel the story Foucault tells about modernity's transformation of economics from a discourse of the home into the "art of government" concerned with coordinating and regulating the social population as a whole. See Foucault, "Governmentality," 92–104.

9. Piven and Cloward, *Regulating the Poor*, 371–72; Theresa Funiciello and Sanford F. Schram, "Post-mortem on the Deterioration of the Welfare Grant," in *The Reconstruction of Family Policy*, ed. Elaine A. Anderson and Richard C. Hula (Westport, Conn.: Greenwood, 1991), 149–64.

10. See Patricia Ruggles, *Drawing the Line: Alternative Poverty Measures and Their Implications for Public Policy* (Washington, D.C.: Urban Institute Press, 1990).

11. See Gordon M. Fisher, "The Development and History of the Poverty Thresholds," *Social Security Bulletin* 55 (Winter 1992): 3–14.

12. Ibid. See Mollie Orshansky, "Counting the Poor: Another Look at the Poverty Profile," *Social Security Bulletin* 28 (January 1965): 3–29. Orshansky's point that resource levels needed to maintain well-being vary with family size and composition was actually something that had been recognized for some time, even if studies done much earlier in the century concentrated on the "average-sized" family. See I. M. Rubinow, "Relief Budgets and Standards of Living," *Jewish Social Service Quarterly* 1 (February 1924): 51–63; B. Seebohm Rowntree and G. R. Laver, *Poverty and the Welfare State* (London: Longmans, Green, 1951). In the 1950s the point was reiterated; see Milton Friedman, "A Method of Comparing Incomes of Families Differing in Composition," *Studies in Income and Wealth* 15 (1952): 9–20; Martin David, "Welfare, Income, and Budget Needs," *Review of Economics and Statistics* 41 (November 1959): 393–99.

13. See Orshansky, "Children of the Poor"; Bradley Schiller, *The Economics of Poverty and Discrimination* (Englewood Cliff, N.J.: Prentice Hall, 1976), 15–22; Harrell R. Rodgers Jr., *Poverty amid Plenty: Political and Economic Analysis* (Reading, Mass.: Addison-Wesley, 1979), 18–30.

14. See Rodgers, *Poverty amid Plenty*, 18; Michael Harrington, *The Other America: Poverty in the United States* (New York: Penguin, 1981), 217.

15. See Orshansky, "Counting the Poor," 5–6.

16. Ibid.

17. See Orshansky, "Counting the Poor"; Schiller, *The Economics of Poverty*, 17–18; Rodgers, *Poverty amid Plenty*, 18–19.

18. Rodgers, *Poverty amid Plenty*, 19.

19. See Mollie Orshansky, *The Measure of Poverty: Technical Paper I, Documentation of Background Information and Rationale for Current Poverty Matrix* (Washington, D.C.: U.S. Department of Health, Education and Welfare, 1976), 233–36, where a July 1, 1970, memo that Orshansky wrote to Daniel Patrick Moynihan, then adviser to President Nixon, is reprinted. Orshansky writes in muted tones: "Originally developed as an overall research tool, not as a means test for determining eligibility for antipoverty programs, the lower SSA measure of minimum income need has been adopted by the OEO and other agencies as a working tool for program eligibility." See also Michael B. Katz, *The Undeserving Poor: From the War on Poverty to the War on Welfare* (New York: Pantheon, 1989), 116.

20. The struggle over the changes in 1969 are documented in Orshansky, *The Measure of Poverty*, 233–36.

21. See U.S. Department of Health, Education and Welfare, *The Measure of Poverty: A Report to Congress as Mandated by the Education Amendments of 1974* (Washington, D.C.: U.S. Department of Health, Education and Welfare, April 1976), 12.

22. In her July 1, 1970, memo to Moynihan, Orshansky wrote: "After much deliberation, the Committee decided to retain the original SSA base year (1963) income criteria for non-farm families but to switch to the CPI as the price inflates for annual inflation. This meant, of course, that the food-income relationship which was the basis for the original poverty measure no longer was the current rationale." See Orshansky, *The Measure of Poverty*, 236; Katz, *The Undeserving Poor*, 116–17. For an early British analysis that stressed food consumption data as the basis for building a poverty standard and that recognized that the poverty standard was something that ought to be understood as inextricably tied to the prevailing standard of living, see Peter Townsend, "Measuring Poverty," *British Journal of Sociology* 5 (June 1954): 130–37.

23. The pull toward mainstream macroeconomic thinking was strong in the Johnson administration and undoubtedly continued into the Nixon administration. See Robert H. Haveman, *Poverty Policy and Poverty Research: The Great Society and the Social Sciences* (Madison: University of Wisconsin Press, 1987), 51–52: "The War on Poverty was conceived of as an economic war; the designs, the debates, and the evaluations were all conducted in economic terms. Economics was the central discipline in both the action and the research components of the war." See also Katz, *The Undeserving Poor*, 79–123.

24. See Jill King, *The Measure of Poverty: Technical Paper V, the Consumer Price Index* (Washington, D.C.: U.S. Department of Health, Education and Welfare, 1976), 8–9.

25. Schwarz and Volgy, *The Forgotten Americans*, 32–65.

26. Rodgers, *Poverty amid Plenty*, 25–30.

27. See Martin Anderson, *Welfare: The Political Economy of Welfare Reform in the United States* (Palo Alto, Calif.: Hoover Institution and Stanford University, 1978), 20–24.

28. See Ruggles, *Drawing the Line*, 180. Note that for food stamps, families with incomes below 130 percent of the poverty line are eligible; for Medicaid, eligibility recently has been extended to mothers and young children in families with incomes below 133 percent of poverty. These eligibility thresholds are tied to the so-called OMB poverty guidelines, which are derived each year by the Department of Health and Human Services using the previous year's official poverty thresholds. See also Schwarz and Volgy, *The Forgotten Americans*, 32–65.

29. Schwarz and Volgy, *The Forgotten Americans*, 35–36.

30. Rodgers, *Poverty amid Plenty*, 24; Betty Peterkin, *The Measure of Poverty: Technical Paper XII, Food Plans for Poverty Measurement* (Washington, D.C.: U.S. Department of Health, Education and Welfare, 1976), 49. Peterkin's report reprints passages of the *Federal Register* that note that "only 10 percent of the 1965–66 survey households that used food at the cost of the economy plan selected nutritionally adequate diets" (p. 93), from *Federal Register* 40 (September 19, 1975): 43404–10.

31. Rodgers, *Poverty amid Plenty*, 36–37.

32. Schwarz and Volgy, *The Forgotten Americans*, 44–45.

33. Fisher, "The Development and History," 5.

34. For a compelling defense of Orshansky's normative approach, see Sharon Oster, Elizabeth Lake, and Conchita Gene Oksman, *The Measure of Poverty: Technical Paper III, a Review of the Definition and Measurement of Poverty*, vol. 1, *Summary Review Paper* (Washington, D.C.: U.S. Department of Health, Education and Welfare, 1976), 7–8. These authors provide a rebuttal of criticism by Rose Friedman, *Poverty Definition and Perspective* (Washington, D.C.: American Enterprise Institute, February 1965): "Friedman argues that the multiplier should be less than 3 because the poor spend a larger fraction of their income on food; in other words, the multiplier should be taken from budget studies of the poor only, not across the income distribution as it is now done. While this is a narrowly correct point, it misses the underlying rationale for the SSA procedure: it seems clear that the large portion spent on food by the poor is a mere expedient of their poverty. Indeed, using a low-

income fraction might only serve to incorporate destitution into a minimum subsistence definition."

35. Schwarz and Volgy, *The Forgotten Americans,* 34–36; Mollie Orshansky, "How Poverty Is Measured," *Monthly Labor Review* 32 (February 1969): 38; Mollie Orshansky, "Who's Who among the Poor: A Demographic View of Poverty," *Social Security Bulletin* 28 (July 1965): 3–32. In "Who's Who among the Poor," Orshansky emphasizes that "the new poverty index represents an attempt to specify the minimum money income required to support an *average* family of given composition at the lowest level consistent with the standards of living prevailing in this country" (p. 8).

36. For a discussion on how a "Poor Price Index" might better capture the rising cost of necessities, see King, *The Measure of Poverty,* 23–25. King rejects such a measure on the grounds that the inflation experience of the poor is not that different from that of everyone else. Again, this sort of orientation misses the point: the poverty index was originally conceived to be not exclusively about isolating the experiences of the poor but about assessing the costs of necessities that the average family would need to achieve a minimally adequate standard of living. From that perspective, a different index might very much be in order, because the costs of necessities such as housing and energy have risen well above the overall inflation rate.

37. See Judith de Neufville, *Social Indicators and Public Policy: Interactive Processes of Design and Application* (New York: Elsevier Scientific, 1975), 86; Fisher, "The Development of the Orshansky Poverty Thresholds," 4. Fisher notes that, technically speaking, "Orshansky did not develop the poverty thresholds as a standard budget—a more precise technical term for what is today commonly called a 'market basket'"; de Neufville notes that Orshansky's threshold, although not a standard budget, is a "related concept" (p. 96).

38. Schwarz and Volgy, *The Forgotten Americans,* 62.

39. Ibid., 61–71.

40. John Schwarz, comment made at a roundtable, "30th Anniversary of Mollie Orshansky's Poverty Line," held at the annual meeting of the American Political Science Association, September 2–5, 1993. See also Lawrence L. Brown III with Renee Miller, *The Measure of Poverty: Technical Paper XVIII, Characteristics of Low-Income Populations under Alternative Poverty Definitions* (Washington, D.C.: U.S. Department of Health, Education and Welfare, 1976), 11–19.

41. The panel was due to issue a report of its findings and recommendations in summer 1994.

42. This and the following section are based on Funiciello and Schram, "Post-mortem on the Deterioration of the Welfare Grant."

43. Although each state is required to assess its welfare grant in terms of how well it meets a "standard of need," states are notorious for doing so infrequently and even then allowing their grants to languish well below need standards. See Adele M. Blong and Timothy J. Casey, *AFDC Program Rules for Advocates: An Overview,* publication no. 160 (New York: Center on Social Welfare Policy and Law, 1993), 8–10.

44. U.S. Department of Health and Human Services, *Characteristics of State Plans for AFDC* (Washington, D.C.: U.S. Government Printing Office, 1989), 375.

45. Frances Fox Piven and Richard A. Cloward, *Poor People's Movements: Why They Succeed, How They Fail* (New York: Pantheon, 1977); Nick Kotz and Mary Kotz, *A Passion for Equality: George Wiley and the Welfare Rights Movement* (New York: W. W. Norton, 1977); Guida West, *The National Welfare Rights Movement* (New York: Praeger, 1981).

46. William Simon, "Legality, Bureaucracy and Class in the Welfare System," *Yale Law Journal* 92 (Fall 1983): 1198–1286.

47. 397 U.S. 412–414 (1970).

48. *RAM v. Blum,* 77 Appellate Division 2nd 278, lst Dept. (1980), Appeal Withdrawn 54 NY 2nd 834, County of New York, Index no. 5550/79, Affidavit of David Gordon.

49. These calculations are based on data from U.S. Department of Labor, *Three Budgets for an Urban Family of Four Persons, 1969–70: Supplement to Bulletin 1570–5* (Washington, D.C.: U.S. Government Printing Office, 1972).

50. For figures on AFDC and food stamp benefits in each state, see Richard A. Kasten and John E. Todd, "Transfer Recipients and the Poor during the 1970s," paper presented at the 2d annual research conference of the Association for Public Policy Analysis and Management, Washington, D.C., 1980), Tables 7, 9. For figures on the proportion of the AFDC budget in each state that went for food in 1979, see U.S. Department of Health and Human Services, *Research Tables Based on Characteristics of State Plans for AFDC* (Washington, D.C.: U.S. Government Printing Office, 1980), 51–52.

51. These calculations are based on AFDC figures from U.S. Department of Health and Human Services, *Research Tables,* 375, and food stamp amounts from the Center on Social Welfare Policy and Law.

52. See New York City Human Resources Administration, *Shelter Policy Options* (New York: New York City Human Resources Administration, 1987).

53. Ibid.

54. Diane L. Baillargeon, *Dependency: Economic and Social Data for New York City* (New York: New York City Human Resources Administration, Office of Policy and Economic Research, June 1986), 62.

55. See Adele M. Blong, *No Relief for the Poor: 1992 State Cutbacks in AFDC, GA and EAF,* pt. 1, publication no. 167, revised (Washington, D.C.: Center on Social Welfare Policy and Law, September, 1992), 4.

56. This estimate comes from the New York State Department of Social Services, Bureau of Data Management, as reported in *1984–1985 New York State Statistical Yearbook* (Albany, N.Y.: Nelson A. Rockefeller Institute of Government, 1985), 86, 95.

57. Timothy J. Casey, *The In-Human Resources Administration's Churning Campaign* (New York: Downtown Welfare Advocate Center, May 1983).

58. See Joel Blau, *The Visible Poor: Homelessness in the United States* (New York: Oxford University Press, 1990), 51.

59. Timothy J. Casey, "Public Assistance Policy and Homelessness," prepared statement for testimony before the New York State Joint Legislative Hearings, "Homeless Families: Causes and Solutions," June 23, 1987.

60. Besides Piven and Cloward, *Regulating the Poor,* 373–81, very few social scientists have studied churning, and those who have have relied largely on a few government studies and the substantial efforts of the Center on Social Welfare Policy and Law to track this phenomenon. Studies by Tim Casey and Mary Mannix at the center have proven critical in trying to maintain understanding of the churning phenomenon. One exception is found in Michael Lipsky, "Bureaucratic Disentitlement in Social Welfare Programs," *Social Service Review* 58 (Winter 1984): 3–27. Also, Theresa Funiciello, in a memoir/analysis on welfare politics, discusses the realities of churning; see *The Tyranny of Kindness: Dismantling the Welfare System to End Poverty in America* (New York: Atlantic Monthly Press, 1993), 168–71.

61. Piven and Cloward, *Regulating the Poor,* 376.

62. Casey, *The In-Human Resources Administration's Churning Campaign.*

63. Ibid.

64. See New York State Department of Social Services, *Administrative Closings in New York City Public Assistance Cases* (Albany: New York State Department of Social Services, April 1984).

65. Anna Lou Dehavenon, *Toward a Policy for the Amelioration and Prevention of Family Homelessness and Dissolution* (New York: East Harlem Interfaith Welfare Committee, May 1987).

66. Doug Lasden et al., *Below the Safety Net: A Study of Soup Kitchen Users in New York City* (New York: Legal Action Center for the Homeless and New York University, April 1987).

67. Additional studies include "Administrative Closings and Churning of Welfare Cases," *The Record* 45 (1990): 379–96; Anna Lou Dehavenon, "Charles Dickens Meets Franz Kafka: The Maladministration of New York City's Public Assistance Programs," *NYU Review of Law & Social Change* 17, no. 2 (1990).

68. Timothy J. Casey and Mary R. Mannix, *Quality Control and the "Churning" Crisis* (New York: Center on Social Welfare Policy and Law, December 1986); Timothy J. Casey and Mary R. Mannix, "Quality Control in Public Assistance: Victimizing the Poor through One-Sided Accountability," *Clearinghouse Review* 22 (April 1989): 1381–85; S. Leiwant and J. Hansen, "Caselaw on AFDC Verification Problems," *Clearinghouse Review* 21 (July 1987): 215–19. For an analysis of how monthly reporting requirements for some recipients do not reduce costs or errors, involve increased administrative costs, and can lead to the termination of otherwise eligible recipients, see Robert Greenstein and Marion Nichols, *Monthly Reporting: A Review of the Research Findings* (Washington, D.C.: Center on Budget and Policy Priorities, February 1989).

69. Timothy J. Casey and Mary R. Mannix, *Quality Control in Public Assistance: Victimizing the Poor through One-Sided Accountability* (New York: Center on Social Welfare Policy and Law, October 1988), 10.

70. See Center on Social Welfare Policy and Law, *Quality Control in Public Assistance: Victimizing the Poor through One-Sided Accountability,* revised (New York: Center on Social Welfare Policy and Law, July 1991).

71. Dehavenon, "Charles Dickens Meets Franz Kafka."

72. For analysis of quality control and its possible effects on churning, see Evelyn Brodkin and Michael Lipsky, "Quality Control in AFDC as an Administrative Strategy," *Social Service Review* 57 (March 1983): 1–34; Lipsky, "Bureaucratic Disentitlement"; Piven and Cloward, *Regulating the Poor,* 373–81.

73. See U.S. Congress, House of Representatives, Committee on Ways and Means, *Background Material and Data on Programs within the Jurisdiction of the Committee on Ways and Means* (Washington, D.C.: U.S. Government Printing Office, 1987), 683–99.

74. See Center on Social Welfare Policy and Law, *Quality Control in Public Assistance.*

75. U.S. Congress, House of Representatives, Committee on Ways and Means, *The Green Book* (Washington, D.C.: U.S. Government Printing Office, 1993), 1591–92.

76. Telephone conversation with Timothy Casey, Center on Social Welfare Policy and Law, October 25, 1993.

77. See Center on Social Welfare Policy and Law, *AFDC: Administration Proposals for Changes in Quality Control System and in Federal Funding for Administrative Costs and Proposed Funding Level For JOBS* (New York: Center on Social Welfare Policy and Law, March 10, 1989).

78. Sandra Hauser and Mary R. Mannix, *The AFDC Optional Fraud Control Program* (New York: Center on Social Welfare Policy and Law, June 1992).

79. A review of the annual publications list of the Center on Social Welfare Policy and Law indicates that the efforts of this welfare rights litigation research office continue to be absorbed by issues related to practices that amount to or are similar to churning.

80. See Center on Social Welfare Policy and Law, *AFDC: HHS Issues Forms to States for Use in Reporting Information Concerning the Periodic Reevaluation of Needs and Payment Standards Which May Sabotage the Statutory Mandate* (New York: Center on Social Welfare Policy and Law, May 31, 1991). For New York's reevaluation, see J. B. Welsh and R. Franklin, *Valuing Basic Needs in New York State: A Methodological Proposal* (Albany: New York State Department of Social Services, 1988); for Minnesota's reevaluation, see Minnesota Department of

Human Services, *A Market Basket Evaluation of the AFDC Standard of Need: A Report to the 1991 Legislature* (St. Paul: Minnesota Department of Human Services, December 15, 1990).

81. By 1993, the maximum value of food stamps and AFDC to a family with no other income rarely rose above four-fifths of the poverty level in any state in the country. Only Alaska, California, and New York brought families above four-fifths of the official poverty level. See Center on Social Welfare Policy and Law, *Living at the Bottom: An Analysis of AFDC Benefit Levels*, publication no. 210 (New York: Center on Social Welfare Policy and Law, 1993), 21. Minnesota, for instance, had not raised its welfare grant for eight years. The state's Department of Human Services estimated that 1990 benefits would have to be raised 65 percent before they reach the "standard of need" estimated by a recent report. That would mean approximately $75 million more in annual payments in Minnesota, a figure that is not likely to be met in any state, given the current fiscal climate. See Minnesota Department of Human Services, *A Market Basket Evaluation*.

6. Rewriting Social Policy History

1. Blaming the War on Poverty of the 1960s for contemporary social ills achieved its most heightened political significance when the Bush administration linked the welfare programs of the Johnson administration to the 1992 Los Angeles riots that followed the acquittal of the police officers who beat Rodney King. See Michael Wines, "White House Links Riots to Welfare," *New York Times*, May 5, 1992, A1. For one of the most explicit statements on how the 1960s engendered cultural changes that helped encourage the development of an irresponsible and promiscuous underclass of misfits, see Myron Magnet, *The Dream and the Nightmare: The Sixties' Legacy to the Underclass* (New York: Morrow, 1993). For a critique, see Meta Mendel-Reyes, *The Sixties as Metaphor* (Ithaca, N.Y.: Cornell University Press, 1994). For an analysis that highlights how the Johnson administration's War on Poverty was an underfunded attempt to reduce welfare taking by offering a "hand up" and not a "handout," see James T. Patterson, *America's Struggle against Poverty: 1900–1985* (Cambridge: Harvard University Press, 1986), 142–70.

2. The leading proponent of this idea was Charles Murray, *Losing Ground: American Social Policy 1950–1980* (New York: Basic Books, 1984), but many others jumped on this bandwagon. See Lawrence M. Mead, *Beyond Entitlement: The Social Obligations of Citizenship* (New York: Free Press, 1986); Leslie Lenkowsky, *Politics, Economics, and Welfare Reform: The Failure of the Negative Income Tax in Britain and the United States* (Landham, Md.: University Press of America, 1986). This reorientation toward indicting public assistance as the primary cause of poverty has continued into the 1990s; see Lawrence M. Mead, *The New Politics of Poverty: The Nonworking Poor in America* (New York: Basic Books, 1992); Mickey Kaus, *The End of Equality* (New York: Basic Books, 1992). Basic Books seems to be trying to monopolize the publication of welfare-bashing tracts that have been written in recent years, although it has also published a moderate defense of the welfare state by Theodore R. Marmor, Jerry L. Mashaw, and Philip L. Harvey, *America's Misunderstood Welfare State: Persistent Myths, Enduring Realities* (New York: Basic Books, 1990).

3. See Douglas J. Bersharov with Amy A. Fowler, "The End of Welfare as We Know It?" *Public Interest* 111 (Spring 1993): 95–108.

4. See Michael J. Shapiro, *Reading "Adam Smith": Desire, History and Value* (London: Sage, 1993), ch. 2.

5. On the narrative character of social statistics, see Joseph Gusfield, *The Culture of Public Problems: Drinking-Driving and the Symbolic Order* (Chicago: University of Chicago Press, 1984).

6. For a discussion of how science in general is not independent of the broader society and its cultural biases, see Helen E. Longino, *Science as Social Knowledge: Values and Objectivity in Scientific Inquiry* (Princeton, N.J.: Princeton University Press, 1990), 3–7.

7. See John E. Schwarz and Thomas J. Volgy, *The Forgotten Americans: Thirty Million Working Poor in the Land of Opportunity* (New York: W. W. Norton, 1992), 3–10; Frances Fox Piven and Richard A. Cloward, *Regulating the Poor: The Functions of Public Welfare*, updated ed. (New York: Vintage, 1993), 343–99.

8. For an analysis on how redescribing dependency has contributed to increased concern about the "nonworking poor," see Nancy Fraser and Linda Gordon, "A Genealogy of *Dependency*: A Keyword of the U.S. Welfare State," *Signs* 19 (Winter 1994): 309–33.

9. The primary proponent of this increasingly popular idea has been Charles Murray; see his *Losing Ground*, 56–68.

10. For an excellent discussion of the political effect of historical narrative, especially when posed as a smooth, linear, legendary, or mythic story that rationalizes the present as predestined natural consequence of the past, see Shapiro, *Reading "Adam Smith"*, 48–59.

11. See William E. Connolly, *Identity\Difference: Democratic Negotiations of Political Paradox* (Ithaca, N.Y.: Cornell University Press, 1991), 183; Michel Foucault, "Question of Method," in *The Foucault Effect: Studies in Governmentality*, ed. Graham Burchell, Colin Gordon, and Peter Miller (Chicago: University of Chicago Press, 1991), 76–78.

12. See Dominick LaCapra, *Soundings in Critical Theory* (Ithaca, N.Y.: Cornell University Press, 1989), 195–98; Michael J. Shapiro, *The Politics of Representation: Writing Practices in Biography, Photography, and Policy Analysis* (Madison: University of Wisconsin Press, 1988), 54.

13. Hayden White, "The Value of Narrativity in the Representation of Reality," *Critical Inquiry* 7 (Autumn 1980): 8.

14. Jean-François Lyotard, *Des Dispositifs Pulsionnels* (Paris: Christian Bourgois, 1980), 170–71; quoted in Shapiro, *Reading "Adam Smith"*, 49.

15. See Edward W. Said, *Beginnings: Intention and Method* (New York: Basic Books, 1975), 50–78.

16. See Michel Foucault, "Of Other Spaces," *Diacritics* 16 (Fall 1986): 22–27; Edward Soja, "History: Geography: Modernity," in *The Cultural Studies Reader*, ed. Simon During (New York: Routledge, 1993), 136.

17. Jacques Derrida, *Positions*, trans. and ann. Alan Bass (Chicago: University of Chicago Press, 1981), 104; LaCapra, *Soundings in Critical Theory*, 186.

18. Jacques Lacan, "Subversion of the Subject and the Dialectic of Desire," in *Ecrits*, trans. Alan Sheridan (New York: W. W. Norton, 1977), 305. Lacan is discussed in LaCapra, *Soundings in Critical Theory*, 32–66; Shapiro, *Reading "Adam Smith"*, 18–19.

19. See Evelyn Z. Brodkin, "The Making of an Enemy: How Welfare Policies Construct the Poor," *Law and Social Inquiry* 18 (Fall 1993): 647–70.

20. See Mimi Abramovitz, *Regulating the Lives of Women: Social Welfare Policy from Colonial Times to the Present* (Boston: South End, 1988), 36–40; Brodkin, "The Making of an Enemy."

21. For an informed analysis on the intentions and motivations of welfare reformers during the last half of the nineteenth century and the early half of the twentieth that suggests that duration in the receipt of assistance of mothers' pensions in particular was not a major issue, see Theda Skocpol, *Protecting Soldiers and Mothers: The Political Origins of Social Policy in the United States* (Cambridge: Harvard University Press, Belknap Press, 1992), 424–79; Linda Gordon, "Welfare Reform: A History Lesson," *Dissent* (Summer 1994): 323–28.

22. For contrasting views on the "new consensus," see Novak et al., *The New Consensus on Family Welfare: A Community of Self-Reliance* (Milwaukee: Marquette University, 1987); Michael B. Katz, *The Undeserving Poor: From the War on Poverty to the War on Welfare* (New York: Pantheon, 1989), 233–35.

23. See Frances Fox Piven and Richard A. Cloward, "The Historical Sources of the Contemporary Relief Debate," in *The Mean Season: The Attack on the Welfare State*, ed. Fred

Block, Richard A. Cloward, Barbara Ehrenreich, and Frances Fox Piven (New York: Pantheon, 1987), 3–44. Piven and Cloward show that the acceptable length of receipt of public assistance historically in English-speaking countries, including the United States, has been a subject of continual political contestation, and that the appropriate duration has almost never been defined explicitly.

24. Housing Act of 1937, as amended, 42 U.S.C.S. sect. 1437d, Pub.L. 93–383 (1992 Supp.).

25. For details on the Housing Act and its effects, see Joel Blau, *The Visible Poor: Homelessness in the United States* (New York: Oxford University Press, 1992), 60–76.

26. Ibid. Christopher Jencks, in *The Homeless* (Cambridge: Harvard University Press, 1994), 94–98, takes issue with the claim that cutbacks during the Reagan-Bush years contributed to a housing shortage that added to the ranks of the homeless. Jencks stresses that "net budget authority" appropriated for housing by Congress continued to rise in real dollars from the late 1970s through the entire decade of the 1980s, and that the number of tenants in public and publicly assisted housing grew from 2.9 million in 1979 to 4.2 million in 1989. Jencks emphasizes the collapse of the private low-cost housing market, including increased abandonment. Yet Jencks overlooks that while federal expenditures and numbers of subsidized tenants continued to grow, increased expenditures were increasingly shifted in the 1980s away from new construction to rental assistance programs, including vouchers, which were for existing housing and therefore did not add to the already inadequate stock of existing low-cost housing (see U.S. Congress, House of Representatives, Committee on Ways and Means, *1992 Green Book* [Washington, D.C.: U.S. Government Printing Office, May 15, 1992], 1673–78). In addition, although Jencks is correct in that housing outlays continued to increase in the 1980s, it is questionable that they increased relative to the growing need for low-cost housing.

27. Blau, *The Visible Poor*, 74.

28. Shawn G. Kennedy, "Applications to Public Housing in New York City Reach Record High," *New York Times*, December 27, 1992, A14.

29. The relationship of lack of access to affordable housing and homelessness is documented in Marjorie Honig and Randall K. Filer, "Causes of Intercity Variation in Homelessness," *American Economic Review* 83 (Winter 1993): 248–55.

30. Jason DeParle, "Government Housing Plan Aims to End Tenants' Dependence on Public Aid," *New York Times*, February 20, 1992, A13.

31. Ibid.

32. Ibid.

33. Mead, *The New Politics of Poverty*, 1–15.

34. Ibid., 133–58.

35. See Frantz Fanon, *The Wretched of the Earth* (London: Hamondsworth, 1968), 223–24. For an examination of how welfare policies themselves help construct "the poor" as a qualitatively distinct group of people, see Brodkin, "The Making of an Enemy."

36. For evidence on how unemployment affects the confidence about work among poor young black males, see John Ballen and Richard B. Freeman, "Transitions between Employment and Unemployment" in *The Black Youth Employment Crisis*, ed. Richard B. Freeman and Harry J. Holzer (Chicago: University of Chicago Press, 1986), 92–95; Richard B. Freeman and Harry J. Holzer, "Young Blacks and Jobs — What We Now Know," *Public Interest*, 78 (Winter 1985): 26. These authors emphasize that poor young black males often have very high expectations about what jobs they should be able to get and therefore can become easily disappointed.

37. See Christopher Jencks, *Rethinking Social Policy: Race, Poverty, and the Underclass* (Cambridge: Harvard University Press, 1992), 165–66. Jencks suggests that economic slowdown has always hit the poorer segments of the population harder, and since the early 1970s this has meant rising joblessness for poor males in particular.

38. See Adolph Reed Jr., "The Underclass as Myth and Symbol: The Poverty of Discourse about Poverty," *Radical America* (January 1992): 21–40.

39. See Stanley Aronowitz, *The Politics of Identity: Class, Culture, Social Movements* (New York: Routledge, 1992), 158–63.

40. For a survey, see Donna J. Haraway, *Simians, Cyborgs, and Women: The Reinvention of Nature* (New York: Routledge, 1991), 183–202.

41. Longino, *Science as Social Knowledge*, 3–7.

42. Haraway, *Simians, Cyborgs, and Women*, 7.

43. See David T. Ellwood, *Targeting the Would-Be Long Term Recipient: Who Should Be Served?* report to the U.S. Department of Health and Human Services (Princeton, N.J.: Mathematica Policy Research, 1986); Mary Jo Bane and David T. Ellwood, *The Dynamics of Dependence: The Routes to Self-Sufficiency*, report to the U.S. Department of Health and Human Services (Cambridge, Mass.: Urban Systems Research & Engineering, 1983); David T. Ellwood and Mary Jo Bane, *The Impact of AFDC on Family Structure and Living Arrangements*, report prepared for the U.S. Department of Health and Human Services under grant no. 92A-82 (Cambridge: Harvard University, March 1984), 1–7. Robert Moffitt, "Work Incentives in Transfer Programs (Revisited): A Study of the AFDC Program," in *Research in Labor Economics*, vol. 8, ed. Ronald G. Ehrenberg (Greenwich, Conn.: Jai, 1986), 389–439; Frank Levy, "The Labor Supply of Female Heads, or AFDC Work Incentives Don't Work Too Well," *Journal of Human Resources* 14 (Winter 1979): 76–97.

44. In particular, see Mead, *The New Politics of Poverty*, 195–98; Kaus, *The End of Equality*, 116–20.

45. Some works that preceded Murray, Mead, and Kaus include Martin Anderson, *Welfare: The Political Economy of Welfare Reform in the United States* (Stanford, Calif.: Hoover Institution Press, 1978); Morton Paglin, *Poverty and Transfers In-Kind* (Stanford, Calif.: Hoover Institution Press, 1980); George Gilder, *Wealth and Poverty* (New York: Basic Books, 1981).

46. See Mead, *The New Politics of Poverty*. Michael Sosin underscores how Mead in an earlier volume exhibited a penchant for citing others' statistics out of context. See Michael Sosin, "Review of *Beyond Entitlement: The Social Obligations of Citizenship* (New York: Free Press, 1986)," *Social Service Review*, 61 (Spring 1987): 378.

47. Mead, *The New Politics of Poverty*, 70.

48. Ibid., 102.

49. See James E. Rosenbaum and Susan J. Poplin, "Employment and Earnings of Low-Income Blacks Who Move to Middle Class Suburbs," in *The Urban Underclass*, ed. Christopher Jencks and Paul E. Peterson (Washington, D.C.: Brookings Institution, 1991), 342–56.

50. Mead, *The New Politics of Poverty*, 96.

51. Ibid., 98.

52. Ibid., 72–84.

53. Michael B. Katz, "The Poverty Debate," *Dissent* (Fall 1992): 550.

54. Mead, *The New Politics of Poverty*, 119–24.

55. Ibid., 117.

56. See Katz, "The Poverty Debate," 549. Katz makes the same point Michael Sosin has made. See note 46.

57. See Murray, *Losing Ground*, 56–84.

58. See Barbara Ehrenreich, *The Fear of Falling: The Inner Life of the Middle Class* (New York: HarperCollins, 1989), 185–95.

59. Murray, *Losing Ground*, 64.

60. Lowell Gallaway and Richard Vedder, *Poverty, Income Distribution, the Family and Public Policy: A Study Prepared for the Use of the Subcommittee on Trade, Productivity, and*

Economic Growth of the Joint Economic Committee of the Congress of the United States (Washington, D.C.: U.S. Government Printing Office, 1986).

61. Sheldon Danziger and Robert D. Plotnick, "Poverty and Policy: Lessons of the Last Two Decades," *Social Services Review* 60 (March 1986): 34–51.

62. Marmor, Mashaw, and Harvey, *America's Misunderstood Welfare State*, 166. Yet, while catching Murray in a misappropriation, Marmor et al. perpetuate their own brand of categorical discrimination. If Murray had limited the latent poor only to those receiving welfare, they would be content. For Marmor, Mashaw, and Harvey, taking some forms of government assistance, such as social security, is not dependency, but taking other forms, such as welfare, is. Murray's problem is therefore their problem. The idea that the latent poor are "dependent" is quite an imaginative leap — one made possible by allowing the prevailing social biases to inform statistical interpretation.

63. See Sheldon Danziger and Peter Gottschalk, *Losing Ground: A Critique*, Special Report Series, no. 38 ed. Sara McLanahan et al. (Madison, Wis.: Institute for Research on Poverty, August 1985).

64. Daniel Patrick Moynihan, "We Can't Avoid Family Policy Much Longer" (interview), *Challenge* (September–October 1985): 11.

65. Daniel Patrick Moynihan, *The Negro Family: The Case for National Action*" reprinted in Lee Rainwater and William L. Yancey, *The Moynihan Report and the Politics of Controversy* (Cambridge: MIT Press, 1967), 74–75.

66. Moynihan claims that he discovered these numbers and then was prompted to write *The Negro Family*. He claims that while on a flight to New York in 1964 he was doing research that suggested a correlation between male unemployment and new welfare cases. Subsequently, he and his staff discovered that the correlation declined in the late 1950s and early 1960s. Moynihan writes: "The data went blooey, and although I knew something had gone wrong, I did not know what to do. Not really. I believe Martin Luther King, Jr. went through some of the same disorientation." See Daniel Patrick Moynihan, *Family and Nation* (New York: Harcourt Brace Jovanovich, 1986), 40–41. Nicholas Lemann, in *The Promised Land: The Great Black Migration and How It Changed America* (New York: Knopf, 1991), 174–77, suggests that Moynihan's staff hit upon the data as they were finishing a draft of the report. Lemann also suggests that Moynihan was hungry for credit and released the report to the press, only to find it made him persona non grata in the liberal social science community.

67. Without emphasizing it, William Julius Wilson and Kathryn Neckerman supply data that indicate that the declines in unemployment for African American males for the period Moynihan examined corresponded with declines in the African American male labor force participation rate. See William Julius Wilson and Kathryn M. Neckerman, "Poverty and Family Structure: The Widening Gap between Evidence and Public Policy Issues," conference paper, Institute for Research on Poverty, Madison, Wis., December 1984, 72.

68. Katz, *The Undeserving Poor*, 44–52.

69. Piven and Cloward, *Regulating the Poor*, 248–82.

70. Piven and Cloward, *Regulating the Poor*, 343–65; Danziger and Plotnick, "Poverty and Policy"; Diana Pearce, "Welfare Is *Not* for Women: Why the War on Poverty Cannot Conquer the Feminization of Poverty," in *Women, the State, and Welfare*, ed. Linda Gordon (Madison: University of Wisconsin Press, 1990), 265–79; Robert Moffitt, "Has Redistribution Policy Grown More Conservative?" *National Tax Journal* 43 (June 1990): 123–42.

71. Theresa Funiciello and Sanford F. Schram, "Post-mortem on the Deterioration of the Welfare Grant," in *The Reconstruction of Family Policy*, ed. Elaine A. Anderson and Richard C. Hula (Westport, Conn.: Greenwood, 1991), 149–64.

72. These data do not, however, strictly indicate the level of poverty in the absence of income transfers or welfare benefits, because undoubtedly under such hypothetical circumstances there would be greater economic productivity, less taxation, and hence less poverty. But they still provide a reliable baseline for comparing changes over time in the level of poverty independent of government benefits. When compared with the official (postwelfare) poverty rate, they are useful for assessing the extent to which government benefits reduce poverty levels. See Danziger and Plotnick, "Poverty and Policy."

73. These data actually are biased in their very construction, and interpretation only compounds the bias. The idea of pretransfer income, at the very least, tacitly accepts the government's invidious distinction regarding sources of income. Only some "transfers" are recognized in this process. The poor's transfers are public; those of many others are private. Already, from the start, the category of transfers highlights government assistance to the poor while backgrounding the benefits the nonpoor gain from the existing system. Take housing assistance. The poor's benefits are expenditures authorized in the federal budget — something highly visible to be retrenched when confronting massive federal deficits. Nonpoor homeowners, however, receive massive tax deductions on the interest on their mortgages and their property taxes — things that survive the budget ax. In 1989, these deductions reached nearly $39 billion and were expected to hit $50 billion by 1993. See Blau, *The Visible Poor*, 62–71.

74. See Danziger and Plotnick, "Poverty and Policy."

75. An additional factor for the declining antipoverty effectiveness of welfare expenditures is the change in the composition of the official poverty population. Since the mid-1970s, the official poverty population has been undergoing rapid change; it is now increasingly made up of female-headed families. The women who head these families often are not prepared to get and keep jobs that can ensure that their families will permanently escape poverty. Under such conditions, there is likely to be a decline in the antipoverty effectiveness of each welfare dollar, and government needs perhaps to spend more per poor person in order to do no more than maintain the previous official poverty reduction rates of welfare expenditures. At the same time, the real value of welfare benefits for this portion of the official poverty population has been, as we have seen, declining dramatically, just when, arguably, we need to spend more per poor person, because of their greater disadvantages, in order to enable them to escape poverty. The net result is that static or even marginally increased levels of welfare expenditures can actually be seen as less relative to the greater need of the official poverty population. See ibid.

76. See Fred Block, "Rethinking the Political Economy of the Welfare State," in *The Mean Season: The Attack on the Welfare State,* ed. Fred Block, Richard A. Cloward, Barbara Ehrenreich, and Frances Fox Piven (New York: Pantheon, 1987), 109–60.

7. The Real Uses of a False Dichotomy: Symbols at the Expense of Substance in Welfare Reform

1. For a positive view that emphasizes how sound implementation of the 1988 legislation has the potential to produce a dramatic departure in welfare, see Richard P. Nathan, *Turning Promises into Performance: The Management Challenge of Implementing Workfare* (New York: Columbia University Press, 1993), 108–21. For a critical view of the 1988 legislation that sees it as a dramatic development that simply ends up reinforcing welfare dependency, see Charles Murray, "New Welfare Bill, New Welfare Cheats," *Wall Street Journal,* October 13, 1988, A22.

2. Nathan, *Turning Promises into Performance,* 108–9.

3. See several of Murray Edelman's books: *Symbolic Uses of Politics* (Chicago: University of Illinois Press, 1964); *Politics as Symbolic Action* (New York: Academic Press, 1971); *Po-*

litical Language (New York: Academic Press, 1977); and *Constructing the Political Spectacle* (Chicago: University of Chicago Press, 1988).

4. Edelman, *Political Language,* 141–55.

5. Edelman, *Politics as Symbolic Action,* 1–30.

6. Edelman, *Constructing the Political Spectacle,* 12–36; see also Nancy Fraser, *Unruly Practices: Power, Discourse, and Gender in Contemporary Social Theory* (Minneapolis: University of Minnesota Press, 1989).

7. See Timothy Smeeding, Michael O'Higgins, and Lee Rainwater, *Poverty, Income Distribution and Comparative Perspective: The Luxembourg Income Study* (Washington, D.C.: Urban Institute Press, 1990). This work provides a recent comparison showing that the United States provides far less in public assistance than do other Western industrialized countries.

8. Deborah A. Stone, *Policy Paradox and Political Reason* (Boston: HarperCollins, 1988), 208–310.

9. Ibid., 106.

10. Ibid., 106–65; see also Michael J. Shapiro, *The Politics of Representation: Writing Practices in Biography, Photography, and Policy Analysis* (Madison: University of Wisconsin Press, 1987), 24.

11. Stone, *Policy Paradox and Political Reason,* 127–46.

12. Frances Fox Piven and Richard A. Cloward, *Regulating the Poor: The Functions of Public Welfare,* updated ed. (New York: Pantheon, 1993), xii.

13. See Frances Fox Piven and Richard A. Cloward, *The New Class War* (New York: Pantheon, 1982), 32–39; James O'Connor, *The Fiscal Crisis of the State* (New York: St. Martin's, 1973).

14. See Frances Fox Piven and Richard A. Cloward, "The Contemporary Relief Debate," in *The Mean Season: The Attack on the Welfare State,* ed. Fred Block, Richard A. Cloward, Barbara Ehrenreich, and Frances Fox Piven (New York: Pantheon, 1987), 85–101.

15. See R. Steven Daniels, "A Matter of Fairness: The Adequacy and Equity of Urban General Assistance," paper presented at the annual meeting of the American Political Science Association, Atlanta, Georgia, September 2, 1989.

16. See the essays in Linda Gordon, ed., *Women, the State, and Welfare* (Madison: University of Wisconsin Press, 1990).

17. Virginia Sapiro, "The Gender Basis of American Social Policy," in *Women, the State, and Welfare,* ed. Linda Gordon (Madison: University of Wisconsin Press, 1990), 44.

18. Fraser, *Unruly Practices,* 155.

19. See Linda Gordon, "What Does Welfare Regulate?" *Social Research* 55 (Winter 1988): 609–30; Linda Gordon, "Single Mothers and Child Neglect, 1880–1920," *American Quarterly* 37 (Summer 1985): 173–92.

20. See Fraser, *Unruly Practices,* 152–53. For another argument on behalf of the concept of "family wage," see Jean Bethke Elshtain, *Power Trips and Other Journeys* (Madison: University of Wisconsin Press, 1991), 61–72.

21. See Gwendolyn Mink, "The Lady and the Tramp: Gender, Race, and the Origins of the American Welfare State," in *Women, the State, and Welfare,* ed. Linda Gordon (Madison: University of Wisconsin Press, 1990), 92–122.

22. See Carol B. Stack, *All Our Kin: Strategies for Survival in a Black Community* (New York: Harper & Row, 1974).

23. See Michael B. Katz, *The Undeserving Poor: From the War on Poverty to the War on Welfare* (New York: Pantheon, 1989), 236–39.

24. See Lisa Peattie and Martin Rein, *Women's Claims: A Study in Political Economy* (New York: Oxford University Press, 1983), 9.

25. Joel F. Handler and Yeheskel Hasenfeld, *The Moral Construction of Poverty: Welfare Reform in America* (Newbury Park, Calif.: Sage, 1991), 11.

26. In her richly detailed, if insufficiently reflective, history of the origins of the welfare state, Theda Skocpol suggests that "soldiers" and "mothers" operated as positive symbols to legitimate the extension in the late nineteenth century of Civil War pensions and in the early twentieth century of mothers' pensions. Skocpol not only minimizes the extent to which these two programs, particularly mothers' pensions, provided minimal benefits in often unreliable ways, she also neglects how the militaristic chauvinism of "soldiers" and the separate-sphere maternalism of "mothers" operated as hegemonic influences that marginalized those who sought assistance on other terms. See Theda Skocpol, *Protecting Soldiers and Mothers: The Political Origins of Social Policy in the United States* (Cambridge: Harvard University Press, Belknap Press, 1992).

27. Welfare therefore is both a form of "social control" and a potential source of empowerment for poor families. See Frances Fox Piven, "Ideology and the State: Women, Power, and the Welfare State," in *Women, the State, and Welfare*, ed. Linda Gordon (Madison: University of Wisconsin Press, 1990), 250–64.

28. Katz, *The Undeserving Poor*, 9–35.

29. For an examination of how foreign policy, just as much as domestic policy, is implicated in the construction of identity for Americans, see David Campbell, *Writing Security: United States Foreign Policy and the Politics of Identity* (Minneapolis: University of Minnesota Press, 1992).

30. See Fraser, *Unruly Practices*, 161–83; Katz, *The Undeserving Poor*, 236–39.

31. For instance, see Michael Novak, *The New Consensus on Family and Welfare* (Washington, D.C.: American Enterprise Institute for Public Policy Research, 1987).

32. Michel Foucault has emphasized that the "art of government" in the modern age involves coordinating exchanges among individuals by inculcating a self of sense predisposed to accept the insistences of such an order. See Michel Foucault, "Governmentality," in *The Foucault Effect: Studies in Governmentality*, ed. Graham Burchell, Colin Gordon, and Peter Miller (Chicago: University of Chicago Press, 1991), 87–104; Michel Foucault, "Afterword: The Subject and Power," in *Michel Foucault: Beyond Structuralism and Hermeneutics*, ed. Hubert L. Dreyfus and Paul Rabinow (Chicago: University of Chicago Press, 1982), 214–15. On welfare narratives, see Nancy Fraser and Linda Gordon, "A Genealogy of *Dependency*: Tracing a Keyword of the U.S. Welfare State," *Signs* 19 (Winter 1994): 309–33.

33. See Fred Block, *Postindustrial Possibilities: A Critique of Economic Discourse* (Berkeley: University of California Press, 1990).

34. Fraser, *Unruly Practices*, 149.

35. See Diana Pearce, "Welfare Is *Not* for Women: Why the War on Poverty Cannot Conquer the Feminization of Poverty," in *Women, the State, and Welfare*, ed. Linda Gordon (Madison: University of Wisconsin Press, 1990), 265–79.

36. See Teresa L. Amott, "Black Women and AFDC: Making Entitlement Out of Necessity," in *Women, the State, and Welfare*, ed. Linda Gordon (Madison: University of Wisconsin Press, 1990), 280–98.

37. See, for example, Charles Murray, *Losing Ground: American Social Policy, 1950–1980* (New York: Basic Books, 1984), 124–34.

38. See William Julius Wilson and Kathryn M. Neckerman, "Poverty and Family Structure: The Widening Gap between Evidence and Public Policy Issues," in *Fighting Poverty: What Works and What Doesn't*, ed. Sheldon H. Danziger and Daniel H. Weinberg (Cambridge: Harvard University Press, 1986), 232–59.

39. For the argument that the prevailing perspective grounded in a commitment to the work ethic marginalizes a care ethic and evaluates women on welfare as unproductive and

irresponsible, see Joan Tronto, *Moral Boundaries: A Political Argument for an Ethic of Care* (New York: Routledge, 1993), 165–66.

40. See Robert D. Reischauer, "Welfare Reform: Will Consensus Be Enough?" *Brookings Review* (Summer 1988): 3–8.

41. For an interpretation that suggests the Family Support Act is based on compromises that produce modest, incremental reform, see Theodore R. Marmor, Jerry L. Mashaw, and Philip Harvey, *America's Misunderstood Welfare State: Persistent Myths, Enduring Realities* (New York: Basic Books, 1990), 231–37.

42. Lawrence Mead, "Principles for Welfare Reform," testimony before the U.S. Senate Finance Committee, Subcommittee on Social Security and Family Policy, February 23, 1987.

43. Irwin Garfinkel, "Welfare: Reform or Replacement: Child Support Enforcement," testimony before the U.S. Senate Committee on Finance, Subcommittee on Social Security and Family Policy, February 20, 1987.

44. See Irwin Garfinkel and Sara S. McLanahan, *Single Mothers and Their Children* (Washington, D.C.: Urban Institute Press, 1987), 181–83.

45. Laurence E. Lynn Jr., "Ending Welfare Reform as We Know It," *The American Prospect* 15 (Fall 1993): 90.

46. For critical reviews of how interpretations of research helped forge the "new consensus," see Piven and Cloward, "The Contemporary Relief Debate," 45–108; Katz, *The Undeserving Poor*, 185–235.

47. See Mary Jo Bane and David T. Ellwood, "The Dynamics of Dependence: Routes to Self-Sufficiency," unpublished report supported by U.S. Department of Health and Human Services grant no. HHS-100–82–0038, John F. Kennedy School of Government, 1983. Earlier studies most often emphasized that the vast majority of recipients received welfare for short periods of time (e.g., less than two years); see Greg Duncan et al., *Years of Poverty, Years of Plenty* (Ann Arbor: University of Michigan, Institute for Social Research, 1983).

48. Piven and Cloward, "The Contemporary Relief Debate," 64.

49. Reischauer, "Welfare Reform," 3–8. For analysis of persistent tensions in the consensus over welfare, see Irene Lurie and Mary Bryna Sanger, "The Family Support Act: Defining the Social Contract in New York," *Social Service Review* 65 (March 1991): 43–67; Mary Bryna Sanger, "The Inherent Contradiction of Welfare Reform," *Policy Studies Journal* 18 (Spring 1990): 664–80.

50. See Sanford F. Schram and Theresa Funiciello, "Post-mortem on the Deterioration of the Welfare Grant," in *The Reconstruction of Family Policy*, ed. Elaine A. Anderson and Richard C. Hula, (Westport, Conn.: Greenwood, 1991), 211–27.

51. Julie Kosterlitz, "The Devil in the Details," *National Journal*, December 12, 1989, 2942–46.

52. Erica B. Baum, "When the Witch Doctors Agree: The Family Support Act and Social Science Research," *Journal of Policy Analysis and Management* 10 (Fall 1991): 603–15; see also Richard P. Nathan, *Social Science and Government: Uses and Misuses* (New York: Basic Books, 1988), 97–121.

53. Ron Haskins, "Congress Writes a Law: Research and Welfare Reform," *Journal of Policy Analysis and Management* 10 (Fall 1991): 616–33.

54. See Joseph Gusfield, *The Culture of Public Problems: Drinking-Driving and the Symbolic Order* (Chicago: University of Chicago Press, 1984), 186–95.

55. Sanford F. Schram and Michael Wiseman, "Should Families Be Protected from AFDC-UP?" discussion paper no. 860-88, Institute for Research on Poverty, Madison, Wis., 1988.

56. See, for example, Harrell R. Rodgers, *Poor Women, Poor Families: The Economic Plight of America's Female-Headed Households* (Armonk, N.Y.: M. E. Sharpe, 1987), 82–83.

57. See John H. Bishop, "Jobs, Cash Transfers, and Marital Instability: A Review and Synthesis of the Evidence," *Journal of Human Resources* 15 (Fall 1980): 301–34; Gilbert Steiner, *The Futility of Family Policy* (Washington, D.C.: Brookings Institution, 1981), 103–4.

58. For a review of these claims, see Schram and Wiseman, "Should Families Be Protected from AFDC-UP?"

59. Piven and Cloward, "The Contemporary Relief Debate," 97.

60. A short questionnaire regarding implementation of the JOBS program was sent to all fifty states and the District of Columbia. Thirty states completed and returned the questionnaire, and twenty of these states, plus one other one, sent copies of their state plans.

61. Center on Social Welfare Policy and Law, *An Explanation of the Federal Rules Governing the Determination of Financial Eligibility for AFDC and the AFDC Payment Amount* (New York: Center on Social Welfare Policy and Law, February 1989).

62. Irwin Garfinkel and Marieka Klawitter, "The Effect of Routine Income Withholding of Child Support Collections," *Journal of Policy Analysis and Management* 9 (Spring 1990): 155–77.

63. See Piven and Cloward, *Regulating the Poor;* Katz, *The Undeserving Poor;* Michael B. Katz, *In the Shadow of the Poorhouse: A Social History of Welfare in America* (New York: Basic Books, 1986); Walter I. Trattner, *From Poor Law to Welfare State* (New York: Free Press, 1979).

64. See Sanford F. Schram, "The Myth of Workfare," *Catalyst* 4 (1982): 49–60.

65. Lawrence M. Mead, "Should Welfare Be Mandatory? What Research Says," *Journal of Policy Analysis and Management* 9 (Summer 1990): 400–404.

66. Lawrence M. Mead, *Beyond Entitlement: The Social Obligations of Citizenship* (New York: Free Press, 1986); Lawrence M. Mead, "The Potential for Work Enforcement: A Study of WIN," *Journal of Policy Analysis and Management* 7 (Spring 1988): 264–88; Wiseman, "Workfare and Welfare Policy," 1–8.

67. U.S. General Accounting Office, *Work and Welfare: Current AFDC Work Programs and Implications for Federal Policy* (Washington, D.C.: U.S. Government Printing Office, 1987); Kathryn H. Porter, *Making JOBS Work* (Washington, D.C.: Center on Budget and Policy Priorities, March 1990).

68. U.S. General Accounting Office, *Work and Welfare,* 3.

69. Porter, *Making JOBS Work,* 53–55.

70. Fred Block and John Noakes, "The Politics of New-Style Workfare," *Socialist Review* 18 (July–September 1988): 31–60.

71. Kathryn Edin and Christopher Jencks, "Reforming Welfare," in Christopher Jencks, *Rethinking Social Policy: Race, Poverty, and the Underclass* (Cambridge: Harvard University Press, 1992), 204–35.

72. See Mead, "The Potential for Work Enforcement," 264–88, *Beyond Entitlement,* ch. 7.

73. See Porter, *Making JOBS Work,* 53–55.

74. Unpublished preliminary data from the U.S. Department of Health and Human Services, Office of Family Assistance, Administration for Children and Families, May 20, 1991.

75. For initial reports on these developments, see Jason DeParle, "Fueled by Social Trends, Welfare Cases Are Rising," *New York Times,* January 10, 1992, A1.

76. See ibid. DeParle quotes Charles Murray as suggesting that he was correct in his original prediction that the 1988 reforms would "backfire" and only make welfare more attractive. Murray's prediction appeared in the *Wall Street Journal* the very day President Ronald Reagan signed the Family Support Act into law. See Murray, "New Welfare Bill," A22. For a criticism of Murray's perspective that puts its faith in workfare, see Nathan, *Turning Promises into Performance.*

77. For more on this development, see chapter 9, see also Adele M. Blong and Barbara Leyser, *Living at the Bottom: An Analysis of AFDC Benefit Levels,* publication no. 210 (New York: Center on Social Welfare Policy and Law, 1993).

78. See Margaret Weir, Ann Shola Orloff, and Theda Skocpol, eds., *The Politics of Social Policy in the United States* (Princeton, N.J.: Princeton University Press, 1988), 25–27.

79. Peter Marcuse, "Neutralizing Homelessness," *Socialist Review* 18 (January–March 1988): 69–96.

80. The self-defeating character of categorical work programs probably more than anything else explains why with program enhancements there is a rise in the welfare rolls. Robert Moffitt and Michael Wiseman both suggest as much when they say that there are "entry" as well as "exit" effects to workfare programs. See Robert A. Moffitt, "The Effect of Work and Training Programs on Entry and Exit from the Welfare Caseload," discussion paper no. 1025-93, Institute for Research on Poverty, Madison, Wis., 1993; Jason DeParle, "Change in Welfare Is Likely to Need Big Jobs Program," *New York Times,* January 30, 1994, A1, A8.

81. For a discussion of the failure of specialized, particularistic social policies as opposed to more universalistic social insurance programs, see Theda Skocpol, "Sustainable Social Policy: Fighting Poverty without Poverty Programs," *The American Prospect* 2 (Summer 1990): 58–70. For arguments on the political value of targeted, especially in-kind, benefit programs, see Robert Greenstein, "Universal and Targeted Approaches to Relieving Poverty: An Alternative View," in *The Urban Underclass,* ed. Christopher Jencks and Paul Peterson (Washington, D.C.: Brookings Institution, 1991), 437–59. For the workfare argument that, given the U.S. political culture, neither universal nor targeted programs will be legitimate unless tied to work, see Mickey Kaus, *The End of Equality* (New York: Basic Books, 1992), 270.

82. See Wendy Sarvasy, "Reagan and Low-Income Mothers: A Feminist Recasting of the Debate," in *Remaking the Welfare State: Retrenchment and Social Policy in America,* ed. Michael K. Brown (Philadelphia: Temple University Press, 1988), 253–76.

83. For a critique of the therapeutic character of U.S. social policy, see Andrew Polsky, *The Therapeutic State* (Princeton, N.J.: Princeton University Press, 1991). For a defense of this approach, see Lawrence M. Mead, "The New Politics of the New Poverty," *Public Interest,* 103 (Spring 1991): 3–20.

84. See Lawrence M. Mead and William J. Wilson, "The Obligation to Work and the Availability of Jobs: A Dialogue between Lawrence M. Mead and William J. Wilson," *Focus* 10 (Summer 1987): 11–20.

85. See Ruth L. Smith, "Order and Disorder: The Naturalization of Poverty," *Cultural Critique* (Winter 1989–90): 209–229.

86. The tendency for reformers to claim that their proposals are grounded in research when that claim is open to contestation was relived recently when David Ellwood testified before a skeptical Representative Robert Matsui (D-Calif.) about the Clinton proposal to limit the receipt of public assistance to two years. See "Welfare Debate: Insults, Attacks, and Accusation," *Minneapolis Star-Tribune,* July 31, 1994, 2A.

8. The Feminization of Poverty: From Statistical Artifact to Established Policy

1. Susan Faludi, *Backlash: The Undeclared War against American Women* (New York: Crown, 1991).

2. Barbara Dafoe Whitehead, "Dan Quayle Was Right," *Atlantic,* April 1993, 47–84.

3. For analysis of how propagandizing the two-parent family accentuates the post-World War II boom in the nuclear family to the neglect of how that was an exceptional countertrend of the past 150 years, see Stephanie Coontz, *The Way We Never Were: Family and the Nostalgia Trap* (New York: Basic Books, 1993).

4. See Charles Murray, "The Coming White Underclass," *Wall Street Journal,* October 29, 1993, A14; Charles Murray, *Losing Ground: American Social Policy* (New York: Basic Books, 1984).

5. E. E. Schattschneider, *Politics, Pressure and the Tariff* (Englewood Cliffs, N.J.: Prentice Hall, 1935); Aaron Wildavsky, *Speaking Truth to Power: The Art and Craft of Policy Analy-*

sis (Boston: Little, Brown, 1979), 62–83; Margaret Weir, *Politics and Jobs: The Boundaries of Employment Policy in the United States* (Princeton, N.J.: Princeton University Press, 1992), 19–26; Frances Fox Piven," Reforming the Welfare State," *Socialist Review* 22 (July–September, 1992): 78. A similar point is made by Theda Skocpol in *Protecting Soldiers and Mothers: The Political Origins of Social Policy in the United States* (Cambridge: Harvard University Press, Belknap Press, 1992), 58: "We must make social policies the starting points as well as the end points of analysis. As politics creates policies, policies also remake politics."

6. For discussion on this issue, see Mary Hawkesworth, *Theoretical Issues in Policy Analysis* (Albany: State University of New York Press, 1988), 190–94; Deborah A. Stone, *Policy Paradox and Political Reason* (Boston: HarperCollins, 1988), 4–10.

7. See Stone, *Policy Paradox and Political Reason*, 106–206; Murray Edelman, *Constructing the Political Spectacle* (Chicago: University of Chicago Press, 1988); Murray Edelman, *Political Language: Words That Succeed and Policies That Fail* (New York: Academic Press, 1977).

8. Anne Schneider and Helen Ingram, "Social Construction of Target Populations: Implications for Politics and Policy," *American Political Science Review*, 87 (June 1993): 334.

9. Nancy Fraser, *Unruly Practices: Power, Discourse, and Gender in Contemporary Social Theory* (Minneapolis: University of Minnesota Press, 1989), 149–53.

10. See Diana Pearce, "Welfare Is *Not* for Women: Why the War on Poverty Cannot Conquer the Feminization of Poverty," in *Women, the State, and Welfare*, ed. Linda Gordon (Madison: University of Wisconsin Press, 1990), 265–79; Maxine Baca Zinn, "Family, Race, and Poverty in the Eighties," *Signs*, 14 (1989): 856–74.

11. Frances Fox Piven and Richard A. Cloward, "The Contemporary Relief Debate," in *The Mean Season: The Attack on the Welfare State*, ed. Fred Block, Richard A. Cloward, Barbara Ehrenreich, and Frances Fox Piven (New York: Pantheon, 1987), 55–57; Teresa L. Amott, "Black Women and AFDC: Making Entitlement Out of Necessity," in *Women, the State, and Welfare*, ed. Linda Gordon (Madison: University of Wisconsin Press, 1990), 280–300.

12. See Christopher Jencks, "Is the American Underclass Growing?" in *The Urban Underclass*, ed. Christopher Jencks and Paul Peterson (Washington, D.C.: Brookings Institution, 1991), 28–100.

13. In particular, see Lawrence M. Mead, *The New Politics of Poverty: The Nonworking Poor in America* (New York: Basic Books, 1992), 7–11.

14. See John E. Schwarz and Thomas J. Volgy, *The Forgotten Americans: Thirty Million Working Poor in the Land of Opportunity* (New York: W. W. Norton, 1992), 61–71: see also the discussion of this issue in chapter 5.

15. See Whitehead, "Dan Quayle Was Right"; Murray, "The Coming White Underclass."

16. See "Mayor Dixon's Call for Action," *Washington Post*, November 29, 1991, A30.

17. Thomas Byrne Edsall with Mary D. Edsall, *Chain Reaction: The Impact of Race, Rights and Taxes on American Politics* (New York: W. W. Norton, 1991), 256–88.

18. Murray, "The Coming White Underclass."

19. Jencks, "Is the American Underclass Growing?"

20. David J. Eggebeen and Daniel T. Lichter, "Race, Family Structure, and Changing Poverty among American Children," *American Sociological Review* 56(1991): 801–17.

21. Murray, "The Coming White Underclass."

22. Jencks, "Is the American Underclass Growing?"

23. Christopher Jencks, *Rethinking Social Policy: Race, Poverty, and the Underclass* (Cambridge: Harvard University Press, 1992), 189–98.

24. Adolph Reed Jr., "The Underclass as Myth and Symbol: The Poverty of Discourse about Poverty," *Radical America* (January 1992): 34.

25. Philip K. Robins and Paul Fronstin, "Welfare Benefits and Family-Size Decisions of Never-Married Women," discussion paper no. 1022-93, Institute for Research on Poverty,

Madison, Wis., September 1993; For the argument that, relative to the black population over-all (as opposed to the number of nonmarried women of childbearing age), the incidence of births outside marriage (as opposed to the ratio relative to all births) consistently increased from the 1950s through the 1980s, see Charles Murray, "Does Welfare Bring More Babies?" *Public Interest* 115 (Spring 1994): 17–30.

26. Kristin Luker, "Dubious Conceptions: The Controversy over Teen Pregnancy," *The American Prospect* 5 (Spring 1991): 73–83.

27. Arlene T. Geronimus, "Black/White Differences in Women's Reproductive-Related Health Status: Evidence from Vital Statistics," *Demography* 27 (1990): 457–66.

28. Luker, "Dubious Conceptions," 81.

29. See Mike Males, "In Defense of Teenaged Mothers," *The Progressive*, August 1994, 22–23; Mike Males, "Public Policy/Infantile Arguments," *In These Times*, August 9, 1993, 18–20.

30. Luker, "Dubious Conceptions," 81.

31. See Eggebeen and Lichter, "Race, Family Structure, and Changing Poverty."

32. In particular, see Martha Hill, "Trends in the Economic Situation of U.S. Families with Children: 1970–1980," in *American Families and the Economy*, ed. Richard R. Nelson and Felicity Skidmore (Washington, D.C.: National Academy Press, 1983), 9–53; Mary Jo Bane, "Household Composition and Poverty," in *Fighting Poverty: What Works and What Doesn't*, ed. Sheldon H. Danziger and Daniel H. Weinberg (Cambridge: Harvard University Press, 1986), 209–31.

33. See Jencks, "Is the American Underclass Growing?"

34. Donald J. Hernandez, *When Households Continue, Discontinue, and Form*, Studies in Household and Family Formation, Series P-23, no. 179 (Washington, D.C.: U.S. Bureau of the Census, 1993), 2.

35. This point is made by Hernandez and reinforced by Bane, "Household Composition and Poverty."

36. Hernandez, *When Households Continue*, 2.

37. This point is reinforced by Hill, "Trends in the Economic Situation of U.S. Families."

38. Ibid.; see also Bane, "Household Composition and Poverty," 231. For a different finding that indicates that black two-parent families are more likely than one-parent families to leave poverty after one year, see Hernandez, *When Households Continue*, 2–3.

39. See Zinn, "Family, Race, and Poverty."

40. For a literature review, see Chong-Bum An, Robert Haveman, and Barbara Wolfe, "Reducing Teen Out-of-Wedlock Births: The Role of Parental Education and Family Stability," discussion paper 944-91, Institute for Research on Poverty, Madison, Wis., 1991.

41. See William Julius Wilson, "Public Policy Research and the Truly Disadvantaged," in *The Urban Underclass*, ed. Christopher Jencks and Paul Peterson (Washington D.C.: Brookings Institution, 1991), 460–81.

42. See Michael B. Katz, *The Undeserving Poor: From the War on Poverty to the War on Welfare* (New York: Pantheon, 1989), 215–23.

43. Linda Gordon, "Welfare Reform: A History Lesson," *Dissent* (Summer 1994): 323–28; Evelyn Z. Brodkin, "The Making of an Enemy: How Welfare Policies Construct the Poor," *Law and Social Inquiry* 18 (Fall 1993): 647–70. Brodkin is paraphrasing Joel F. Handler and Yeheskel Hasenfeld, *The Moral Construction of Poverty: Welfare Reform in America* (Newbury Park, Calif.: Sage, 1991).

44. See Pearce, "Welfare Is *Not* for Women," 265.

45. Linda Gordon, "What Does Welfare Regulate?" *Social Research* 55 (1988): 609–30.

46. Pearce, "Welfare Is *Not* for Women."

47. See Fraser, *Unruly Practices*, 144–87; Nancy Fraser, "Clintonism, Welfare, and the Antisocial Wage: The Emergence of a Neoliberal Political Imaginary," *Rethinking Marxism* 6 (Spring 1993): 9–23.

48. Gordon, "What Does Welfare Regulate?"

49. Barbara J. Nelson, "The Origins of the Two-Channel Welfare State: Workmen's Compensation and Mothers' Aid," in *Women, the State, and Welfare*, ed. Linda Gordon (Madison: University of Wisconsin Press, 1990), 123–51; Mimi Abramovitz, *Regulating the Lives of Women: Social Welfare Policy from Colonial Times to the Present* (Boston: South End, 1989).

50. Sheldon Danziger and Jonathan Stern, *The Causes and Consequences of Child Poverty in the United States*, research report no. 90-194 (Ann Arbor: University of Michigan, Population Studies Center, 1990).

51. Ibid.

52. See Gordon, "What Does Welfare Regulate?"; Nelson, "The Origins of the Two-Channel Welfare State." For a view that recognizes but de-emphasizes the significance of differences between programs concentrated on female-headed families and male-identified programs, see Skocpol, *Protecting Soldiers and Mothers*, 525–39; Ann S. Orloff, "Gender and the Social Rights of Citizenship: The Comparative Analysis of Gender Relations and Welfare States," *American Sociological Review* 58 (June 1993): 303–28.

53. For a debate over whether welfare was more in service of sexist subordination of women than of capitalist subordination of workers, see Gordon, "What Does Welfare Regulate?"; Frances Fox Piven and Richard A. Cloward, "Welfare Doesn't Shore Up Traditional Family Roles: A Reply to Linda Gordon," *Social Research* 55 (Winter 1988): 631–45.

54. For a summation of a convincing analysis of how the federalization of welfare programs since the New Deal has served to construct welfare recipients as second-class citizens, see Linda Gordon, *Pitied but Not Entitled: Single Mothers and the History of Welfare* (New York: Free Press, 1994), 293–306.

55. See Joan Tronto, *Moral Boundaries: A Political Argument for an Ethic of Care* (New York: Routledge, 1993), 165–66. Tronto argues that the breadwinner system of a family wage is premised on the work ethic in a way that marginalizes the care ethic so as to devalue women's responsibility, competence, and productivity as members of society.

56. See, for instance, Murray, "The Coming White Underclass."

57. See Susan L.Thomas, "From the Culture of Poverty to the Culture of Single Motherhood: A New Poverty Paradigm," paper prepared for the annual meeting of the Western Political Science Association, San Francisco, March 19–22, 1992.

58. There has been what seems to be growing acceptance of the calls by Charles Murray for the outright abolition of public assistance. The increased interest in the Clinton two-year time limit for receipt of welfare is one indicator. See Murray, "The Coming White Underclass." Wisconsin has adopted legislation calling for the abolition of public assistance by 1999. For a polemic on behalf of this legislation from Charles Murray of Wisconsin, see Charles J. Sykes, "Good Reasons to Kill Welfare," *Isthmus*, December 3, 1993, 12.

59. See William E. Connolly, *Identity\Difference: Democratic Negotiations of Political Paradox* (Ithaca, N.Y.: Cornell University Press, 1991), 206–10.

60. Improvements in child support collection and a growing interest in getting unemployed noncustodial parents into work programs, including the nationwide experimental project Parents' Fair Share, are laudable developments that should not be overrated. Many poor absent fathers lack not only employment but the skills that would enable them to get jobs that would provide enough child support to remove their families from welfare. See Jean Hopfensperger, "Anoka, Dakota Counties Target 'Welfare Dads' in New Jobs Program," *Minneapolis Star Tribune*, March 21, 1994, 1A, 7A. For a plan to replace welfare with an assured child support system that routinely collects child support payments, works to improve the

earnings of noncustodial parents, and supplements support payments of the low-income with government assistance, see Irwin Garfinkel, *Assuring Child Support: An Extension of Social Security* (New York: Russell Sage Foundation, 1992).

61. For analyses of how treating women the same and treating them differently — providing equality *and* protection, in the parlance of social policy — are not mutually exclusive and can be combined in ways that protect women against risks special to them as equally as men are insured by the state, see Wendy Sarvasy, "Postsuffrage Feminism, Citizenship, and the Quest for a Feminist Welfare State," *Signs* 17 (Summer 1992): 329–62; Orloff, "Gender and the Social Rights of Citizenship," 322–24.

62. It is interesting that the extent to which welfare taking is associated with women's attempts to escape abusive relationships remains a phenomenon rarely studied by welfare analysts. This suggests that welfare analysis most often at least implicitly invokes a gendered conception of citizenship that relegates welfare to that status of something less than an entitlement. Correspondingly, welfare taking is not affirmed as an attempt to act responsibly. Seeing welfare as a women's resource that enables them to act publicly to redress private problems would put welfare taking in a different light. See Sarvasy, "Postsuffrage Feminism"; Orloff, "Gender and the Social Rights of Citizenship"; Kathleen Jones, "Citizenship in a Woman-Friendly Polity," *Signs* 15 (Fall 1990): 781–812; Linda Gordon, "The New Feminist Scholarship on the Welfare State," in *Women, the State, and Welfare*, ed. Linda Gordon (Madison: University of Wisconsin Press, 1990), 26–30.

63. See Tronto, *Moral Boundaries*, 165–66. Tronto argues that the ascendant work ethic's emphasis on independence evaluates welfare taking as a dependency, whereas an alternative care ethic's emphasis on interdependence recognizes welfare taking as an attempt to fulfill responsibilities to care for others under difficult circumstances. In addition, a care ethic's emphasis on interdependence recognizes that poverty is a community problem, not an individual problem, and that concentrating on individual behavior to the neglect of creating a supportive community with sufficient economic opportunities will lead to failed welfare policies.

9. Waltzing with the Rapper: Industrial Welfare Policy Meets Postindustrial Poverty

1. See Daniel Patrick Moynihan, "Toward a Postindustrial Social Policy," *Public Interest* 96 (Summer 1989): 16–27. For a historically informed critique of Moynihan's attempt to make "dependency" into a central pathology of postindustrialism, see Nancy Fraser and Linda Gordon, "A Genealogy of *Dependency*: Tracing a Keyword of the U.S. Welfare State," *Signs* 19 (Winter 1994): 309–36.

2. See Richard L. Berke, "Moynihan Makes Public Example of His 'Student': Clinton," *Minneapolis Star-Tribune*, January 17, 1993, 4A.

3. Like all denial, "postindustrial social policy" denies reality in multiple ways. It denies the commonality between what it has identified and the "other" from which it is distinguished. *New* postindustrial social policy denies the extent to which it perpetuates the *old* stigmatization of welfare taking. It also denies how "dependency" shares much with its alleged opposite — "self-sufficiency." Like all claims about what is real, it additionally denies how "dependency" is an effect of discursive practices rather than a condition of their possibility. On denial in discourse, see Jacques Derrida, *Of Grammatology*, trans. by Gayatri Chakravorty Spivak (Baltimore: Johns Hopkins University Press, 1974), 141–64.

4. For an examination of how discursive practices in policy help constitute the ostensibly pregiven reality against which they are directed, see David Campbell, *Writing Security: United States Foreign Policy and the Politics of Identity* (Minneapolis: University of Minnesota Press, 1992), 18. Campbell notes that the "danger" addressed in foreign policy is an "effect of political practices rather than the condition of their possibility." The same could be said of "depen-

dency" — that it is an "effect" of policy discourse more than a preexisting reality that can be assumed to be given as a ready-standing reservoir of deleterious behavior in need of eradication.

5. As an enactment of a culture in denial, postindustrial social policy is an exemplary instance of public policy "written under erasure." It cancels its own signifier. The phrase is from Derrida, *Of Grammatology*, 43, and suggests how terms imply their opposite. Postindustrial social policy's emphasis on "self-sufficiency" implies the extent to which individuals in the deindustrializing United States of postindustrialism cannot be expected to be self-sufficient just by taking manual jobs as much as before, no matter how much the discourse of postindustrial social policy insists. Denial here involves resisting the extent to which the "self-sufficient" are dependent upon the state to ensure their economic security in the postindustrial era. This is a denial that conveniently reinforces "self-sufficiency" as a coherent identity and thereby allows the state to claim that welfare recipients are the "other" — (in this case) "dependents" when both welfare recipients and workers both are highly dependent upon the state to ensure their self-sufficiency.

6. For an analysis of how "the 'able-bodied poor' present a 'moral dilemma' to the modern state because their mere existence poses a threat to the legitimacy of the economic and civic order" (p. 654), see Evelyn Z. Brodkin, "The Making of an Enemy: How Welfare Policies Construct the Poor," *Law and Social Inquiry* 18 (Fall 1993): 647–70. Brodkin is paraphrasing Joel F. Handler and Yeheskel Hasenfeld, *The Moral Construction of Poverty: Welfare Reform in America* (Newbury Park, Calif.: Sage, 1991), 7.

7. See Douglas J. Besharov with Amy A. Fowler, "The End of Welfare as We Know It?" *Public Interest* 111 (Spring 1993): 95–108; Jason DeParle, "Momentum Builds for Cutting Back Welfare System," *New York Times*, November 13, 1994, 1.

8. Even critical commentary that makes many other good points sometimes risks idealizing postindustrialism. See Fred Block, *Postindustrial Possibilities: A Critique of Economic Discourse* (Berkeley: University of California Press, 1990), 189–218.

9. Frances Fox Piven and Richard A. Cloward, *Regulating the Poor: The Functions of Public Welfare*, updated ed. (New York: Vintage, 1993), 344–65.

10. See David Wessel and Daniel Benjamin, "In Employment Policy, America and Europe Make Sharp Contrast: U.S. Spawns Jobs, but Often Ill-Paid; Germany Offers High Pay, Few Openings," *Wall Street Journal*, March 14, 1994, 1.

11. Barry Bluestone and Bennett Harrison, *The Deindustrialization of America* (New York: Basic Books, 1982); Thomas Ferguson and Joel Rogers, *Right-Turn* (New York: Pantheon, 1986); Piven and Cloward, *Regulating the Poor*, 344–65.

12. Doug Henwood, "Clinton and the Austerity Cops," *The Nation*, November 23, 1992, 628.

13. John E. Schwarz and Thomas J. Volgy, *The Forgotten Americans: Thirty Million Working Poor in the Land of Opportunity* (New York: W.W. Norton, 1992), 70.

14. Laurence Lynn Jr., "Ending Welfare Reform as We Know It," *The American Prospect* 15 (Fall 1993), 86–88.

15. Block, *Postindustrial Possibilities*, 189–218.

16. See Jeremy Brecher, "After NAFTA: Global Village or Global Pillage?" *The Nation*, December 6, 1993, 685–88. For specifics on how NAFTA legitimates corporate restructuring in a global context of capital mobility, see Elaine Bernard, "What's Wrong with NAFTA," *New Politics* (Winter 1994): 80–90.

17. Stanley Aronowitz, *The Politics of Identity: Class, Culture, Social Movements* (New York: Routledge, 1992), 225–52; Herbert J. Gans, "Scholars' Role in Planning a 'Post-Work Society,'" *Chronicle of Higher Education*, June 9, 1993, B3. For the idea that centrality of the work ethic displaces the care ethic and devalues other forms of responsibility, competence, and productivity, see Joan Tronto, *Moral Boundaries: A Political Argument for an Ethic of Care* (New York: Routledge, 1993), 165–66.

18. For a report on how Europeans, particularly the Germans and French, who already have a shorter work week on average than U.S. workers, are seriously discussing shorter work hours as a postindustrial necessity, see Roger Cohen, "Europeans Consider Shortening Workweek to Relieve Joblessness," *New York Times,* November 22, 1993, A1

19. The phrase "postindustrial economy of limited choice" comes from Jerome Skolnick, "Gangs in the Postindustrial Ghetto," *The American Prospect* 8 (Winter 1992): 109–20.

20. See Herbert J. Gans, *People, Plans, and Policies: Poverty, Racism, and Other National Urban Problems* (New York: Columbia University Press, 1991).

21. See Center on Social Welfare Policy and Law, *Living at the Bottom: An Analysis of AFDC Benefit Levels,* publication no. 210 (New York: Center on Social Welfare Policy and Law, 1993).

22. Schwarz and Volgy, *The Forgotten Americans,* 133.

23. Jason DeParle, "Whither on Welfare: Even Though They Please Moynihan, Clinton's Actions Are Far from Bold," *New York Times,* February 3, 1993, A9; and DeParle, "Momentum Builds for Cutting Back Welfare System," 1.

24. Paul E. Peterson and Mark C. Rom, *Welfare Magnets: A New Case for a National Standard* (Washington, D.C.: Brookings Institution, 1990), 50–83.

25. See Robert B. Moffitt, "Has State Redistribution Policy Grown More Conservative?" *National Tax Journal* 43 (Summer 1990): 123–42.

26. See Center on Social Welfare Policy and Law, *1991 State Budgets and Welfare: A Bad Year for the Poor* (Washington, D.C.: Center on Social Welfare Policy and Law, 1991), 3.

27. See Center on Social Welfare Policy and Law, *Living at the Bottom,* 21–26.

28. Charles Murray claims that benefits have declined from highs in the early 1970s but remain well above the real value of benefits in the 1960s. Yet he includes estimates of housing subsidies for AFDC recipients along with AFDC, food stamps, and Medicaid while failing to mention that only about one-fifth of AFDC families receive housing subsidies. See Charles Murray, "Does Welfare Bring More Babies?" *Public Interest* 115 (Spring 1994): 17–30. See also Robert Moffitt, "Incentive Effects of the U.S. Welfare System: A Review," *Journal of Economic Literature* 30 (March 1992): 5; U.S. House of Representatives, Committee on Ways and Means, *Background Material and Data on Programs within the Jurisdiction of the Committee on Ways and Means* (Washington, D.C.: U.S. Government Printing Office, 1989), 570.

29. See Christopher Jencks, *The Homeless* (Cambridge: Harvard University Press, 1994), 95; Moffitt, "Incentive Effects," 5.

30. See Richard Nathan, *Turning Promises into Performance: The Management Challenge of Implementing Workfare* (New York: Columbia University Press, 1993), 3–5; Center on Social Welfare Policy and Law, *The Rush to Reform* (Washington, D.C.: Center on Social Welfare Policy and Law, November 7, 1993).

31. For a survey of state waivers, see Michael Wiseman, "Welfare Reform in the States: The Bush Legacy," *Focus* 15 (Spring 1993): 18–36.

32. See Center on Social Welfare Policy and Law, *Living at the Bottom,* 4.

33. For a survey of state efforts on programs to promote the use of Norplant, see Martha F. Davis, *The New Eugenics: A Legal and Policy Analysis of State Proposals to Control Poor Women's Reproduction through Norplant* (New York: NOW Legal Defense and Education Fund, April 1993).

34. Center on Social Welfare Policy and Law, *The Rush to Reform.*

35. Sheldon Danziger and Jonathan Stern, *The Causes and Consequences of Child Poverty in the United States,* research report no. 90-194, (Ann Arbor: University of Michigan, Population Studies Center, 1990).

36. See John Karl Scholz, "The Earned Income Tax Credit: Participation, Compliance,

and Antipoverty Effectiveness," discussion paper no. 1020-93, Institute for Research on Poverty, Madison, Wis., 1993.

37. See John Karl Scholz, "Tax Policy and the Working Poor: The Earned Income Tax Credit," Focus 15 (Winter 1993–94): 1–12.

38. Lynn, "Ending Welfare Reform as We Know It," 83–92.

39. David T. Ellwood, Poor Support: Poverty in the American Family (New York: Basic Books, 1988), 236–41.

40. Theda Skocpol, "Sustainable Social Policy: Fighting Poverty without Poverty Programs," The American Prospect 1, no. 3 (1990): 58–70.

41. For an example, see Thomas Byrne Edsall with Mary D. Edsall, Chain Reaction: The Impact of Race, Rights and Taxes on American Politics (New York: W. W. Norton, 1991). For criticism of this perspective, see Richard A. Cloward and Frances Fox Piven, "Race and the Democrats," The Nation, December 9, 1991, 737–40; Robert Greenstein, "Universal and Targeted Approaches to Relieving Poverty: An Alternative View," in The Urban Underclass, ed. Christopher Jencks and Paul Peterson (Washington, D.C.: Brookings Institution, 1991), 437–59.

42. See Lawrence M. Mead, The New Politics of Poverty: The Nonworking Poor in America (New York: Basic Books, 1992); Charles Murray, "The Coming White Underclass," Wall Street Journal, October 29, 1993, A14; Charles Murray, Losing Ground: American Social Policy 1950–1980 (New York: Basic Books, 1984).

43. Katharine G. Abraham, "Structural/Frictional vs. Deficient Demand Unemployment: Some New Evidence," American Economic Review 73 (1983): 708–24.

44. The primary proponent of this view is Lawrence Mead. See The New Politics of Poverty, 252–61.

45. Schwarz and Volgy, The Forgotten Americans, 92–106.

46. Fraser and Gordon, "A Genealogy of Dependency," 311.

47. Nancy Fraser, "Clintonism, Welfare, and the Antisocial Wage: The Emergence of a Neoliberal Political Imaginary," Rethinking Marxism 6 (Spring 1993): 9–23.

48. Ibid. Fraser has identified six points on which any political imaginary might differ when it comes to social policy. First is commitment to the "social wage," or the idea that the state has an obligation to ensure all individuals and families access to resources that will enable them to make lives for themselves. Second is the distinction between "commodities" provided through the market and "public goods" provided through the state. Third is the distinction between "contract," which implies one has earned benefits and is contractually due them, and "charity," which implies that any benefits one gets are a handout. Fourth is the distinction between "independence" and "dependence," with the receipt of selected government benefits implying that one is not independent and the receipt of other benefits not implying that stigma. Fifth is the idea that ensuring rights to "entitlements" in the form of government benefits has been overemphasized, and it is now time to enforce "obligations" that are allegedly entailed when one receives such entitlements. Sixth is the idea of "mutual responsibility," or the notion that the individual and the community have reciprocal responsibilities toward each other—the community is committed to ensuring all of its members access to the resources needed to create the "capacity" to participate in society, and the individual in return must exhibit the "competence" that is assumed of well-functioning members of the society.

49. See Barbara J. Nelson, "The Origins of the Two-Channel Welfare State: Workmen's Compensation and Mother's Aid," in Women, the State, and Welfare, ed. Linda Gordon (Madison: University of Wisconsin Press, 1990), 123–51.

50. Mead, The New Politics of Poverty, 259–61.

51. See Isaac Shapiro and Robert Greenstein, *Making Work Pay: The Unfinished Agenda* (Washington, D.C.: Center on Budget and Policy Priorities, May 1993), 19; Wendell Primus, "The Clinton Administration and Child Support," paper presented at the 1993 Summer Workshop on Low-Income Populations, Institute for Research on Poverty, University of Wisconsin-Madison, June 25, 1993; "Welfare Reform Sure to Add Zeros to Budget," *Minneapolis Star Tribune,* January 27, 1994, 7A. See also Besharov, "The End of Welfare as We Know It?"

52. See Aronowitz, *The Politics of Identity,* 225–52.

53. See Jason DeParle, "Change in Welfare Is Likely to Need Big Jobs Program," *New York Times,* January 30, 1994, A1, A8; Richard P. Nathan, "Welfare, Work and the Real World," *New York Times,* January 31, 1994, A11.

54. "Poverty Policy Priorities for President Clinton," *Focus* 14 (Winter 1992–93): 13.

55. See Jean Hopfensperger, "State Begins Experiment Aimed at Helping Parents Work Free of Welfare," *Minneapolis Star Tribune,* March 29, 1994, 1A, 14A. The Minnesota Family Investment Plan also allows those who take jobs to keep most of their cash benefits, food stamps, and medical insurance.

56. See Robert B. Moffitt, "The Effect of Work and Training Programs on Entry and Exit from the Welfare Caseload," discussion paper no. 1025-93, Institute for Research on Poverty, University of Wisconsin-Madison, 1993; DeParle, "Change in Welfare."

57. See "Welfare Reform Sure to Add Zeros." Clinton is willing to stress targeting teen mothers for workfare programs even though such programs may be inappropriate and rarely effective in the case of young mothers of young children. See Betsy Reed, "Welfare Programs That Work, and Those That Win," *Dollars and Sense,* 196 (November/December): 137.

58. Primus, "The Clinton Administration and Child Support."

59. Some states have received funding for limited experimental projects to place noncustodial parents in jobs. See Jean Hopfensperger, "Anoka, Dakota Counties Target 'Welfare Dads' in New Jobs Program," *Minneapolis Star Tribune,* March 21, 1994, 1A, 7A.

60. See Fraser and Gordon, "A Genealogy of *Dependency,*" 323–31.

61. "Clinton May Seek to Cut Welfare for Immigrants," *Minneapolis Star Tribune,* December 20, 1993, 5A; and DeParle, "Momentum Builds for Cutting Back Welfare," 1.

62. See Aronowitz, *The Politics of Identity,* 225–52; Gans, "Scholars' Role in Planning a 'Post-Work Society.'" Eugene McCarthy and William McGaughey, *Non-Financial Economics: The Case for Shorter Hours of Work* (New York: Praeger, 1989).

63. Using their own "self-sufficiency threshold," Schwarz and Volgy found that "in March 1990, when the nation was still four months from the end of its record-breaking recovery, 9.3 million workers in full-time jobs (10.3 percent of all full-time workers) found themselves ... in households, which contained 24 million persons, [that] all had total incomes beneath the self-sufficiency threshold." Limiting the analysis to those employed full-time for the entire year, "5.9 million workers (7.4 percent of all fully employed Americans) worked full-time the whole year during 1989 and yet lived beneath the threshold of self-sufficiency." *The Forgotten Americans,* 64.

64. Fraser, "Clintonism, Welfare, and the Antisocial Wage" Mimi Abramovitz and Frances Fox Piven, "Scapegoating Women on Welfare," *New York Times,* September 2, 1993, A14.

65. Fraser and Gordon, "A Genealogy of *Dependency,*" 325–27.

66. See Piven and Cloward, *Regulating the Poor,* 365–99.

67. See Mark Robert Rank, *Living at the Edge: The Realities of Welfare in America* (New York: Columbia University Press, 1994), 1–8, 197–204.

68. "Although public policies have contributed to the alleviation of poverty as a social condition, they also have tended to construct the poor as society's enemy.... the recently ex-

panded earned income tax credit will supplement the incomes of poor adults who are able to work but will more sharply differentiate them from those less able or unable to engage in wage work.... In this sense, poverty policy presents a Hobson's choice. The policies formulated to relieve poverty simultaneously institutionalize a moral construction of the poor as society's enemy." Brodkin, "The Making of an Enemy," 670.

69. See Linda Gordon, "What Does Welfare Regulate?" *Social Research* 55 (1988): 609–30.

70. William E. Connolly, *Identity\Difference: Democratic Negotiations of Political Paradox* (Ithaca, N.Y.: Cornell University Press, 1991), 206–8.

71. See Gans, "Scholars' Role in Planning a 'Post-Work Society.' "

72. For a novel approach to "investing" in the poor, see Michael Sherraden, *Assets and the Poor: A New American Welfare Policy* (Armonk, N.Y.: M. E. Sharpe, 1991).

73. See Frances Fox Piven, "Reforming the Welfare State," *Socialist Review* 22 (July–September 1992): 69–82.

Index

Compiled by Douglas J. Easton

Sanford F. Schram is associate professor of political science at Macalester College. He has been a visiting professor at the La Follette Institute of Public Affairs at the University of Wisconsin and also a visiting affiliate at the Institute for Research on Poverty at the University of Wisconsin. Author of more than thirty articles on issues of poverty and welfare, he has worked with various community groups during the past twenty years to promote social science research that serves ordinary people rather than just policy makers.

Frances Fox Piven is distinguished professor of political science at the Graduate School and University Center of the City University of New York. She is the coauthor of *Poor People's Movements: Why They Succeed, How They Fail* (1977) and coeditor of *Regulating the Poor: The Functions of Public Welfare* (1993).